Waterscapes

New Historical PERSPECTIVES

New Historical Perspectives is an open access book series for early career scholars, commissioned, edited and published by the Royal Historical Society and the University of London Press in association with the Institute of Historical Research. Submissions are encouraged relating to all historical periods and subjects. Books in the series are overseen by an expert editorial board to ensure the highest standards of peer-reviewed scholarship, and extensive support and feedback for authors is provided.

The series is supported by the Economic History Society.

ISSN 3049-5091 (Print)
ISSN 3049-5105 (Online)

INSTITUTE OF HISTORICAL RESEARCH | SCHOOL OF ADVANCED STUDY UNIVERSITY OF LONDON

ECONOMIC HISTORY SOCIETY

Waterscapes

Reservoirs, Environment and Identity in Modern England and Wales

Andrew McTominey

UNIVERSITY OF LONDON PRESS

Available to purchase in print or download
for free at https://uolpress.co.uk

First published 2025 by
University of London Press
Senate House, Malet St, London WC1E 7HU

A CIP catalogue record for this book is available from The British Library.

ISBN 9781915249104 (hardback)
ISBN 9781915249111 (paperback)
ISBN 9781915249128 (.epub)
ISBN 9781915249142 (.pdf)
ISBN 9781913002220 (.html)

DOI https://doi.org/10.63674/cxiv5434

Cover image: Thruscross Reservoir, Harrogate, UK. 2023.
Photo by Matthew Inamdar on Unsplash.

Cover design for University of London Press by Nicky Borowiec.
Book design by Nigel French.
Text set by Westchester Publishing Services UK
in Meta Serif and Meta, designed by Erik Spiekermann.

Contents

List of illustrations

Figures

Maps

Tables

Acknowledgements

This work would not have been possible without the help of a number of people. First, I'd like to thank the Royal Historical Society's New Perspectives series, particularly the lead editors, Elizabeth Hurren and Heather Shore, and my mentor, Catherine Clarke, for supporting the project from its inception. I'd like to thank Matthew Kelly for his incredibly detailed and helpful feedback at the workshop stage of this project. I'd also like to thank Emma Gallon at University of London Press for her support throughout the project, and the copy-editing teams at University of London Press and Westchester Publishing Services for all their hard work.

This project would not have happened without PhD funding, for which I'm extremely grateful to the Arts and Humanities Research Council and to the Heritage Consortium. Further funding to do extra research to turn my thesis into a manuscript was provided by the Royal Historical Society, the Economic History Society and Leeds Beckett University, to whom I'm very grateful. I'm also grateful to the Marc Fitch Fund for providing funding for image rights.

My appreciation goes to the archivists of the West Yorkshire Archives Service, Leeds branch, where I completed the majority of my archival research. I'd also like to thank the staff of Leeds Central Library and the Leeds Library, as well as the archivists and staff of the British Library, the Library of Birmingham, Liverpool Record Office, the National Archives, North Yorkshire County Record Office and Otley Museum. Special mention goes to the volunteers of Washburn Heritage Centre, particularly Janet Fox and Sally Robinson, for their help and support with the project from the outset.

I'm grateful to the professional associations I have been able to make over the years that have helped to develop this work. My colleagues in the School of Humanities and Social Sciences at Leeds Beckett University have, in the space of around ten years, morphed from teachers to friends, and have continuously provided support and encouragement. Special thanks go to Shane Ewen, who has been guiding me for nearly thirteen years and without whom this project would not exist. I'd also like to thank colleagues at the University of Huddersfield, especially Rob Ellis for his support and expertise during my PhD thesis.

I'm grateful for the feedback and discussions that have helped to shape this book, as well as inspire ideas, at the various conferences I have attended and presented work at. Special mention goes to the attendees of the Urban History Group, which has provided an accommodating and sociable atmosphere for many years, and the editorial team of *Urban History*. In particular I'd like to thank Tom Hulme, who was very supportive in the early stages of this book.

I would not have been able to complete this book without the support of friends, both professional and personal. As well as colleagues past and present at the University of Leeds Library service, special thanks go to Aaron Andrews, Olly Bowling, Dan Broadbent, Chris Burgess, Mark Butterfield, Chris Hatton, Maddie Hewitson, Michael Hewitson, Matt Joy, Miranda Lickert, Simon Lickert, Sabina Peck, Rob Piggott, Elliot Reay, Michael Reeve, Simon Sandison, and Tosh Warwick.

Finally, I would like to thank my parents, Daniel and Di McTominey, my sister Nicole, and Ariadne Deverson-Pavlidou for their support and encouragement that has helped me reach this point.

Introduction: waterscapes

The summer of 2022 was marked by hot weather and dry grass. Temperatures in excess of 30°C were recorded across Europe for a sustained period of time, demonstrating that climate has no regard for national borders. On 19 July 2022, a temperature of 40.3°C was recorded and verified by the Met Office in the United Kingdom. Record temperatures and a lack of rain resulted in the driest July since 1935. The Environment Agency declared drought in eleven of its fourteen areas, with hosepipe bans brought into effect by Thames Water, South East Water, South West Water, Southern Water and Yorkshire Water. In and of itself, drought is not a new phenomenon, even to a temperate country like Britain. However, record temperatures and a lack of rain point to the effects of anthropogenic climate change being felt with more regularity. Hosepipe bans were retained by South East Water in response to a dry February 2023 and increased consumption, while the hosepipe ban instigated by South West Water continued until September 2023.[1]

In response to the growing threat of drought and an ever-greater demand for water supply as populations grew, the water regulator Ofwat greenlit the development of three new reservoirs in Cambridgeshire, Oxfordshire and Lincolnshire in June 2023. The combined cost of the three schemes is projected to be around £6.17 billion, aiming to be completed in the 2040s. In contrast to the reservoir projects of the 1960s and 1970s, which were seen as threats to local communities and ecology, Ofwat anticipated that the projects would have wider 'social, environmental and economic benefits', including a net gain to biodiversity as well as the potential to develop leisure pursuits.

These schemes, though, have not lacked for opposition. Historic England noted with regards to both the Fens reservoir in Cambridgeshire and the South Lincolnshire reservoir that, when planning the projects, little reference seemed to have been made to the historic environment.

While some engagement with Historic England had taken place in Oxfordshire, there is more to be done.[2] These comments pale in comparison with the opposition to the eloquently named South East Strategic Reservoir Option. A number of opponents, including local pressure groups, parish and county councils, preservationist groups and local members of the public, have expressed concerns over the need for the reservoir, citing financial worries, the risk of floods and the lack of input from those most affected by the project: local residents. Indeed, some questioned whether the reservoir would be needed at all if Thames Water carried out maintenance of existing systems to stop leakage.[3]

While some of the factors involved in reservoir development had changed, such as embracing the potential for reservoirs to act as sites of biodiversity, it is striking how much of the opposition to reservoir development has remained the same: the burdensome costs, the opposition of preservationists concerned with the effects on the natural landscape, but also the potential for reservoirs to have social and cultural impacts, becoming sites of leisure for urbanites. Ultimately, *Waterscapes* is concerned with tracing these links between the past and the present, exploring undervalued rural landscapes to emphasise how much waterworks management, mainly to supply urban areas, has affected landscape and people both negatively and positively.

There is also a pressing need for urban-environmental historical research of this kind in Britain. Environmental histories have traditionally focused on the macro scale or on specific geographic entities, such as rivers that cross national borders. While there is a rich base of research on environmental history in Britain, the development of waterworks systems and their impacts on local areas and local people, as well as what this means for the urban–rural hinterland exchange, has been neglected. Urban history has the benefit of bringing broader environmental issues back to the local level, emphasising the impact of larger socionatural processes in specific locations to specific people. It also helps to shed light on local decision-making processes that are vital to understanding the conceptualisation of nature during the nineteenth and twentieth centuries – unlike other utilities, water was not nationalised by the Atlee government after the Second World War and remained in the hands of local authorities until the creation of regional water boards in 1973.

Water has always been of vital importance to sustain human life. The nineteenth century saw unprecedented urban growth, and with it an increased demand for water. This continued into the twentieth century as urban areas and populations continued to grow. As we enter a period in which there is increased pressure on available water sources due to anthropogenic climate change, we need to understand how we have conceptualised our relationships with these waterscapes. How have local landscapes and communities been affected by the quest to fulfil urban need, and how have waterscapes provided a space for urban development, not just in terms of the water they supply but in how they have subsequently been utilised by urban authorities and urban residents? This monograph sets out to address this lack of attention on waterscapes, taken here to mean landscapes that have been inextricably altered and affected by their relationship with water. As reservoirs are man-made, this relationship is multifaceted and socionatural; the landscapes examined here have not just been shaped by their interaction with humans but also by the agency of nature to create a new, hybrid type of landscape. In focusing on the examples of Leeds, Liverpool and Birmingham, this monograph sets out to explore neglected landscapes, those landscapes that have been underexplored due to their lack of exceptionalism – these waterworks are not in national parks or areas historically thought to be of outstanding natural beauty but are, nonetheless, illuminating.

This monograph also shows how the local increasingly became entangled with the national. While water supply was not nationalised after the Second World War, this is a period in which the supply of water became increasingly conceptualised within a national rather than local or regional framework.[4] These waterscapes also intersect with nationalist politics to an increasing degree – the projects at Claerwen and, especially, Llyn Celyn (Tryweryn) invoked increased nationalist opposition. These are difficult histories – the purpose here is to help understand these difficult histories and to better understand the connections between local and national tensions when they arose.

Key terms

Waterscapes engages with a number of concepts that have long formed part of urban-environmental historical discourse. One such idea is taming the wilderness, an idea that has been associated with efforts to modify the rural landscape in the Western world. William Cronon has demonstrated these attitudes in regard to the settlement and transformation of American plains, which was framed by historians like Frederick Jackson Turner as a step towards creating an egalitarian and democratic nation. These progressive narratives of environmental change helped situate the role of society within national development as fighting against an old and obstinate enemy, one that was overcome by greater scientific and technical knowledge and skill.[5] This is something that continued well into the twentieth century, particularly in arid regions of the United

States such as Texas, where new waterworks helped to facilitate new towns.[6] While the taming of the countryside in Britain was less emphatically celebrated, it was stressed by certain key actors like engineers and local authorities and helped to perpetuate a sense of modernity.

This is linked to Maria Kaika's idea of the 'Promethean project', defined as the quest to 'tame, control, and discipline nature' in order to facilitate the expansion of towns and cities and, therefore, modern urban society.[7] Like Prometheus, who stole fire from the Greek gods and, therefore, provided humanity with technology and knowledge, structures like waterworks fundamentally altered the countryside to improve urban civilisation. This is also linked to the idea of second nature, a concept that essentially refers to the ways in which humanity remakes nature. For Theodor Adorno, second nature presents itself as meaningful but illusionary.[8] A good example of this paradigm was Frederick T. Olmstead's Central Park, which included scenery that was meant to invoke the Catskill Mountains, from where New York derives its water supplies.[9] This scenery looks natural, particularly in the wider context of a green space, but is entirely man-made. This is a remaking of nature for sociocultural purposes, a process that also occurred with the creation of lake-like reservoirs. Like other forms of second nature, this form of nature was illusionary: it was real but not real. This is a key concept to consider when looking at accounts of the countryside provided by journalists and guidebook writers who saw the landscape as improved by what would we term as second nature.

This leads into another key term: amenity. In short, this refers to the ways in which the appearance of the rural landscape has been altered and the attempt to preserve a more natural aesthetic. This is a term with a long and charged history, infused by Romanticism, preservation and, latterly, legislative and modernist narratives. As Katrina Navickas has noted, narratives around landscape in the post-war period became entwined with debates around ecology and wilderness; for some, the rural wilderness was not there to be tamed but to be preserved, a forerunner to more recent debates around rewilding.[10] While the post-war period is when issues of amenity came to be defined in legislative terms, it had long been associated with waterworks and changes to the rural environment. The Thirlmere Defence Association, formed to stop Manchester from extracting water from Lake Thirlmere in the Lake District, essentially rooted its opposing argument in ideas around amenity: the importance of preserving the natural appearance of the Lake District.[11] Before then, Wordsworth had led campaigns against the coming of the railway to the Lake District, an area that he had done so much to define in his poetry.[12] Matthew Kelly has also noted the use of amenity in opposition to a waterworks project on Dartmoor to supply London, which focused on utility rather than notions of Romanticism, showing that even in the nineteenth century the term encapsulated different meanings.[13]

Amenity in the twentieth century, though, took on a more nuanced meaning. As John Sheail has noted in his analysis of the amenity clause, the term came to reflect the ultimate paradox of technology: 'namely that the most effective way of tackling the disruption caused to the environment by technology is through further advances in technology'.[14] While less obvious than examples of rural modernism like concrete dams or electric pylons, authorities had been engaging in this paradox for decades. The construction of Victorian reservoirs was an exercise in masking changes to the landscape, their earthen-embankment design helping to cover their technological nature and allowing them to blend in to appear as natural lakes, a central feature of guidebook descriptions in this period. As Chapter 3 highlights, the concept of amenity could also be malleable, used to defend changes to the landscape that were seen even by preservationists as tasteful. *Waterscapes* engages with this more nuanced understanding of amenity, focusing less on the outright instincts of preservationists to highlight the ways in which forestry and cultural depictions of the landscape following reservoir construction could add to understandings of amenity: understandings that were, as Navickas, Sheail and others have shown, developing after the Second World War.

The growth of water history

The ways in which historians approach the history of water supply has changed significantly over the past forty years, moving from viewing water solely as a medium for discussions on public health to considering the cultural importance of water and supply systems. Much work has concentrated on the way in which the water industry operated politically. The governance of the water industry remained remarkably stable over the course of the nineteenth and twentieth centuries, at least until the 1970s. Before the 1840s, private companies provided water to urban areas, given statutory powers by Parliament to supply specific areas, the most prominent example of this being the thirteen water boards that supplied the London metropolitan area.[15] Several issues came to the fore during the early to mid-nineteenth century that resulted in municipal governments becoming more involved in managing the water industry. Public health was a large issue, not just in terms of the increasingly recognised effects of polluted water but also the means of solving this problem, as espoused by Edwin Chadwick, requiring greater quantities of water. In addition to this, consumer dissatisfaction with the quality of water supply and what was deemed as profiteering by private water companies provided municipal government with the opportunity to purchase waterworks and bring them under public control.[16] Sally Sheard has argued that private water companies in Liverpool failed to provide a fit and proper water supply, were driven by profit and held irresponsible attitudes towards public health.[17] This ties into a broader historiography of water during the 1980s and 1990s, which focused predominantly on water as a medium for histories of public health.[18]

From the 1840s onwards, more towns and cities followed the example of Liverpool in bringing their water supply under municipal control. Among other reasons for municipalisation, it was felt that local government could raise necessary funds for large-scale infrastructure projects more easily than private water companies, although this was by no means easy for many smaller towns.[19] Towns and cities, as well as private water companies that had the means to do so, applied to Parliament for the statutory powers, as well as funds, to construct reservoirs in rural areas. This involved gaining legal rights to land as well as arbitrating private land rights in the targeted area. While an expensive process, it was largely straightforward for many who had done their due diligence; indeed, water engineers employed by municipal governments to plan and construct reservoirs, like Frederick Bateman and Thomas Hawksley, also became extremely adept at providing expert testimony to parliamentary committees.[20] Thirlmere was a point of contrast to this process. Parliamentary bills often faced opposition that was then heard and arbitrated or resolved privately. The strength of feeling behind the opposition to Thirlmere, as well as its more organised nature, meant that Parliament took the unusual step of establishing a special committee to hear all arguments and judge whether the bill should progress.

With some notable exceptions, such as Bristol and Newcastle, many towns and cities had brought their water supplies under municipal control by the twentieth century. Even London, with its sprawling thirteen water boards, brought a level of centralised control with the creation of the Metropolitan Water Board in 1903. Municipalisation also demonstrates that the governance of water in this period was mirrored across the Atlantic. The history of Manchester's water supply has been compared by Harold L. Platt to Chicago, the 'shock cities' of the late nineteenth and early twentieth centuries. He has argued that the political culture of both cities was vital in shaping narratives of water supply and sanitation.[21] The attitudes of city aldermen in Chicago, who saw their position within municipal government in a self-serving manner aided by heavy devolution of power and universal male suffrage, were indicative of their approach to the environment. They did not want investment into the city to be harmed by issues around water usage, despite warnings from progressive reformers that the city's water supply was not inexhaustible.[22] The municipal governance of Manchester, affected by limited suffrage and strong centralised government, was driven more by a sense of social and moral duty, which informed attitudes towards water supply.[23] William Kahrl has highlighted a similar approach to the environment in his study of dam construction in the Owens Valley, California. He has shown that the waterworks system built in the valley to service Los Angeles during the twentieth century was undoubtedly positive for the city, as water authorities were able to predict future demand and construct ahead of time.[24] This, however, came at the expense of the agriculture of the valley, which was destroyed during construction. It also affected the valley's residents, who were left displaced and marginalised by the scheme, with many of the vital decisions that affected their future made in Los Angeles where they had no representation.[25]

While the parliamentary process for Thirlmere was more complex, the standard water bill procedure broadly remained in place well into the twentieth century, a process that could be costly as well as drawn-out. This changed with the implementation of ministerial orders during the interwar and post-war period, which made it easier to pass uncontroversial local government legislation.[26] Ultimately, straightforward waterworks projects were decided by the minister for housing and local government, on the advice and evidence of civil servants, rather than a lengthy and expensive parliamentary committee. This speaks to the ways in which the water industry was reformed during the twentieth century, ostensibly to provide more power to centralised figures and bodies. However, this was not a simple process. Water was not nationalised by post-war Labour governments despite it being a part of Labour policy up until 1965.[27] As Christine McCulloch notes, due to the nature of water ownership, nationalisation may have antagonised both municipal and private providers.[28] Robert Millward has also pointed to various other stakeholders in water supply that made nationalisation unfeasible, such as landowners, industrialists and river conservancy boards to name a few.[29] Despite this, John Hassan has highlighted attempts by central government to improve the water industry amid increased demand, leading to the 1963 Water Resources Act, which sought to radically reorganise the water industry, implementing centralised river authorities to directly manage and sustain rivers across the country.[30] The establishment of the river authorities under this act, followed by the establishment of the regional water boards in 1973, saw central government play an increasingly interventionist role in the governance of water without fully nationalising the industry. As Glen O'Hara has highlighted, though, post-war governments of both colours struggled to fully manage the water industry, meaning that confusion was often the end result.[31]

Political histories and histories of public health remain vitally important, particularly for areas of the world where colonial power structures affected the development of infrastructure and health environments.[32] However, they can only illuminate a part of the broader impact of water to society and culture in the nineteenth and twentieth centuries in the United Kingdom. As Andrea Gaynor has argued, historians of public health have failed 'to trace the co-evolution of cultures, technologies, and environments as they relate to water over time'.[33] Embracing a cultural approach to these issues can help shed light on these wider themes, an approach that historians of water have increasingly taken to the subject.

In part, this has been aided by the broader cultural turn, which has shifted the focus from water as a medium of public health to the different cultural and semiotic associations that water can hold.[34] More recently, this has moved beyond the study of water itself to the technologies involved in the supply of water, such as pipes and reservoirs. This has attracted the attention of historians interested in the development of liberalism and power during the nineteenth century. Influenced by Michel Foucault's idea of governmentality, the ways in which individuals self-govern through the practices of power enacted by the state and experts, they have analysed the implementation of infrastructure in the city as an example of how expertise influenced the practices of self-rule.[35] Surveillance was a key element in maintaining liberal governmentality, with civic institutions like newspapers helping to control and mediate urban space during the nineteenth century. Under the guise of anonymity provided by pseudonyms, writers could report instances of poor behaviour, thereby utilising the newspaper as an apparatus of surveillance and as a method of shaming.[36] Urban space, though, was also mediated by technology. Chris Otter has argued that the state implemented large engineering projects in order to impose a state of governability, the management of which constituted a large part of the growth of government during the nineteenth century.[37] While city councils began to appoint experts such as borough surveyors and medical officers of health to inform on how to govern aspects of the city, Otter has argued that it was the engineers employed by local government who built the networks that governed everyday life.[38] Patrick Joyce has complemented this argument by illustrating that Chadwickian public health and sanitary reform was used in order to mediate urban space by regulating the installation of infrastructure such as water pipes and water closets in the home.[39] Thus, it was through the implementation of technology that the idea of freedom (and, ergo, self-rule) was secured. This approach has been criticised by historians, not least because of the denial of individual agency. This is the case with Vanessa Taylor and Frank Trentmann's work on drought in London and Sheffield in the late nineteenth century, the first drought in the United Kingdom to occur following the widespread implementation of high-pressure water supply to homes. Rather than be disciplined into self-rule, water became a consumer issue, with consumers demonstrating against water companies who were seen to be denying access to a resource that had become part of everyday life, further demonstrating the importance of taking cultural approaches to the history of water.[40]

Embracing a cultural approach can also help to develop local political studies of waterworks, particularly by engaging in ideas around civic identity. The attachment to one's town or city and their municipal achievements were an important part of urban life in the nineteenth century. The opening of key civic institutions, such as Leeds Town Hall, or the ceremonies to celebrate new waterworks became hallmarks for civic pride.[41] As such, a certain pageantry was engaged with on such occasions, such as the presence of members of the royal family to bestow the event with national patronage. There was also an engagement with processional culture, with members of the procession to open a new venture ranked according to their social standing. Gunn has argued that the celebration of civic pride reached a zenith in large industrial cities in 1870, with a slow decline in participation until 1914, when national and imperial identities took precedence. In the interwar period, the prominence of events like the British Empire Exhibition and the opening of the British Empire Stadium (more commonly known as Wembley Stadium) in 1924 were believed to have turned the attention of urbanites away from civic achievements.[42]

The predominance and privileging of national identities on the urban stage has been questioned in recent years, though. Events like pageants and civic anniversaries in the 1920s and 1930s help to demonstrate the continued importance of civic identity.[43] As historians like Charlotte Wildman have shown, this continued into the post-war period. Although the post-war context was different to the interwar years, as the interwar years were different to the late nineteenth century, municipal endeavours like the civic film *A City Speaks* (1947) continued to be used to express faith in the city's aspirations.[44] While this may have been the province of the industrial middle classes in the nineteenth century, by the post-war period civic pride was taken up by architects and developers who saw new, dynamic cities on the horizon. As Peter Shapely has convincingly argued, the design and construction of new buildings in cities that embraced post-war consumerism, such as the Merrion Centre in Leeds, designed by Arnold Ziff, became symbols of what cities could achieve.[45] Civic pride and identity, then, adapted to time and place, becoming increasingly inclusive and participatory, a revisionist argument that *Waterscapes* looks to contribute to.

The interest in cultural history has also developed within environmental history, which sees water as representation as well as environmental asset.[46] Environmental historians like Richard White have long recognised human alterations to landscapes like the Colorado River as a remaking of nature.[47] Changes made to the river impacted not only its flow but also how the river was utilised by others, especially salmon that could not swim up a dammed river. Thus, in the remaking of nature to suit human needs, ecosystems were often adversely affected. Similarly, environmental historians also began to consider the effects of cities on the environment, which had previously been dismissed by established scholars like Donald Worster.[48] Cronon argued that by focusing on socio-economic modes of production at the expense of culture, towns and cities, which Worster viewed as products of culture and separate from nature, were excluded from his environmental history agenda.[49] In order to produce an inclusive environmental history, the impact of towns and cities on nature, endogenously and exogenously, had to be integrated, as Christine Meisner Rosen and Joel Arthur Tarr argued, to better understand society's impact on the natural environment.[50]

In a pioneering study that sought to highlight the benefits of incorporating cities into environmental history, Cronon examined the development of Chicago during the nineteenth century. He explored Chicago's geographic position as a 'gateway' to the American West and the subsequent development of transport links with the city as a port, flows of goods such as meat, lumber and grain from surrounding states, including Michigan, Illinois, Iowa and Wisconsin, and further flows of capital, manufactured goods and culture.[51] This illustrates that Chicago did not develop just as a city, an area with a clear boundary demarcating urban and rural, but as a city intimately connected with its hinterlands, an example of how cities were not just shaped by their physical environments but helped to shape the environments around them. Thus, urban and rural environments cannot be considered as separate; they shape and are shaped by each other. The demands of the city for resources, food and capital are drawn from rural and semi-urban hinterlands, which are themselves shaped by these demands. While Cronon does not discuss water supply, his work can help an environmental history of water. The ways in which British towns and cities like Leeds and Liverpool went to their rural hinterlands for sources of water, thereby shaping the rural environment through the construction of dams and reservoirs, and, indeed, further policies of land management, is another way in which the relationship that he describes is evident, a relationship that is explored in this book.

Cities, therefore, cannot be considered as wholly expressions of culture, as Worster has argued, but as an integral element in the shaping of rural environments, gaining resources from rural areas while simultaneously remaking the natural environment.

This approach has been developed by historical geographers interested in structures like reservoirs as sites of socionature, the nexus of social and natural forces that work in tandem to create an assemblage that is neither social nor natural but a hybrid of both.[52] Kaika has examined the dialectic of nature and the city that has influenced urban planners through the nineteenth and twentieth centuries. Both nature and the city have been coded as 'good' – as places untouched by the horrors of urban industrialism and as the pinnacle of civilised society – and 'bad' – as a foreboding wilderness that requires control and as harbouring the evils of modern society. This has impacted on how planners have approached the design of urban public spaces: for example, F. L. Olmsted's aforementioned incorporation of wild nature into the design of New York City's Central Park in the 1850s.[53] This dialectic was expressed in the construction of the Marathon Dam, Athens, in the 1920s, as evidence of the ability of humans to tame nature while reconceptualising the city as a modern, constructed space removed from the influence of nature.[54] Gaynor has built upon Kaika's work in exploring the need for water to maintain residential lawns in Perth, Western Australia, during the early twentieth century. While water was always at a premium due to the heat experienced in Australian summers, residents continued to water lawns, which provided Perth with a picturesque suburban image that could be compared with other cities within the British Empire.[55] Thus, water as a socionatural product held important social and cultural values; indeed, some residents used their domestic supply in order to maintain their lawn.[56] This can be further seen in Taylor and Trentmann's analysis of constant water supply and the fitting of fixed baths and water closets in Sheffield, which increased the material value of water in the home as water became a part of everyday life.[57] Analysing sites of socionature like the Marathon Dam or New York can illustrate the power dynamics between the city and nature, and the centrality of water to those relationships.

Indeed, across the Atlantic, the study of water has moved beyond groundbreaking work on municipalisation and public health by historians like Martin Melosi to study the more holistic impact of water to areas like Texas, where towns were created by the construction of reservoirs in more than one sense.[58] Waterworks in this region also helped to facilitate spaces for leisure, becoming synonymous with days that celebrated water-based activities.[59] This speaks to the ways in which studies of waterworks are becoming increasingly entwined into histories of leisure and tourism.

Australian environmental historians have also sought to use cultural approaches to water management, highlighting how historic floods and droughts have shaped urban living in a country that, at times, struggles for potable water supplies. Additionally, they highlight the importance of indigenous beliefs around water and how those beliefs can inform water management in the present.[60] The focus on areas of the world that struggle for potable water supplies, like Texas and Australia, speaks to the increasing interest of water historians in parts of the world that will be affected by anthropogenic climate change more quickly than others; arguably, some of these areas already are.

While some have concentrated on drought, others have focused on flooding. Historians in Australia have explored flooding in relation to drought, particularly in urban areas that have suffered from periodic flooding due to their proximity to major rivers. They take flooding to be a symptom of the wider hydrological cycle that has been adversely affected by climate change. There are also cultural associations with flooding that are being increasingly focused on. Lotte Jensen's work on the cultural history of water in the Netherlands demonstrates the paradoxical attitudes that the Dutch hold towards water in a country that has been ravaged by floods for centuries: water is linked to traumatic events that illustrate the country's geographical vulnerabilities, while simultaneously being a reminder that through technical innovations they have overcome such vulnerabilities. This sense of fear and national pride is at the heart of the country's relationship with water, a duality that will once again come to the fore in a time of climate crisis.[61] Recent works, then, have focused on the role of water, both its abundance and its absence, in a time of crisis inspired by the current context. In focusing on a more temperate climate, *Waterscapes* looks to contribute to these cultural histories of water by analysing the different – sometimes complementary, sometimes conflicting – relationships society had with rural water taken for urban needs, as we deal with questions around water supply in the present.

Rethinking waterscapes

The ways in which historians think about changes to rural places by urban authorities has been influenced by a number of ideas. One such idea is socionature, developed by cultural geographers like Erik Swyngedouw. Socionature is a way of conceptualising changes to the environment by social forces, the results of which are neither fully social nor natural but a socionatural hybrid.[62] Reservoirs are a good example of socionatural hybridity, constructed by urban authorities, built by human labour, but within the contours of the rural landscape.[63] Waterworks can be viewed as urban/rural hybrids, rather than within an urban/rural binary relationship.

Another useful theoretical underpinning is the idea of rural modernity. Landscape historians have, in the past, tended to neglect the impact that waterscapes have made on the landscape. Tom Williamson, a landscape archaeologist, has argued that landscape history 'is concerned with the historical interpretation of the physical structures and spaces which make up the environment', yet this has often concentrated on fields, agriculture, gardens and woodlands rather than waterscapes that have been reconfigured by urban needs.[64] Furthermore, Williamson has also suggested that landscape history has not fitted well with ecological or natural histories owing to their respective focus on social or natural historical processes.[65] This, perhaps, speaks to the lack of impact of environmental history in Britain in some disciplinary circles. It also highlights the importance of taking a socionatural approach to studying waterscapes in order to view these social and natural historical processes simultaneously. This is especially the case in the North of England and Wales, where, as this monograph demonstrates, waterscapes like reservoirs were adapted not just for the purpose of water supply but for leisure and tourism.

Conceptualising these waterscapes as sites of rural modernity can help to shift this lens, taking in the wider social, cultural, environmental and political issues they impacted upon. Traditionally, landscape in England has been seen within a specific framework, crystallised by W. G. Hoskins who sought to show the depth of history of the English landscape – the countryside of the 1950s was not just a product of the Victorian or Georgian period but had been formed over centuries. As such, the countryside that Hoskins venerated was one of hedgerows, streams and small stone churches; he had little time for the activities of post-war planners or changes to the countryside at large since 1914. (He was, though, quite complimentary about the aesthetic qualities of reservoirs in the North and Midlands.)[66] While the term rural modernism has been associated with the time in which Hoskins was writing, given the influence of modernist architecture in the countryside through pylons and transmission stations, Navickas has argued that nineteenth-century waterworks structures, as well as canals, are also examples of this process.[67] Furthermore, an engagement with ideas around rural modernism can, as Navickas has done, highlight the historic tensions with utilising land that was deemed to be not outstanding. Historiographically and contemporaneously, certain landscapes have been privileged over others due to their apparent aesthetic value, a trait pushed by poets and writers and then, in the twentieth century enshrined in legislation, the creation of national parks, and

Areas of Outstanding Natural Beauty. There is much to be gained by focusing on what Navickas refers to as areas of non-outstanding natural beauty, as she has done in her examination of debates around amenity and preservation of the industrial Pennines.[68] Similarly, many of the case studies examined here focus on areas not typically associated with Areas of Outstanding Natural Beauty or what would become national parks: Washburn Valley is a little-known area of North Yorkshire between Harrogate and Leeds; Lake Vyrnwy and the Elan Valley were conceptualised by what they could provide to English cities rather than for their aesthetic value. How ideas of aesthetics, amenity and interaction from both local and urban people combined in these areas is of central interest here.

Taking influence from ideas like socionature and rural modernity means that, by its very nature, *Waterscapes* is an interdisciplinary endeavour. Indeed, an engagement with the idea of waterscapes is inherently interdisciplinary, given that waterscapes are hybrid spaces that encompass intersecting social, cultural, political, economic and environmental factors. As such, this monograph examines a number of different themes such as social and cultural histories of the environment, politics and leisure among others. To do so, it takes in a broad range of sources, from traditional historical sources such as archival records and historical newspapers, to novels, photographs and film. Incorporating a diverse set of sources allows for a more holistic and nuanced analysis of the impact of waterworks projects across England and Wales, providing scope to assess this impact from a number of different angles and themes. In so doing, this monograph engages with ideas related to the environmental humanities, a growing field that recognises the need to incorporate a greater variety of sources and analytical frameworks in order to fully comprehend historical attitudes to the environment.

Chapter outlines

This monograph thus contributes to historical debates in two novel ways: first, by emphasising that the hinterland relationship was reciprocal, seen in the activities of writers and city dwellers in remaking and experiencing urban waterscapes; second, by showing that municipal water provision continued to be associated with civic identity well into the post-war period, tied to a wide variety of everyday activities.

Water was a necessity for towns and cities to survive and grow, but the process of procuring water was rarely straightforward. The first chapter highlights a number of case studies, in particular water schemes undertaken by Leeds, Liverpool and Birmingham, to demonstrate what, at times, could be a tumultuous process. It took time for water authorities to find suitable locations to construct reservoirs, only to be faced by the opposition of local landowners and other interested parties. Once parliamentary permission had been secured, the difficulties of engineering the landscape came to the fore. A series of incidents occurred during the construction of Leeds's Washburn Valley scheme that led to one reservoir, Thruscross, being postponed for nearly one hundred years. The construction of Liverpool's Vyrnwy waterworks was beset with conflict between the waterworks committee and the consultant water engineer Thomas Hawksley. In the twentieth century, the opposition of the landed gentry was increasingly replaced with that of ecology and, in the case of Wales, nationalism. While engaging in detail with the various waterworks projects that feature throughout this book, what runs through all the chapters is the strong sense of civic pride that was attached to these projects. It was expressed differently in 1866 than in 1966, but it was present nonetheless and consistently so across time.

In Chapter 2, the consequences of the long, drawn-out processes of construction are examined from an environmental perspective. Some of these consequences became apparent during construction, some shortly after. Having to address landslips and cracks in the earth brought into question the expert knowledge of the engineers and their ability to tame the wilderness. This ability was brought into further focus when environmental incidents occurred after construction had been completed. Dam collapses at Bilberry, Holmfirth and Dale Dyke, Sheffield were well chronicled in the nineteenth century and certainly played into fears around potential environmental disaster as more reservoirs were built. Changes in engineering practice and design did develop as the nineteenth and twentieth centuries progressed and ever more water was required. Although the appearance of reservoirs had changed over the hundred years covered here, attitudes to the environment by water authorities and engineers had not. The belief in the engineer's ability to tame the wilderness was as strong in 1966 as it was in 1866, despite the incidents in between covered in Chapter 2.

Chapter 3 explores the importance of trees and forestry to managing waterscapes. It was not enough to build reservoirs on rivers that had good quality water: that quality had to be maintained. This was a hard task in rural areas as farming effluent often found its way into the water and farmers washed their sheep in the river. Municipal government, then, had to be more interventionist to protect the purity of the water supply. Historians have paid little attention to afforestation in England and Wales before the First World War, but notable schemes at Lake Vyrnwy and in Washburn

Valley were undertaken, with varying degrees of success. In the case of the latter, unemployed men with little training were used, which resulted in the politics of water management becoming intertwined with the politics of unemployment. After the First World War, although forestry policy became more centralised with the creation of the Forestry Commission, municipal government remained vital to successful tree-planting efforts, with Liverpool in particular at the forefront of afforestation. Successful afforestation thus became tied to ideas of civic identity. It seemed to provide evidence of the positive role the city could play in developing timber stocks and protecting water supply, intertwining the urban and rural closely.

The fourth chapter examines the impact of reservoirs on the cultural landscape. The rural areas targeted by water authorities were not just altered in a physical sense, but in a cultural sense too. Many nineteenth-century reservoirs were built into the landscape, effectively giving them the appearance of natural lakes. To some, this was perceived as heightening the beauty of the rural idyll. Despite narratives of urban encroachment or negative portrayals of the city more generally, these rural areas had been *improved* by urban engineering. The influence of Romanticism was strong in depictions of these rural areas, as was the cultural legacy of the Lake District. Indeed, the Washburn Valley scheme was dubbed by local newspapers and guidebooks as the 'Leeds Lake District', with all of the cultural associations of that label. What is explored here is how the cultural landscapes of rural areas affected by reservoir construction were remade, once more highlighting the link between positively altering the appearance of the countryside and civic pride.

The construction of reservoirs did not just alter how the landscape was consumed from afar but also how it was used for leisure, the focus of Chapter 5. Newly developed lakes provided opportunities for angling and, in some cases, boating, while the rich descriptions analysed in the previous chapters brought ramblers, first from the middle class and then from the 1920s onwards from the working class, to these areas. As with construction, afforestation and cultural depictions, leisure also became tied to ideas of civic identity. Fishing in municipal reservoirs could be seen to contribute to the good health of the city's water supply; by helping to stop reservoirs becoming overstocked with fish, anglers were fulfilling their civic duty. The engagement of urbanites with rural areas that had been altered by urban engineering, essentially becoming a part of the city in the countryside, again was a way to participate in civic pride. On the surface, this seems to have reflected ideas of inclusion and citizenship; however, class continued to be a factor in who could and could not properly participate in the achievements of the city. The forms of angling that developed in reservoirs, typically fly fishing, was associated with middle-class leisure, while the growth of working-class rambling led in some quarters to unease about unruly elements in the countryside. In an age where civic identity was becoming more democratic and participatory, examining leisure in waterscapes can help us to assess how democratic this identity actually was. Rights of way around waterscapes are part of this untold story.

The predominant focus of the preceding chapters is on the impact of waterworks to the rural environment, how the urban affects the rural for resource extraction. When chapters focus on the reciprocal nature of this relationship, as in Chapters 4 and 5, they nevertheless centre on the experiences of urban residents. The penultimate chapter switches focus to those most affected by the construction of reservoirs in rural areas: local communities. Some villages on the edges of reservoir development, such as St John's in the Vale in the Lake District, were largely depopulated when construction began. Others were literally washed away, submerged by dammed river water only to be seen again in times of severe drought. A number of people, though, lived alongside reservoirs as water management continued to impinge on their lives. Chapter 6 will explore how the lives of residents in the valleys explored here were affected by the management of water. The first half focuses on Washburn Valley, looking at the ebbs and flows of community life as residents acclimatised to their new role as tenants of Leeds Corporation. The second half looks at the flooding of villages, a common aspect of many reservoir projects. Here, two in particular will be highlighted: Leeds's Thruscross reservoir, which flooded the village of West End, and the more famous Llyn Celyn reservoir, controversially flooded by Liverpool in spite of an outpouring of Welsh nationalist sentiment.

The concluding chapter brings together the themes of the book, while placing the findings within the wider context of urban waterworks in England and Wales during the nineteenth and twentieth centuries. Similarities and differences are highlighted between the main case studies, showing the importance of taking a local, urban angle when considering the national importance of reservoir provision. There was no consensus on design, implementation or management of reservoirs; however, there were commonalities as authorities sought to supply the best source of water they could to towns and cities. The overall conclusion thus incorporates the myriad forms of identity we will encounter in the chapters, in terms of civic, class and gender, and how they intersect with the provision and management of water, pointing to the importance of incorporating cultural and urban-environmental history. Other themes such as the role of citizenship and environment will also be highlighted to demonstrate the novel findings of the book. Finally, the importance of this research to the contemporary politics of water will be discussed, stressing the need for policymakers to consider a more holistic interpretation of urban waterscapes.

Notes

1. 'Driest July in England since 1935', Met Office, 1 August 2022, https://www.metoffice.gov.uk/about-us/press-office/news/weather-and-climate/2022/driest-july-in-england-since-1935.

2. Ofwat, *Strategic Regional Water Resource Solutions: Standard Gate Two Final Decision for Fens Reservoir*, 28 June 2023, 8–9, 12, https://www.ofwat.gov.uk/consultation/strategic-regional-water-resource-solutions-standard-gate-two-draft-decision-for-fenland-reservoir/; Ofwat, *Strategic Regional Water Resource Solutions: Standard Gate Two Final Decision for South Lincolnshire Reservoir*, 28 June 2023, 8, https://www.ofwat.gov.uk/consultation/strategic-regional-water-resource-solutions-standard-gate-two-draft-decision-for-south-lincolnshire-reservoir/.

3. Ofwat, *Strategic Regional Water Resource Solutions: Standard Gate Two Final Decision for South East Strategic Reservoir Option*, 28 June 2023, 7–26, https://www.ofwat.gov.uk/consultation/strategic-regional-water-resource-solutions-standard-gate-two-draft-decision-for-south-east-strategic-reservoir-option/.

4. Denis Cosgrove, Barbara Roscoe and Simon Rycroft, 'Landscape and Identity at Ladybower Reservoir and Rutland Water', *Transactions of the Institute of British Geographers* 21, no. 3 (1996): 534–51, https://doi.org/10.2307/622595.

5. William Cronon, 'A Place for Stories: Nature, History, and Narrative', *Journal of American History* 78, no. 4 (1992): 1352, https://doi.org/10.2307/2079346.

6. Andrew M. Busch, 'Dams and the Age of Abundance: Hydraulic Boosterism, Regional Growth, and the Reemergence of Water Scarcity in Central Texas', *Journal of Urban History* 49 no. 2 (2023): 309–34, https://doi.org/10.1177/00961442211008865.

7. Maria Kaika, 'Dams as Symbols of Modernization: The Urbanization of Nature Between Geographical Imagination and Materiality', *Annals of the Association of American Geographers* 96, no. 2 (2006): 276, https://doi.org/10.1111/j.1467-8306.2006.00478.x.

8. Theodor W. Adorno, 'The Idea of Natural History', *Telos* 1984, no. 60 (1984): 123–4, https://doi.org/10.3817/0684060111.

9. Matthew Gandy, *Concrete and Clay: Reworking Nature in New York City* (MIT Press, 2003), 93.

10. Katrina Navickas, 'Building Amenity in Areas of Non-Outstanding Natural Beauty in the Southern Pennines', in *New Lives, New Landscapes Revisited: Rural Modernity in Britain*, ed. Linda M. Ross et al. (British Academy, Oxford University Press, 2023), 96.

11. Harriet Ritvo, *The Dawn of Green: Manchester, Thirlmere, and Modern Environmentalism* (University of Chicago Press, 2009).

12. Keith Hanley, 'The Imaginative Visitor: Wordsworth and the Romantic Construction of Literary Tourism in the Lake District', in *The Making of a Cultural Landscape: The English Lake District as Tourist Destination, 1750–2010*, ed. John K. Walton and Jason Wood (Ashgate, 2013), 113–32.

13. Matthew Kelly, *Quartz and Feldspar: Dartmoor – A British Landscape in Modern Times* (Vintage, 2016), 99.

14. John Sheail, 'The "Amenity" Clause: An Insight into Half a Century of Environmental Protection in the United Kingdom', *Transactions of the Institute of British Geographers* 17, no. 2 (1992): 163, https://doi.org/10.2307/622543.

15. Joseph Hillier, 'Implementation Without Control: The Role of the Private Water Companies in Establishing Constant Water in Nineteenth-Century London', *Urban History* 41, no. 2 (2014): 228–46, https://doi.org/10.1017/S0963926813000278.

16. Christopher Hamlin, *Public Health and Social Justice in the Age of Chadwick: Britain, 1800–1854* (Cambridge University Press, 1998), 13–14; Sally Sheard, 'Water and Health: The Formation and Exploitation of the Relationship in Liverpool, 1847–1900', *Transactions of the Historic Society of Lancashire and Cheshire* 143 (1994): 151, https://www.hslc.org.uk/wp-content/uploads/143-8-Sheard.pdf; John Hassan and Peter Taylor, 'The Politics of Water in Early and Mid-Victorian Britain: The Experience of Bolton', *Transactions of the Historical Society of Lancashire and Cheshire* 148 (1998): 133.

17. Sheard, 'Water and Health', 151.

18. Bill Luckin, *Pollution and Control: A Social History of the Thames in the Nineteenth Century* (Adam Hilger, 1986); Hamlin, *Public Health and Social Justice*; Anthony S. Wohl, *Endangered Lives: Public Health in Victorian Britain* (J. M. Dent and Sons, 1983); Christopher Hamlin, 'Muddling in Bumbledom: On the Enormity of Large Sanitary Improvements in Four British Towns, 1855–1885', *Victorian Studies*, 32, no. 1 (1988): 55–83, https://www.jstor.org/stable/3828289.

19. Robert Millward and Sally Sheard, 'The Urban Fiscal Problem, 1870–1914: Government Expenditure and Finance in England and Wales', *The Economic History Review* 48, no. 3 (1995): 526, https://doi.org/10.2307/2598179.

20. G. M. Binnie, *Early Victorian Water Engineers* (Thomas Telford, 1981), 136.

21. Harold L. Platt, *Shock Cities: The Environmental Transformation and Reform of Manchester and Chicago* (University of Chicago Press, 2005), 406.

22. Platt, *Shock Cities*.

23. Platt, *Shock Cities*, 406–7.

24. William L. Kahrl, *Water and Power: The Conflict over Los Angeles' Water Supply in the Owens Valley* (University of California Press, 1982), 438.

25. Kahrl, *Water and Power*, 443.

26. John Sheail, 'Local Legislation: Its Scope and Context', *Archives* 30, no. 113 (2005): 48, https://doi.org/10.3828/archives.2005.3.

27. Christine S. McCulloch, 'The Water Resources Board: England and Wales' Venture into National Water Resources Planning, 1964–1973', *Water Alternatives* 2, no. 3 (2009): 462, https://www.water-alternatives.org/index.php/alldoc/articles/vol2/v2issue3/59-a2-3-10.

28. McCulloch, 'Water Resources Board'.

29. Robert Millward, 'The Political Economy of Urban Utilities', in *The Cambridge Urban History of Britain, Volume 3: 1840–1950*, ed. Martin Daunton (Cambridge University Press, 2001), 348.

30. John Hassan, *A History of Water in Modern England and Wales* (Manchester University Press, 1998), 86; Glen O'Hara, *The Politics of Water in Post-War Britain* (Palgrave Macmillan, 2017), 89.

31. O'Hara, *Politics of Water*.

32. Aditya Ramesh, 'Indian Rivers, "Productive Works", and the Emergence of Large Dams in Nineteenth-Century Madras', *The Historical Journal* 64, no. 2 (2021): 281–309, https://doi.org/10.1017/S0018246X20000163.

33. Andrea Gaynor, 'Lawnscaping Perth: Water Supply, Gardens, and Scarcity, 1890–1925', *Journal of Urban History* 46, no. 1 (2020): 65, https://doi.org/10.1177/0096144217692991.

34. Jean-Pierre Goubert, *The Conquest of Water: The Advent of Health in the Industrial Age*, trans. Andrew Wilson (Polity Press, 1989); Veronica Strang, 'Fluidscapes: Water, Identity, and the Senses', *Worldviews* 10, no. 2 (2006): 147–54, https://www.jstor.org/stable/43809682.

35. Shane Ewen, *What Is Urban History?* (Polity, 2016), 70.

36. Andy Croll, *Civilising the Urban: Popular Culture and Public Space in Merthyr, c.1870–1914* (University of Wales Press, 2000), 89–90.

37. Chris Otter, *The Victorian Eye: A Political History of Light and Vision in Britain, 1800–1910* (University of Chicago Press, 2008), 14.

38. Otter, *Victorian Eye*, 15.

39. Patrick Joyce, *The Rule of Freedom: Liberalism and the Modern City* (Verso, 2003), 70.

40. Vanessa Taylor and Frank Trentmann, 'Liquid Politics: Water and the Politics of Everyday Life in the Modern City', *Past & Present* 211, no. 1 (2011): 199–241, https://doi.org/10.1093/pastj/gtq068.

41. Owen G. Roberts, 'Waterworks and Commemoration: Purity, Rurality, and Civic Identity in Britain, 1880–1921', *Continuity and Change* 22, no. 2 (2007): 305–25, https://doi.org/10.1017/S0268416007006352.

42. Simon Gunn, *The Public Culture of the Victorian Middle Class: Ritual and Authority in the English Industrial City 1840–1914* (Manchester University Press, 2000), 163–82.

43. Tom Hulme, *After the Shock City: Urban Culture and the Making of Modern Citizenship* (Boydell Press, 2019); Charlotte Wildman, *Urban Redevelopment and Modernity in Liverpool and Manchester, 1918–1939* (Bloomsbury Academic, 2016).

44. Paul Rotha, dir. *A City Speaks*, Manchester Corporation, 1947, https://player.bfi.org.uk/free/film/watch-city-speaks-1947-online

45. Peter Shapely, 'Civic Pride and Redevelopment in the Post-War British City', *Urban History* 39, no. 2 (2012): 310–28, https://doi.org/10.1017/S0963926812000077.

46. Stephen Mosley, 'Common Ground: Integrating Social and Environmental History', *Journal of Social History* 39, no. 3 (2006): 915–33, https://doi.org/10.1353/jsh.2006.0007.

47. Richard White, *The Organic Machine: The Remaking of the Columbia River* (Hill and Wang, 1995), 59.

48. Donald Worster, 'Appendix: Doing Environmental History', in *The Ends of the Earth: Perspectives on Modern Environmental History*, ed. Donald Worster (Cambridge University Press, 1998), 292; Matthew Evenden, 'Beyond the Organic Machine? New Approaches to River Historiography', *Environmental History* 23, no. 4 (2018): 698–720, http://dx.doi.org/10.1093/envhis/emy054.

49. William Cronon, 'Modes of Prophecy and Production: Placing Nature in History', *Journal of American History* 76, no. 4 (1990): 1122–31, https://doi.org/10.2307/2936590.

50. Christine Meisner Rosen and Joel Arthur Tarr, 'The Importance of an Urban Perspective in Environmental History', *Journal of Urban History* 20, no. 3 (1994): 307, https://doi.org/10.1177/009614429402000301.

51. William Cronon, *Nature's Metropolis: Chicago and the Great West* (Norton, 1991).

52. Erik Swyngedouw, 'Modernity and Hybridity: Nature, *Regeneracionismo*, and the Production of the Spanish Waterscape, 1890–1930', *Annals of the Association of American Geographers* 89, no. 3 (1999): 445, https://doi.org/10.1111/0004-5608.00157.

53. Maria Kaika, *City of Flows: Modernity, Nature, and the City* (Routledge, 2005), 14; Gandy, *Concrete and Clay*, 93.

54. Kaika, *City of Flows*, 107.

55. Gaynor, 'Lawnscaping Perth', 63–78.

56. Gaynor, 'Lawnscaping Perth', 63–78.

57. Taylor and Trentmann, 'Liquid Politics', 214.

58. Busch, 'Dams and the Age of Abundance', 309–34.

59. Busch, 'Dams and the Age of Abundance', 309–34.

60. Margaret Cook, Lionel Frost, Andrea Gaynor, Jenny Gregory, Ruth A. Morgan, Martin Shanahan, and Peter Spearritt, *Cities in a Sunburnt Country: Water and the Making of Modern Australia* (Cambridge University Press, 2022), https://doi.org/10.1017/9781108917698.

61. Lotte Jensen, *Water: A Dutch Cultural History* (Radboud University Press, 2024), 12–14, https://doi.org/10.54195/ASQH4249.

62. Swyngedouw, 'Modernity and Hybridity'.

63. Swyngedouw, Erik. '"Not a Drop of Water …": State, Modernity, and the Production of Nature in Spain, 1898–2010', *Environment and History* 20, no. 1 (2014): 67–92, https://doi.org/10.3197/096734014X13851121443445.

64. Tom Williamson, 'Landscape: The Configured Space', in *History Beyond the Text: A Student's Guide to Approaching Alternative Sources*, ed. Sarah Barber and Corinna M. Peniston-Bird (Routledge, 2009), 137.

65. Williamson, 'Landscape', 140.

66. William George Hoskins, *The Making of the English Landscape* (Hodder and Stoughton, 1955), 298–303.

67. Navickas, 'Building Amenity', 112.

68. Navickas, 'Building Amenity', 99–100.

Chapter 1

Remaking the countryside: urban engineering and the pursuit of water

In his writings on the future supply of water for Birmingham in 1891, the councillor Thomas Barclay proclaimed that: 'Perhaps the heaviest responsibility resting on any local government is the establishment and maintenance of a proper supply of water for those under its care. How unpardonable a failure in this all-important matter! Yet how vast the task!'[1] In this short quote, Barclay aptly demonstrates two important facets of municipal water supply: the vital role of water delivery to the prosperity of residents and industry; and just how enormous a task that delivery was. Water supply was foundational to the continued health and prosperity of urban areas. As the nineteenth and twentieth centuries progressed, and as cities grew, larger and more expensive schemes were required to keep up with demand. In a city like Birmingham, so wedded to the civic gospel, spending large amounts on an excellent water supply was permissible – a meeting of ratepayers in 1891 overwhelmingly backed the city's Elan Valley scheme, with 7,837 votes for and 997 votes against, roughly a ratio of 8:1.[2] In other cities, such as Leeds and Liverpool, hawkish councillors and a critical local press wanted the best return for the ratepayers. It was not enough to provide pure, soft water: finances also had to be well managed. As the twentieth century progressed, some attitudes to water supply changed: schemes were so much bigger even than those of the late nineteenth century. However, some attitudes remained the same, particularly the confidence in urban engineering to overcome and tame the rural wilderness. When Barclay wrote of the vastness of the task, he was also referring to the magnitude of the Promethean project, the ability of modern urban society to tame and conquer the vast wilderness of nature.

This first chapter provides an overview of some notable waterworks projects, particularly those of Leeds, Liverpool and Birmingham, in order to establish context for the case studies developments going forward. Some prominent works, such as Manchester's Thirlmere scheme, have been covered elsewhere, so will not be referred to in detail here.[3] Given the essence of water supply in the nineteenth and twentieth centuries, until the establishment of the regional water boards in 1973, schemes were markedly individual, undertaken by specific towns and cities or private companies in distinct parts of rural England and Wales. As such, each scheme was, in some way, unique. However, there are some commonalities that can be drawn out. In mapping out a number of key works in England and Wales from the 1860s to the 1960s, the chapter will show changes in the industry over time and the ways in which these waterworks intersected with a number of themes and issues, most notably here politics, economics and expertise, all of which are tied to the wider ideas of second nature, amenity and rural modernism highlighted in the Introduction.

Water supply across England and Wales

The nineteenth century was the time in which a number of municipal authorities took control of their water supplies, as well as other utilities such as gas and, towards the end of the century, electricity. Before this point, water was supplied to towns and cities by private water companies run by shareholders. For example, the Leeds Waterworks Company supplied the town from 1837, taking over from the improvement commissioners who had overseen supply since 1790.[4] In a period of liberal, laissez-faire economics, it was natural for the private sector to provide resources for towns and cities. However, there were a number of reasons that prompted local governments to become involved in water supply. As populations and industries grew, demand for water increased, meaning that water companies had to contemplate more ambitious schemes. Companies faced two key issues in this regard: first, it was difficult for them to raise the necessary funds to finance such schemes; and second, it was increasingly difficult for them to enact infrastructural improvements to urban areas. Municipal authorities were better placed to address both of these issues – it was easier for municipal authorities to apply to Parliament to raise funds and to use the rates to help finance large-scale projects, while they were also in a position to facilitate digging up roads to lay pipes.[5] There were also issues around water supply and public health: the cholera epidemic of 1832, the publication of Edwin Chadwick's *The Sanitary Condition of the Labouring Population* in 1842, and the Royal Commission on the Health of Towns (1843–45) all resulted in an increased recognition of the problems polluted water posed to urban health.[6] Furthermore, accusations of profiteering were often levelled at private water companies. An example of this was in Liverpool, where the water company was accused of prioritising profits over water quality and constant supply.[7] For a number of reasons, municipal authorities were deemed to be better equipped to deliver pure water to residents and industries.

The process of municipalisation, though, was quite uneven. Because the impetus for reform came from local governments, it was local factors that determined the successful acquisition of waterworks. In the aforementioned case of Liverpool, concerns over the quality and quantity of supply meant that the town's corporation was able to purchase the waterworks by 1847.[8] Leeds was able to benefit from a clause inserted into the Act of Parliament authorising the creation of the Leeds Waterworks Company in 1837 that provided its corporation with an opportunity to purchase the works after a twelve-year period had elapsed, which the corporation did in 1852.[9] Other towns and cities struggled to acquire their waterworks. Propelled by the zeal of the civic gospel, Birmingham acquired its waterworks in 1876; while, despite the collapse of Dale Dike reservoir in 1864 – a disaster laid firmly at the feet of the private water company – Sheffield was not able to purchase its waterworks until 1887.[10] London's supply was made up of a patchwork of private companies brought under one umbrella organisation in 1903 with the creation of the Metropolitan Water Board.[11] Despite the advantages municipal government had over private companies, some towns and cities continued to be supplied by private companies until the creation of the regional water boards in the 1970s. In cities such as Bristol and Newcastle, private companies were deemed to work well, which meant that the drive for municipalisation never gained momentum.[12] This uneven approach to water supply, predicated on local factors, was frustrating to some in the water industry. By the time consensus had shifted to a more centralised approach to water management in the twentieth century, successive governments had failed to successfully reform the sector to implement a singular vision.[13] With the privatisation of the water industry in 1989 and the perpetuation of regional private water companies, the sector continues to lack a singular approach to water supply.

The remainder of this chapter will focus on a number of key waterworks projects that broadly outline the development of the industry from the 1860s until the 1960s, focusing on Leeds, Liverpool and Birmingham, with reference to other important works during this period.

Leeds and the Washburn Valley

The state of water supply in Leeds was not in a good place by 1866. As noted, Leeds Corporation had gained control of the waterworks in 1852. One of the main drivers of municipalisation in Leeds was an inadequate supply of water due to unforeseen growth in demand. Despite the construction of Eccup reservoir in 1842, members of the waterworks committee were soon on the lookout for new sources of water. The corporation initially targeted the upper Wharfe Valley, West Yorkshire, but were beaten to that source by Bradford in the mid-1850s. They settled for the lower Wharfe Valley, constructing a pumping station on the river at Arthington in 1855.[14] It was not long, though, before the corporation was once again looking for new sources of water. Although Bradford profited from pure water in the upper Wharfe Valley, a number of mills along the river meant that by the time water reached Arthington it was quite badly polluted. A *Leeds Mercury* article from 1865 detailed a report from Dr. Hunter of the Privy Council that outlined the poor quality of water in Leeds: 'It is certain that the River Wharfe [...] receives large and constantly increasing quantities of filth'.[15] A much greater scheme would be needed to supply the town with the quantity and quality needed to meet demand.

The borough surveyor for Leeds, Edward Filliter, presented a report on a new source of water for the town to the corporation in September 1866.[16] He looked at four potential sources of water: the River Washburn, the River Nidd, the River Ure, and the rivers Burn and Laver, all in North Yorkshire. Of the four proposed sites, the Ure was discounted immediately due to the hardness of its water, which would not have been beneficial to the textile industry; the River Nidd possessed water that was soft but of questionable purity; but the rivers Washburn, Burn and Laver possessed soft and pure water. They also received a good amount of rainfall and were well located in relation to the already established Eccup reservoir, which meant that they could be connected to the town's existing water system more conveniently. Four reservoirs were proposed as part of the Washburn scheme: Lindley Wood, a reservoir to compensate for loss of water to the River Wharfe; Swinsty, a service reservoir; Fewston and Thruscross, both storage reservoirs. As the Washburn was the nearest geographically to Leeds and was the cheapest scheme at approximately £150,000, Filliter recommended the Washburn 'in respect of both economy and quality'.[17]

The scheme was not universally popular. Some of the opposition that centred on concerns with the landscape will be returned to in Chapter 2, but there were also concerns both within and outside the corporation regarding the finances of the scheme. Editorials in the *Yorkshire Post*, a fiscally conservative newspaper, called for a better use of public finances than costly public works such as the Washburn scheme. When the estimated cost of the scheme was revised by Thomas Hawksley, who acted as a consultant engineer, from £150,000 to £410,000, the *Yorkshire Post* criticised the corporation for the unforeseen costs, adding that these criticisms were not made in political partisanship, 'but on the knowledge of facts in our possession'.[18] On the other hand, some criticised the corporation for being too frugal. William Wheelhouse, a former Conservative town councillor, pointed to how Filliter's recommendation was based on fiscal prudency, and suggested taking water from the Nidd as it would provide a larger and purer supply than what he deemed to be the temporary Washburn solution.[19] Within the council chamber, the Liberal councillor George Linsley argued that Leeds should not waste money on such a small stream as the Washburn and put their resources towards a scheme from the Lake District. His characterisation of the Lake District summed up how many saw the area in terms of water supply in the nineteenth century: 'the lakes were natural reservoirs – God's reservoirs – for the supply of the large towns of England'.[20]

The scheme also encountered opposition from local landowners, who registered their feelings during the parliamentary process. A number of petitions were submitted opposing the scheme; however, the main opposition came from the local landowner F. H. Fawkes. Fawkes owned land around the proposed Lindley Wood reservoir and, as a landowner in the south of the valley, had previously opposed waterworks in the area. He campaigned against the waterworks, writing several missives published in the Leeds newspapers. One such letter in 1866 lambasted the chairman of the waterworks committee, R. M. Carter, for suggesting in public that he supported a gravitation scheme in the valley, which he had been opposed to since 1851.[21]

Fawkes was one of the few opponents of the scheme who had the resources to object to the Leeds waterworks bill in Parliament. Municipal authorities and private water companies needed the permission of Parliament to build large structures outside their municipal boundaries: indeed, one of the reasons why municipal government took responsibility of water supply was because they were better placed financially and legally to gain statutory powers.[22] Water authorities and their engineers would put the case to parliamentarians, with opponents of the bill bringing reasons as to why schemes should not be allowed to progress. Due to the vast amount of money needed to oppose a bill in Parliament, legal opposition was beyond many who would be affected by the scheme.[23] As such, opposition in Parliament usually rested on pre-existing land ownership and riparian rights, those who claimed to hold land adjacent to rivers who would be impacted by loss of water or land. In the case of some opponents, like Lady Franklin Russell who asserted riparian rights to a section of the River Washburn, claims were dismissed as lands did not quite touch the edge of rivers.[24] Other opponents proved to be more difficult to remove. Ultimately, the corporation entered into private negotiations with Fawkes – in return for dropping his opposition, Fawkes gained control over the location and general specifications of Lindley Wood reservoir, sole sporting rights around Farnley and Lindley Wood, and £45,000 for the use of land at Lindley Wood.[25] With Fawkes's opposition removed, the way was clear for the passing of the Leeds Corporation Waterworks Act 1867, which empowered the corporation to build four reservoirs in the Washburn Valley within a ten-year period and granted the powers to raise £400,000.

It would take another two years for work on the Washburn scheme to begin. The *Leeds Times* reported on the breaking of ground by the mayor, Alderman T. W. George, in August 1869 at Lindley Wood, the site of the first reservoir to be built: 'The first sod of the new reservoir was turned on the bank of the Washburn, and in as lovely a valley as it is possible to find even in this picturesque county of ours'.[26] The positive reporting of the event from the *Leeds Times* contrasts with that of the *Yorkshire Post*, which had been against the Washburn scheme from its inception. Using the inscribed silver spade presented to him by the waterworks committee for the event, 'the Mayor then formally excavated the first sod, and in doing so he unfortunately bent and considerably spoiled the symmetrical shape of the silver spade'.[27] The article continued: 'the Mayor then said he was exceedingly sorry that any mishap should have occurred [...] but he felt quite sure it would be no augury at all as to the progress of their undertaking'.[28] How much of an ill omen this turned out to be will be discussed in the following chapter.

Needless to say, construction was not particularly straightforward. There were a number of issues with the landscape that made construction more difficult than anticipated, including cracks in the land and difficulty forming a stable foundation. It also made the project more expensive. As Table 1.1 shows, the costs of the scheme had outstripped the £400,000 estimate by 1873, before substantive work had begun on Fewston and Thruscross reservoirs.[29] An editorial in the *Leeds Mercury* noted somewhat optimistically that £250,000 would 'probably' be required to finish the works, a number that foreshadowed 'an unpleasant increase in local taxation'.[30] The waterworks committee requested a report from Hawksley and Filliter 'without a day's unnecessary delay' on the suitability of moving the proposed Thruscross reservoir, and how much further capital would be required to complete the scheme. A report was submitted by the engineers at the following meeting, stating that £200,000 would be required to complete the existing works, citing money spent on the purchase of land,

Table 1.1: Costs of the Washburn Valley scheme, 1870–1875.

	Cost of Act of Parliament, wages, purchase of land	Washburn Foot	Lindley Wood reservoir	Swinsty reservoir	Fewston reservoir	Valuation of Pool Mill	Gravitation mains	Total
1870	£109,102	£10,560	£27,392	£495	£854	£4,026	-	£152,429
1873	£131,993	£10,609	£121,836	£61,929	£1,720	-	£76,924	£405,011
1875	£143,626	£12,325	£175,453	£121,417	£7,066	-	£90,593	£550,480

the increase in costs of labour and materials since 1866, and problems with the land at Lindley Wood. They suggested if powers of borrowing were to be sought from Parliament that £400,000 should be requested in order to build a system capable of supplying water to the town for twenty years. This discussion, however, led to another proposal two years later. Filliter suggested to the committee to suspend the building of Thruscross reservoir indefinitely, and instead enlarge the already established Eccup reservoir.[31] An Improvement Act was secured in 1877 granting Leeds the ability to enlarge Eccup and, crucially, secure an extra £200,000 to finish the works.

With work moved over to Eccup, the Washburn scheme finished in 1879 with the opening of Fewston reservoir. At a small ceremony the civic value was stressed, an attempt to build an early link between the countryside and the town. The mayor and waterworks committee member Alderman Robert Addyman responded to criticism received over the expenditure of the scheme, stating that: 'those stupendous works had been carried out without a single penny of rate having been levied upon the town [...] there ought to be no more grumbling heard from the ratepayers about the expense of the scheme, because they had not paid one farthing towards it'.[32] The mayor further noted that it was an important day in the history of Leeds, 'which would be of interest when all present at the ceremony were gone'.[33] Hawksley proclaimed that when the enlargement of Eccup reservoir was completed, 'Leeds would be in possession of one of the finest, if not the very finest, waterworks in the United Kingdom'.[34] While Leeds had, indeed, secured a fine gathering grounds, grander waterworks elsewhere in the country were yet to come.

Liverpool and Vyrnwy

Unlike Leeds and the Washburn Valley, the construction of Liverpool Corporation's Vyrnwy reservoir was long in the making. After becoming one of the first large municipal authorities to take ownership of their town's waterworks in 1847, Liverpool proceeded to investigate several potential sources of water, with Rivington reservoir on the West Pennine Moors in Lancashire completed in 1856. However, the town was soon looking for new sources of water. With daily consumption around thirty gallons per day by 1864, the resources of Rivington were put under strain, resulting in the disruption of constant supply. While Yarrow reservoir, a supplementary reservoir to Rivington on the River Yarrow, was undertaken in 1867, it was clear that a new source of water was needed to fulfil increasing demand.[35] In 1866, the same year that the Washburn scheme was proposed in Leeds, the water engineer for Liverpool, Thomas Duncan, prepared a report on potential sites of water. Duncan looked at a number of sites including: Windermere, Haweswater and Ullswater in the Lake District; the Rivers Hodder and Ribble in the Forest of Bowland, Lancashire; and a number of rivers and bodies of water in Wales, including Bala Lake (Llyn Tegid) and the River Dee. After examining all of these proposed sites, Duncan concluded that the only viable site was Bala Lake, favourable because of the quality of the water it held and the geology of the lake that meant it could be engineered effectively.[36]

Despite the pressing need for more water, the water committee did not act on Duncan's report. Duncan died in 1866, so the committee turned to Joseph Jackson to prepare a new report in 1873. As J. F. Bateman outlined in his 1875 report for the committee on potential water sources, Liverpool had managed to maintain a water supply from Rivington due to greater than average rainfall during the late 1860s, as well as the introduction of infrastructural improvements by the corporation's engineer George Deacon, that helped to tackle waste.[37] However, supply was far from constant, sometimes only available for three hours a day. This clearly renewed the vigour of the water committee to find a more permanent and sustainable solution.

Joseph examined the same sites that Duncan had in 1866, with the addition of the River Wyre near Blackpool. Unlike Duncan, Brown dismissed Bala Lake as a potential source, citing a number of changes that had taken place between 1866 and 1873, including the construction of a railway along one side of the lake that would make engineering work difficult. Brown advocated for the River Wyre, which held water of a similar quality to Rivington and, being closer to the Liverpool, represented a cheaper scheme than other proposed sites, such as Haweswater.[38] Clearly unsure as to which route to take, in 1875 the water committee commissioned further reports from two of the most renowned water engineers of the nineteenth century: J. F. LaTrobe Bateman and Thomas Hawksley. Liverpool Corporation had experience working with Hawksley, having employed him to design and construct Rivington reservoir, while during the 1870s Bateman was employed by, among other authorities, Manchester, to help plan the waterworks at Thirlmere.

Having reviewed the sites and the conclusions of Duncan and Brown, Bateman concurred with Brown that Bala Lake would be unsuitable owing to the changes that had taken place in the area, as well as concluding that Bala Lake would not offer as much water to Liverpool as Duncan had suggested. Bateman, though, also dismissed Brown's endorsement of the River Wyre, taking exception to Brown's proposal to build one large reservoir at Bleasdale that would collect both pure and turgid water running down the hillsides. He also questioned Brown's estimates regarding water supply and the cost of the scheme, which Bateman adjusted to be around £2.3 millon, as well as Brown's assertion that the corporation should compensate local stakeholders with money rather than water, an unusual proposal given that manufacturers depended on reliable supplies of water to power their mills. Muddying the waters further, Bateman suggested that Liverpool should look to the Lake District, particularly Haweswater and Ullswater. Indeed, he proposed that Liverpool should bid jointly for this water with Manchester, an unrealistic proposition given the levels of civic rivalry at play during the second half of the nineteenth century.[39] As for Hawksley, he also dismissed Bala Lake because of the presence of railways in the area, as well as the proposed cost, which he placed at around £3 million. While Hawksley did not consider Haweswater and Ullswater, he did investigate Windermere, which he considered to be too expensive. Ultimately, Hawksley favoured the River Wyre, which he deemed to be able to provide Liverpool in excess of twenty million gallons per day, the estimated amount needed to supply the town comfortably, for around £2 million.[40]

After commissioning four reports by 1875, Liverpool Corporation was no closer to settling on a new source of water. Time was also against the town. Hawksley noted in his report that if the corporation acted in 1875, given the state of supply, the earliest the new works would be ready would be 1881, 'the latest period to which the introduction of an additional supply of water can be advisably deferred'.[41] One source of water that had not been considered, though, was the River Vyrnwy. Following a resolution by a subcommittee of the water committee, Deacon compiled a report on the suitability of Vyrnwy in 1877, noting that it was 'hitherto unknown except to the angler'.[42] Vyrnwy had previously been suggested by Bateman as a potential source in evidence he had given to the 1869 Royal Commission on water supply for London, but no town or city had seriously considered it up until this point.[43] Vyrnwy offered the possibility of, in time, delivering up to fifty million gallons of water a day to Liverpool.[44] The quality of the water was excellent, with little to no filtering required, while there were few riparian interests that would offer resistance to the proposal. Most importantly, Deacon estimated the cost of the scheme at £1.2 million, cheaper than other proposed sites.[45] Further endorsement was given by Dr J. Campbell Brown, who conducted tests on the purity of the Vyrnwy waters, remarking that

> it is superior to the present Rivington water, and would be a much safer supply. It is superior to the present supply of Manchester, Birmingham, and many other towns receiving water from sources of similar character. It is superior to Windermere, and practically as good as Ullswater and the main feeders of Bala Lake.[46]

A final report by Alderman W. B. Forwood for the water committee summarised the positives and negatives of both schemes – ultimately, both Haweswater and Vyrnwy would provide ample, good quality water, with minor interference from riparian landowners. The difference between the two was the cost – Haweswater was estimated to cost around £1.5 million, whereas Vyrnwy was estimated at around £1.2 million.[47] At a time when councils consisted of a number of hawkish members mindful of overzealous municipal expenditure, as with Leeds, the lower cost of the scheme won the day for Vyrnwy.

While the proposal faced opposition in Parliament, as did most waterworks schemes, Liverpool managed to successfully progress their bill in 1880, which gave them powers to purchase land compulsorily for seven years in order to build the reservoir. As with Leeds, there were concessions in the bill, most notably that a new school and church was to be built by the corporation in Llanwddyn, as well as sporting rights over the reservoir being given to the Earl of Powis.[48] The construction of the reservoir, which began in 1881, went more smoothly than those in the Washburn Valley. The scheme was most notable for being the first in the United Kingdom to include a masonry dam, which allowed for a greater and stronger structure. The issues that arose with Vyrnwy, though, came behind the scenes. Liverpool Corporation had employed Thomas Hawksley as chief engineer on the project. Hawksley was one of the predominant water engineers of his day, having worked with Liverpool on its Rivington waterworks among some 120 other schemes during his career. However, four years into the Vyrnwy project, Hawksley announced his resignation from the scheme.

Concerns had been growing within the corporation about the ever-increasing cost of the waterworks, which was starting to surpass the estimate given to Parliament. In response, Hawksley told the waterworks committee that the estimate given was just that, an estimate, and that costs often increased during construction, as they had in the Washburn Valley. An incendiary meeting of the corporation took place on 4 March 1885.

It started with the explanation that the project costs had increased to around £2 million from £1.2 million. The chairman of the waterworks committee, Councillor Bower, noted some reasons for this increase: the corporation had been forced to compensate a number of stakeholders in the area, whose opposition had been raised in Parliament after the initial estimate had been submitted, while the embankment was higher than originally planned and the tunnel lower, which again added to the costs.[49]

This explanation did not satisfy some members of the corporation. Councillor Thomas Hughes raised a salient point for many – the Vyrnwy scheme had been chosen over Haweswater because it was cheaper. As noted earlier, the lower cost of Vyrnwy was the primary reason why the water committee, and ergo the corporation, chose that site, with Haweswater the more favoured site before costs were taken into account. Hughes continued that the original estimate for the embankment was around £300,000, while Hawksley now put the cost at around £800,000. Alderman A. B. Forwood was more forthright in his opinions, stating that Hawksley had deceived the corporation. After questioning the disparities between the original estimates and the current figures, he implored the chairman of the water committee 'to say whether an engineer who could so mislead the council did not require bringing before the committee for an explanation and whether they ought to endorse that further expenditure until a satisfactory explanation was given of the deceit that had been practised on the Council'. After refusing to retract the accusation of deceit, Forwood put forward an amendment to compel Hawksley and Deacon to compile separate reports on the reasons why expenditure had exceeded the estimates by so much.[50]

While this amendment was rejected, the criticism endured during this meeting was enough for Hawksley to resign. In a letter to the waterworks committee reprinted in the *Liverpool Mercury*, Hawksley took exception to the allegations, stating that:

> With these incidents and accidents past, present, and to come, I have no further concern than that it seems to be wished – a not very uncommon practice – to fasten upon the absent and unheard man – as a scapegoat, perhaps – the sins, if they be sins, of promoters, of opponents, of Parliament, of the Council, of the committee, and even of Nature herself.[51]

The criticism endured from councillors, though, was not the only reason that Hawksley stood down from his position. It was then revealed that the relationship between Hawksley and Deacon had been somewhat misrepresented. Hawksley had agreed to work for the corporation on the understanding that he would be chief engineer and that Deacon would be resident engineer and his subordinate. As later discovered by Alderman Forwood, the water committee had altered a committee resolution and changed the wording of Deacon's contract so that he would work 'in conjunction with' Hawksley; in other words, they would jointly be chief engineer. In a series of scathing articles published in the *Liverpool Mercury* following Hawksley's successful arbitration in 1888 against the corporation over his resignation, accusations were made on the relationship between Deacon and the chair of the water committee, Councillor Bower, which may have involved business dealings.[52] It also emerged that Hawksley had complained numerous times to Bower over the conduct of Deacon, who he deemed to be overstepping his mark and, at times, not displaying the requisite engineering knowledge for such a large project.[53]

In spite of the turmoil behind the scenes, the Lake Vyrnwy project was completed by Deacon and opened in 1892. In time, the waterworks would become a key civic landscape for Liverpool, an area utilised to promote civic identity, examined further in Chapter 3. But attitudes to Vyrnwy were not particularly optimistic when the scheme was completed. The *Liverpool Echo* reported that the scheme had cost around £2.5 million, in contrast to the projected £1.25 million. For the *Liverpool Mercury*, the incident with Hawksley showcased the worst aspects of municipal government: 'we venture to think, and we express our thoughts unreservedly, that no Corporation, great or small, ever committed itself so lamentably to its own honour and so disastrously to the interests of the ratepayers as has the Liverpool Corporation [...] over this Vyrnwy scheme'.[54] The scheme had become an acid test for the governance of the city, showing the importance of waterworks to the wider health of the council. Vyrnwy would go on to successfully supply the city with good quality water for decades, but its behind-the-scenes troubles highlight how fractious the execution of these great waterscapes could be.

Birmingham and the Elan Valley

Birmingham, the second city of the United Kingdom, joined other large towns and cities towards the end of the nineteenth century in sourcing a new and large watershed. Impetus was given to finding a new water supply in the 1870s due to the corporation finally purchasing the city's private waterworks. The water engineer Robert Rawlinson, in his report to the corporation on new sources of water for the city in 1871, urged the council to purchase the Birmingham Waterworks Company so that it could properly facilitate the large-scale project the city needed. Of the sources surveyed by Rawlinson for Birmingham, the rivers Elan and Claerwen in

Radnorshire, Wales, were deemed to be the most suitable, offering excellent quality water and enough quantity to supply the city for many years. Indeed, as the *Birmingham Daily Post* noted, 'As a gathering ground, Mr Rawlinson thinks nothing better could be found in the country, nor could better be desired.'[55]

The waterworks, though, were not purchased by the corporation until 1876. Unlike other towns and cities, the process of identification was more straightforward. Works were subsequently undertaken to sink new wells and to construct Shustoke reservoir on the River Bourne, meaning that the need for a large-scale waterworks did not arise until the late 1880s. By this point, population, as well as industrial demand, was rising in Birmingham. Additionally, like much of England, the city had undergone the drought of 1887 that threatened the ability of the corporation to offer constant water supply.[56] There was also another reason for haste: London. As noted in the case of Liverpool and Vyrnwy, various metropolitan authorities and engineers had been eying the Welsh gathering grounds for a number of years by 1890. While the Royal Commission into water supply for London had settled for the River Thames despite the presence of cholera, following Bateman's recommendations in 1869, future works in Wales to supply the capital had not been dismissed.[57] In targeting the rivers Elan and Claerwen, Birmingham was potentially making itself a rival to London, and any parliamentary process would no doubt favour the capital.[58] For a number of reasons, then, Birmingham had to act with some urgency by 1891 to secure the waters of the Elan Valley.

Unlike Liverpool, which sought multiple experts that provided different, competing visions, Birmingham employed James Mansergh to inspect the area recommended by Rawlinson nearly twenty years earlier. Mansergh concurred with Rawlinson's views on the Elan Valley and designed a plan to abstract water. The plan would be split into two. The first phase of the plan would concentrate on the River Elan, starting with the construction of Caban Coch reservoir at the confluence of the rivers Elan and Claerwen, two storage reservoirs at Pen y Garreg and Craig Goch, and a further submerged reservoir at Garreg Ddu. The second phase of the scheme would be built as and when required in the future, consisting of three reservoirs on the River Claerwen: Dol y Mynach, Cil-Oerwynt, and Pant y Beddau. Indeed, it was envisioned that Pant y Beddau would not be needed for another fifty years. Ultimately, the second phase of the scheme would never be built as originally conceived, but it highlights the forward planning of Mansergh and the Birmingham Corporation that such a scheme was devised.[59]

One of the intriguing aspects of the Elan Valley, so far as members of the corporation were concerned, was the almost virginal quality of the landscape. In passing judgement on the proposal, Sir Thomas Martineau, the former Lord Mayor of Birmingham and chairman of the water committee, spoke of his visit to the area:

> He stood on the hills and saw for a great distance all in the area of the watershed, and there was not a house, or an enclosure, or even a tree. The whole district was about as absolutely wild as any member of the Council had ever seen, and coming back to Birmingham and walking into our crowded streets it was difficult to believe that a district of that kind so free from habitations so absolutely wild in its character, existed within 90 miles of the city.[60]

There are several aspects to note here. First, the distinction between the wild but calm ambiance of the Elan Valley and the busy but chaotic nature of the city perfectly illustrates Maria Kaika's urban/rural dialectic: that to urban authorities the urban and the rural could embody competing characteristics simultaneously.[61] Second, the way in which the Elan Valley is defined as wild implies the ability of the corporation to tame the wilderness through urban engineering, a quality highlighted in American contexts by William Cronon.[62] Third, the picture of wilderness and isolation presented by Martineau was simply not true. As David Lewis Brown has highlighted, there were a number of residents and local interests affected by the proposed reservoir, so many that the bill to approve the Elan scheme took five months to ratify and included a hybrid select committee to hear all opposition, including those petitioning on behalf of the rural poor of the area. The bill was passed in June 1892 with no fewer than sixty clauses attached to help protect local interests.[63] Far from being an area untouched by humanity that Martineau depicted, the reservoirs would have a great impact on the local communities of Radnorshire, an impact that will be returned to in Chapter 6.

The construction of the reservoirs themselves was relatively straightforward. Work on Caban Coch began in 1894, while excavations for Pen y Garreg and Garreg Ddu started a year later. The landscape did provide problems for engineers to solve – Caban Coch is situated on Silurian grit, while the reservoirs further up the valley were built on a foundation of slate. One journalist praised the work of Mansergh in dealing with these issues effectively – as will be shown in Chapter 2, foundations could be very problematic for engineers both during and after construction.[64] By the time King Edward VII and Queen Alexandra came to open the works in 1903, Birmingham had managed to construct their enormous chain of reservoirs in just under ten years. The royal procession that opened the waterworks shared similarities with the opening of Leeds Town Hall – opened by Queen Victoria in 1857 – and other civic processions in the nineteenth century city that Simon Gunn has highlighted: the royal party was accompanied by the Lord Mayor and Lady Mayoress of Birmingham, who would be met at the filter beds by, in order, the Lord Bishop of St. David's, the chairman of the waterworks committee, members of the waterworks committee, then the engineer James Mansergh and the resident engineer. Despite not being in the city and, therefore, away from the urban arena, as Gunn has noted, this procession still gave physical form to social authority – members of the corporation were given precedence over the men who actually designed the scheme, and, therefore, we can see continuity with expressions of urban authority within the city itself.[65]

The interwar years

The quest to fulfil urban thirst did not stop after the First World War. Despite the harsh economic milieu of these years, several notable waterworks projects were undertaken and completed. Water projects during this period were predicated on two prominent factors: predictions of urban growth that required more water sooner rather than later, and issues with existing water supplies. On the former factor, it seems that a number of changes to living standards influenced the supposed growth of water usage: namely, tapped supply to individual homes and a decline in communal facilities.[66] A related factor was the development of suburban council housing in many English cities during the interwar years: Liverpool rehoused 140,000 residents into around 33,000 new houses, while in Manchester nearly 22,000 suburban council houses had been built by 1933.[67] The 1930s also saw the development of major municipal housing projects such as the Wythenshawe estate in Manchester and Quarry Hill in Leeds, all of which required more water for plumbed baths and toilets.

Issues with existing water supplies were felt particularly keenly during the drought years of the 1920s and 1930s: 1921, 1929 and 1933–34, which showed up inefficiencies in cities like Leeds. A number of large projects were either initiated or progressed during these years, including Manchester's Haweswater scheme, Ladybower reservoir serving the East Midlands, and Leeds's Leighton reservoir among others. Haweswater and Leighton are illustrative of the issues that water authorities encountered during this period. Parliamentary approval was given to Manchester to abstract water from Haweswater in 1919, in spite of opposition similar to that of Thirlmere, if not as voracious.[68] After a lengthy parliamentary process, which resulted in Manchester being compelled to share water from Haweswater with other municipalities in the local area, the chairman of the water committee, Sir Edward Holt, remarked that:

> It was a Bill that was an absolute necessity, for Manchester must have an adequate supply of water. The city had secured a supply for at least sixty years, and Manchester, if it had to progress, would need all the water it could get.[69]

This was not quite the case, though. Due to the impact of the First World War, the population of cities like Manchester did not increase at the expected rate. Additionally, Ritvo has argued that the estimates for water usage put forward by proponents of Haweswater were overgenerous, predicated on an ideology of ever-increasing demand.[70] Although there were changes in standards of living, many of the changes such as reliable piped supply to each house became more widespread towards the end of the 1930s and the start of the 1940s, meaning that this rise in living standards did not seriously affect water usage until after the Second World War.[71] By the time construction actually began, some ten years after Parliament had approved the project, the reservoir was not quite as necessary as first thought. Water from Haweswater did not reach Manchester until 1941.[72]

Leeds had to wait just as long as Manchester for their Leighton reservoir to bear fruit. First proposed in the 1890s and subject to parliamentary approval in 1901, a series of mishaps and mismanagement meant that the Ure Valley project was delayed by a number of years. Initially featuring five reservoirs including Leighton, it came to light that the landscape near Masham, North Yorkshire, was not suitable for reservoir development, with £300,000 wasted on Colsterdale reservoir, a site that was never finished. Attention turned to Leighton reservoir, but the interruption of the First World War and the poor economic environment of the 1920s meant that primary work on the reservoir was not finished until 1926, while water did not flow regularly to the city until the 1930s. As in Manchester, Leeds discovered that its much needed scheme was not, in fact, much needed because of infrastructural improvements that had been made before the First World War, as well as an unexpected decline in population growth during the interwar period. While towns and cities continued to eye the urban hinterland as a space of further expansion predicated on continued and sustained urban growth, a number of factors interceded to suggest that continued growth was not the only way to manage water supply.

The post-war years

Issues related to water supply reappeared after the Second World War. John Hassan has highlighted that, in contrast to the interwar years, demand after the Second World War increased at an unprecedented rate, particularly as the complex and growing requirements of heavy industry in parts of the North East, Yorkshire and South Wales needed to be met.[73] Additionally, water shortages were ever present throughout the 1950s, culminating in the drought of 1959.[74] It is within this context that the building of Rutland Water in the East Midlands, completed in 1976, was seen by local residents as aiding the provision of water for the nation. This, though, was not the case, as water continued to supply the local area even after the regional water boards were established.[75]

The state of the water industry was much changed from the second half of the nineteenth century. Water was not nationalised by post-war Labour governments despite it being Labour policy up until 1965.[76] There were various stakeholders in water supply that made nationalisation unfeasible, such as landowners, industrialists and river conservancy boards, to name a few.[77] Despite this, Hassan has highlighted attempts by central government to improve the water industry amid increased demand, leading to the 1963 Water Resources Act, which sought to radically reorganise the water industry, implementing centralised river authorities to directly manage and sustain rivers across the country.[78] The establishment of the river authorities under this act, followed by the establishment of the regional water boards in 1973, saw central government play an increasingly interventionist role in the governance of water without fully nationalising the industry.

The development of ministerial orders during the interwar and post-war periods made it easier to pass uncontroversial local government legislation. This had a large impact on water legislation, which often fell into this category, at least in the eyes of policy makers. Additionally, austerity following the end of the Second World War meant that central government did not have the resources to fund municipal authorities to build waterworks.[79] Indeed, Glen O'Hara has noted that in 1959 over fifty ministerial orders were passed that allowed authorities to slow or halt the release of water from reservoirs, indicating that measures were needed other than impounding more water.[80] However, growing demand mixed with dry weather led to the severe water shortage of 1959 that left the resources of cities like Leeds 'strained "to the limits"'. As time went by and economic recovery from the Second World War had taken hold, central government was more willing to invest in water schemes to combat shortages.[81]

The Leeds Corporation's waterworks committee began to move towards securing an additional source of water as early as 1952, perhaps prompted by the water shortage of 1949 that had seen storage levels fall to as low as a thirty-day supply.[82] Drought, a scarcity often produced as much by infrastructural frameworks of water management as by rainfall, often acted as an instigator for debate and reform, particularly regarding the inception of a national water grid in the twentieth century.[83] This can be seen in the political debates that took place within the waterworks committee during the 1950s, as Labour members used the issue of water shortages to homes and industry for political gain against the Conservative-led corporation.[84] In July 1952 the waterworks committee returned to the Washburn Valley, visiting the proposed site for a reservoir at Thruscross. A memorandum on the development of a new impounding reservoir in the Washburn Valley was subsequently approved by the committee later that year.[85] It was made clear during the 1950s that, unlike earlier plans for Thruscross reservoir from the 1870s, construction would require flooding the village of West End, the impact of which is explored in more detail in Chapter 6.

Soil tests were carried out in 1953; however, it was not until 1959 that affirmative action was taken by the corporation to request powers from Parliament to construct the reservoir for an estimated £1,600,000.[86] An editorial in the *Yorkshire Evening News* highlighted this drawn-out process, noting the lack of funding from central government during the immediate post-war period, which changed after the drought of 1959, illustrated in the deficiencies in the country's water supplies.[87] Due to the development of ministerial orders, there was no need to attempt a costly local government bill. Although Thruscross required the flooding of West End, much of the land had already been purchased by the Leeds Corporation in the early twentieth century in an attempt to abate pollution. There was, though, opposition to the scheme from local interests and members of Parliament, who were particularly concerned about access for farmers across the valley.[88] Negotiations between the corporation and the respective objectors led to all concerns being addressed, in particular the construction of a new road and the reconstruction of the local church, resulting in the passing of the Leeds Corporation (Thruscross Reservoir) Water Order in December 1960.[89]

Leeds was not the only city to return to watersheds that had provided in the past. Undergoing the same pressures as those in the West Riding of Yorkshire, Liverpool sought a new water supply in the 1950s. After once again considering a supply from the Lake District, they turned to the River Tryweryn, near Bala in Wales. Tryweryn had been mentioned as a potential source of water in the 1870s; however, its relative proximity to Lake Vyrnwy, which was already connected to Liverpool, made the scheme attractive. Liverpool proposed an eight-hundred-acre reservoir that required flooding the village of Capel Celyn. While Liverpool successfully completed construction of Llyn Celyn reservoir in 1965, the project stimulated a level of opposition not seen in Wales until that point. As noted above, taking water from Wales to supply English towns and cities was not novel by the 1960s, but Llyn Celyn helped to crystallise the intersection between water politics and emergent Welsh nationalism, becoming a bitter symbol of Welsh identity and complicating the idea of a national water story.[90]

A much less controversial return to Wales was undertaken by Birmingham. The second part of the Elan and Claerwen project was to construct three reservoirs on the River Claerwen. However, due to technological advancements, Birmingham Corporation decided to build one large reservoir. Parliamentary approval for Claerwen reservoir was given in 1946, with the reservoir classified as a high priority project following the Second World War. Construction started in the same year – not a moment too soon, given that Birmingham was struggling with supply for the first time since the 1880s. In 1952, the reservoir was officially opened by Queen Elizabeth II, mirroring the opening of the Elan Valley reservoirs by her great-grandfather in 1903.[91] While there was only one reservoir instead of the originally planned three, the enormous size of Claerwen reservoir compensated for this. The dam has a depth of 184 feet and is four miles in length, meaning that it stored 21.8 billion gallons of water, approximately the same as the three original Elan reservoirs combined.[92]

Manchester also tried to return to a profitable gathering ground, eyeing up Ullswater in the Lake District to add to Thirlmere and Haweswater. In an example of the cyclical nature of history, though, Manchester faced stringent opposition from local and regional interests who were concerned with the impact the reservoir would have on the local aesthetic. There were also increasing concerns in the 1960s about the ecological effects of reservoirs, seen most prominently in the opposition to Teesside's Cow Green reservoir.[93] Unlike the efforts of the Thirlmere Defence Association just under one hundred years previously, the defenders of Ullswater won the day, with the Ullswater bill defeated in Parliament in 1961. Manchester would eventually take water from Ullswater, gaining permission to abstract water from that lake and Windermere, but the use of underground pumps rather than the construction of a dam meant that both lakes remained untouched to the naked eye.[94]

To return to the case of Leeds, the construction of Thruscross reservoir was not as tumultuous as the building of the other reservoirs. The Thruscross reservoir built in the 1960s was quite different from the one originally envisioned by Edward Filliter in the 1860s, largely due to advances in engineering and water technology but also due to differences in design.[95] The original reservoir was due to have a watershed of 4,500 acres and a storage capacity of 540 million gallons, which was comparable with the other contemporary reservoirs.[96] The revised proposal saw the watershed increase to 7,120 acres and the storage capacity to 1,725 million gallons.[97] As such, the reservoir is much larger than the original three;

while the surface area is less than that of Swinsty and Fewston reservoirs, the greater depth means that the storage capacity dwarfs the reservoirs in the lower valley.

Although little detail of progress is provided by the committee minutes, the *Yorkshire Evening Post* provided infrequent reports on the development of the reservoir, which are examined in more detail in Chapter 2. Despite not being completed by the original target of 1965, construction was completed by January 1966, when a civic ceremony with the waterworks committee took place. After the chairman of the committee, Alderman William Hemmingway, had shut the dam valve, the *Evening Post* reporter Malcolm Barker brought him a cup with water from the reservoir, 'the first water from Thruscross'.[98] The official opening by the Lord Mayor, Alderman J. S. Walsh, took place on 7 September 1966, with sentiment echoing the completion of Fewston reservoir in 1879: 'Its completion is a notable occasion not only for all connected with the city's waterworks committee and the Leeds City Council but also for everyone living within the undertaking area of supply'.[99] Both occasions marked an important milestone in the history of Leeds, as well as the completion of the work Edward Filliter had set out to undertake in 1866, one hundred years prior, showing that the provision of water remained an important part of civic identity.[100]

Conclusion

The water industry changed greatly in the one hundred years covered in this chapter. It is almost impossible to cover all aspects of the industry in detail – there were great changes in sanitation and approaches to water and public health. But in introducing some of the larger waterworks undertaken in England and Wales in the late nineteenth and twentieth centuries, it is possible to see the broad strokes of development. There was change over this period: reservoirs and waterworks projects became increasingly larger owing to technological developments and increased demand. As seen after the Second World War, opposition to waterworks projects in certain areas was beginning to be successful, the start of a sea change in how authorities would approach water management that was not solely predicated on building ever more reservoirs. There was also continuity: as will be explored in more detail in future chapters, the belief in the engineer's ability to tame the wilderness remained resolute. Communities were affected as badly in the 1960s as they were in the 1860s, as seen in the number of examples cited in the twentieth century that included flooding villages. It is also clear that, until the 1970s, waterworks were driven by local authorities and dictated by local needs and local factors. This sense of the local and its placement in a national context is critical to how reservoirs and waterworks were conceptualised as extensions of the city in the countryside and a key theme of the book. To paraphrase Thomas Barclay, whose quote opened this chapter, the task would remain vast well into the twentieth century.

This chapter has provided an introduction to the main case studies looked at in *Waterscapes*. It is possible to see that the impact of reservoir projects was not just consigned to the delivery of water. In future chapters, themes such as the cultural landscape, recreation and environment will further expand on this, but this chapter has shown how politics, economics and expertise all intersected with and helped to shape urban waterworks. The impact of waterworks was also not uniform – while Birmingham was able to establish a successful waterworks without many issues, Liverpool's Vyrnwy project was quite unpopular during and immediately after its construction due to the amount of money that had been spent on the project as well as the clear mismanagement of the project by the water committee, which led Thomas Hawksley to resign. As with criticisms of Leeds's Washburn Valley scheme, Vyrnwy would, in time, become more popular with urban residents. The reservoir would form a key link with the city and become an emblem of civic identity. How civic identity intersected with changes to the environment is the subject of the following chapter.

Notes

1. Thomas Barclay, *The Future Water Supply of Birmingham* (Cornish Brothers, 1892), 1.
2. Barclay, *Future Water Supply of Birmingham*, 29.
3. Harriet Ritvo, *The Dawn of Green: Manchester, Thirlmere, and Modern Environmentalism* (University of Chicago Press, 2009).
4. Richard Samuel Pepperd, 'The Growth and Development of Leeds Waterworks Undertakings, 1694–1852' (unpublished doctoral thesis, University of Leeds, 1973), 58.
5. Robert Millward, *Private and Public Enterprise in Europe: Energy, Telecommunications and Transport, 1830–1990* (Cambridge University Press, 2005), 44.
6. Bill Luckin, *Pollution and Control: A Social History of the Thames in the Nineteenth Century* (Adam Hilger, 1986). For a wider debate on the development of infrastructure and public health, see Christopher Hamlin, *Public Health and Social Justice in the Age of Chadwick: Britain, 1800–1854* (Cambridge University Press, 1998).
7. Sally Sheard, 'Water and Health: The Formation and Exploitation of the Relationship in Liverpool, 1847–1900', *Transactions of the Historic Society of Lancashire and Cheshire* 143 (1994): 151.
8. Sheard, 'Water and Health', 142.
9. Leeds Waterworks Act 1837, 7 Will. 4 & 1 Vict. c. lxxxiii. Available at https://www.legislation.gov.uk/ukla/Will4and1Vict/7/83/contents/enacted.

10. Shane Ewen, 'Sheffield's Great Flood of 1864: Engineering Failure and the Municipalisation of Water', *Environment and History* 20, no. 2 (2014), 205, https://doi.org/10.3197/096734014X13941952680954.

11. John Broich, *London: Water and the Making of the Modern City* (University of Pittsburgh Press, 2013), 142.

12. Judith Thornton and Peter Pearson, 'Bristol Water Works Company: A Study of Nineteenth Century Resistance to Local Authority Purchase Attempts', *Water History* 5, no. 3 (2013), 307–30, https://doi.org/10.1007/s12685-013-0083-1.

13. Glen O'Hara, *The Politics of Water in Post-War Britain* (Palgrave Macmillan, 2017).

14. Andrew McTominey, 'Bad Neighbours? Water Supply and the Civic Rivalry of Leeds and Bradford, *c.*1850–1887', *International Journal of Regional and Local History* 12, no. 1 (2017), 31, https://doi.org/10.1080/20514530.2017.1353769.

15. 'The Health of Leeds: Dr. Hunter's Report', *Leeds Mercury*, 1 December 1865, 4.

16. Leeds Corporation, 'Leeds Waterworks Committee Minutes, volume 2, 1861–1870', West Yorkshire Archive Service (WYAS), LLC22/1/2, 223.

17. Edward Filliter, 'Report on the Best Mode of Obtaining an Additional and Purer Supply of Water for the Borough of Leeds' (1866), 9–13.

18. 'Editorial', *Yorkshire Post*, 26 January 1867, 4.

19. William St James Wheelhouse, 'The Washburn Scheme', *Yorkshire Post*, letter to the editor, 5 October 1866, 3.

20. 'Leeds Town Council', *Yorkshire Post*, 11 October 1866, 4.

21. F. H. Fawkes, 'Leeds Water Supply', *Leeds Mercury*, letter to the editor, 2 October 1866, 7.

22. Millward, *Private and Public Enterprise in Europe*, 44.

23. 'Private Bill in Parliament', *The Yorkshire Post*, 21 February 1867, 2.

24. 'Local News', *Leeds Times*, 29 June 1867, 3

25. Marion Sharples, *The Fawkes Family and Their Estates in Wharfedale, 1819–1936* (Thoresby Society, 1997), 51.

26. 'Local News: The Future Water Supply of Leeds', *Leeds Times*, 28 August 1869, 3.

27. 'The Future Water Supply of Leeds', *Yorkshire Post*, 24 August 1869, 3.

28. 'The Future Water Supply of Leeds', *Yorkshire Post*, 24 August 1869, 3.

29. Information for this table was collected from the following sources: costs for 1870 are from 'The Undertaking of the Leeds Corporation', *Leeds Mercury*, 4 May 1871, 7; costs for 1873 are from 'Leeds Water Supply', *Leeds Mercury*, 31 May 1873, 11; and costs for 1875 are from 'The Progress of the Waterworks', *Leeds Mercury*, 3 April 1875, 10.

30. 'Editorial', *Leeds Mercury*, 16 May 1873, 2.

31. Leeds Corporation, 'Leeds Waterworks Committee Minutes, volume 3, 1870–1878', WYAS, LLC22/1/3, 129–130, 132–36, 226–7.

32. 'The Leeds Water Supply: Completion of the Washburn Scheme', *Yorkshire Post*, 4 November 1879, 5.

33. 'The Leeds Water Supply: Completion of the Washburn Scheme', *Yorkshire Post*, 4 November 1879, 5.

34. 'The Leeds Water Supply: Completion of the Washburn Scheme', *Yorkshire Post*, 4 November 1879, 5.

35. John Frederick Bateman, 'New Water Supply: Report of Mr John Frederick Bateman C.E., F.R.S.', 1875, Liverpool Record Office (LRO) 352.6 WAT, 3–7.

36. Bateman, 'New Water Supply', 7–8.

37. Bateman, 'New Water Supply'.

38. Bateman, 'New Water Supply', 8–12.

39. Bateman, 'New Water Supply', 14–31.

40. Thomas Hawksley, 'New Water Supply: Report of Mr. T. Hawksley, C.E.', 1875, LRO 352.6 WAT.

41. Hawksley, 'New Water Supply', 23.

42. George Deacon, 'Report of the Borough and Water Engineer as to a Supply from the Upper Waters of the Vyrnwy in North Wales', 1877, LRO 352.6 WAT, 9.

43. Broich, *London: Water*, 49.

44. Deacon, 'Report', 11.

45. Deacon, 'Report', 17.

46. J. Campbell Brown, 'Appendix to Supplementary Report of the Borough and Water Engineer as to a Supply of Water from the Upper Waters of the River Vyrnwy in North Wales', 1878, LRO 352.6 WAT, ii.

47. W. B. Forwood, 'Water Supply: Notes and Observations', 1879, LRO 352.6 WAT.

48. Liverpool Corporation Waterworks Act 1880, 43 & 44 Vict. c. cxliii, 7–32. Available at https://www.legislation.gov.uk/ukla/Vict/43-44/143/contents/enacted.

49. 'Liverpool City Council', *Liverpool Mercury*, 5 March 1885, 3.

50. 'Liverpool City Council', *Liverpool Mercury*, 5 March 1885, 3.

51. 'The Cost of the Vyrnwy Scheme', *Liverpool Mercury*, 30 March 1885, 6.

52. 'The Vyrnwy Scandal: Hawksley v. the Corporation I. Introduction', *Liverpool Mercury*, 19 Sept 1888, 5.

53. 'The Vyrnwy Scandal: Hawksley v. the Corporation III. Mr Deacon's Agreement', 21 Sept 1888, 5.

54. 'The Vyrnwy Scandal: Hawksley v. the Corporation I. Introduction', *Liverpool Mercury*, 19 Sept 1888, 5.

55. 'Birmingham Water Supply: Report of Mr. Rawlinson, C.B.', *Birmingham Daily Post*, 18 May 1871, 5.

56. 'Birmingham City Council', *Birmingham Mail*, 7 April 1891, 3.

57. Broich, *London: Water*, 50.

58. Broich, *London: Water*, 50.

59. 'The Birmingham Water Scheme', *Birmingham Daily Post*, 13 October 1891, 4; David Lewis Brown, *The Elan Valley Clearance* (Logaston Press, 2019), 41.

60. 'Birmingham City Council', *Birmingham Mail*, 7 April 1891, 3.

61. Maria Kaika, *City of Flows: Modernity, Nature, and the City* (Routledge, 2005), 14.

62. William Cronon, 'Modes of Prophecy and Production: Placing Nature in History', *The Journal of American History* 76, no. 4 (1990), 1122–31, https://doi.org/10.2307/2936590.

63. Brown, *Elan Valley Clearance*, 22–38.

64. 'Feat of Engineering: Three Great Dams at Elan Valley', *Birmingham Newspaper Scrapbook, part 2, 1867–1907*, Library of Birmingham, LF 71.061 243371.

65. City of Birmingham Waterworks Department, 'Visit of Their Majesties the King and Queen to the Elan Valley Works, Rhayader: Official Programme', 1904, Library of Birmingham, L/./45/31; 202633.

66. John Hassan, *A History of Water in Modern England and Wales* (Manchester University Press, 1998), 53–5.

67. Charlotte Wildman, *Urban Redevelopment and Modernity in Liverpool and Manchester, 1918–1939* (Bloomsbury Academic, 2016), 22–3.

68. Ritvo, *Dawn of Green*, 163–4.

69. 'Manchester Water: Supply Assured for Sixty Years', *Manchester Evening News*, 3 December 1919, 4.

70. Ritvo, *Dawn of Green*, 164. Also see Andrew McTominey, 'Waterworks, Municipal Government and the Environment in Twentieth-Century Britain', *Urban History* 51, no. 3 (2024): 600–615, https://doi.org/10.1017/S0963926823000597.

71. Hassan, *History of Water*, 55.

72. Ritvo, *Dawn of Green*, 168.

73. Hassan, *History of Water*, 85, 87.

74. Vanessa Taylor et al., 'Drought Is Normal: The Socio-Technical Evolution of Drought and Water Demand in England and Wales, 1893–2006', *Journal of Historical Geography* 35, no. 3 (2009): 568–91, https://doi.org/10.1016/j.jhg.2008.09.004.

75. Denis Cosgrove et al., 'Landscape and Identity at Ladybower Reservoir and Rutland Water', *Transactions of the Institute of British Geographers* 21, no. 3 (1996): 545, https://doi.org/10.2307/622595.

76. Christine S. McCulloch, 'The Water Resources Board: England and Wales' Venture into National Water Resources Planning, 1964–1973', *Water Alternatives* 2, no. 3 (2009): 462.

77. Robert Millward, 'The Political Economy of Urban Utilities', in *The Cambridge Urban History of Britain, Volume 3: 1840–1950*, ed. Martin Daunton (Cambridge University Press, 2001), 348.

78. Hassan, *History of Water*, 86; O'Hara, *Politics of Water*, 89.

79. John Sheail, 'Local Legislation: Its Scope and Context', *Archives* 30 no. 113 (2005): 48, https://doi.org/10.3828/archives.2005.3.

80. O'Hara, *Politics of Water*, 31.

81. O'Hara, *Politics of Water*, 90.

82. Leeds Corporation, 'Leeds Waterworks Committee Minutes, volume 12, 1949–1961', WYAS, LLC22/1/12, 24.

83. Taylor et al., 'Drought Is Normal', 578.

84. 'Aldermen Clash on Waterworks "Lost Years" Criticism: Ministry Asked Leeds to Defer New Schemes', *Yorkshire Post*, 3 November 1949, 6.

85. Leeds Corporation, 'Leeds Waterworks Committee Minutes, volume 12', 121, 131.

86. Leeds Corporation, 'Leeds Waterworks Committee Minutes, volume 12', 142, 335–6.

87. Hassan, *History of Water*, 90.

88. W. A. Evans to Messrs Sharpe, Pritchard and Company, 27 June 1960, Leeds CB Thruscross Reservoir: Water Order 1960, National Archives, HLG 127/29; Parliamentary correspondent, 'Minister May Visit Doomed Village', *Yorkshire Evening Post*, 2 June 1960, 3.

89. Church commissioners to secretary of ministry of housing and local government, 15 August 1960, Leeds CB Thruscross Reservoir: Water Order 1960, National Archives, HLG 127/29; Leeds municipal correspondent, 'Work on New Dam Starts in Spring', *Yorkshire Post*, 9 December 1960, 13.

90. Ed Atkins, 'Building a Dam, Constructing a Nation: The "Drowning" of Capel Celyn', *Journal of Historical Sociology* 31, no. 4 (2018): 455–68, https://doi.org/10.1111/johs.12186.

91. Birmingham Corporation, *City of Birmingham Waterworks* (James Upton Ltd, 1967), 16–18.

92. Birmingham Corporation, *The Elan Valley Works of the Birmingham Corporation* (Birmingham Corporation, 1968), 2.

93. Christine S. McCulloch, 'Political Ecology of Dams in Teesdale', in *Long-Term Benefits and Performance of Dams*, ed. Henry Hewlett (Thomas Telford, 2004), 49–58.

94. Ritvo, *Dawn of Green*, 168–70.

95. Norman Smith, *A History of Dams* (Peter Davies, 1971), 234.

96. The Architect, 'New Waterworks in Yorkshire', *Leeds Mercury*, 18 September 1871, 4.

97. Local government correspondent, '300 Years of Progress: Population Supplied by Undertaking Has Increased Hundredfold', *Yorkshire Post*, 7 September 1966, 11.

98. Malcolm Barker, 'First Cup from New Reservoir', *Yorkshire Evening Post*, 5 January 1966, 10.

99. Dennis Bolton, 'Thruscross Reservoir Holds Extra 50 Days' Supply: Safeguard for Leeds Consumers', *Yorkshire Post*, 7 September 1966, 10; Local government correspondent, 'Reservoir Opened in the Sunshine: Delayed Scheme Comes to Fruition', *Yorkshire Post*, 8 September 1966, 14.

100. Debates around the decline of civic pride have developed over recent years. Following Simon Gunn's assertion that civic pride peaked in the 1870s and declined up until 1914, historians such as Tom Hulme, Charlotte Wildman and Peter Shapely have argued that civic pride remained an important feature of urban life beyond the First World War and, indeed, into the post-Second World War period. See Simon Gunn, *The Public Culture of the Victorian Middle Class* (Manchester University Press, 2000), 163–86; Tom Hulme, '"A Nation of Town Criers": Civic Publicity and Historical Pageantry in Inter-War Britain', *Urban History* 44, no. 2 (2017): 270–92, https://doi.org/10.1017/S0963926816000262; Charlotte Wildman, '*A City Speaks*: The Projection of Civic Identity in Manchester', *Modern British History* 23, no. 1 (2012): 80–99, https://doi.org/10.1093/tcbh/hwr067; Peter Shapely, 'Civic Pride and Redevelopment in the Post-War British City', *Urban History* 39, no. 2 (2012): 310–28, https://doi.org/10.1017/S0963926812000077.

Chapter 2

Slips and spillages: reservoirs and the environment

One evening, a reservoir outside Sheffield gave way, spilling water down towards the town. The physical damage of the event is hard to overstate: several villages and suburbs were submerged by the rampaging water, while over two hundred people lost their lives.[1] Another incident saw a town evacuated as the reservoir above the area began to give way. Both incidents were caused by neglect: the former being poorly built, the latter poorly designed and maintained.[2] The difference between the two was in their timing – the first refers to the collapse of Dale Dyke reservoir in 1864, which led to the largest 'natural' disaster in Victorian Britain. The second refers to Toddbrook reservoir, which began to collapse in August 2019. While they occurred over one hundred and fifty years apart, both incidents point to the dangers inherent in water engineering. Gravitation reservoirs, the predominant form of reservoir for water supply, are built at a higher altitude so that water will gravitate down towards the area of supply. Any weakness in the structure could be damaging and deadly. Both incidents highlight the continued need to properly maintain water engineering structures after construction. They also illustrate that second nature and the Promethean project – humanity's supposed ability to successfully tame nature – were never absolute.[3]

It is a testament to the ability of engineers throughout the nineteenth and twentieth centuries that many waterworks projects were well built and have, so far, stood the test of time. However, that does not mean that taming the wilderness was ever easy, or that nature never fought back. Despite the assertions of engineers and municipal authorities, nature could never be fully tamed. This chapter builds on the previous by examining the environmental aspects of reservoir construction in more detail to show the importance of focusing on the environmental impact of infrastructural development. In highlighting some of the concerns and troubles that engineers encountered during and after construction in the Washburn Valley, Vyrnwy Valley and Claerwen Valley, it challenges the inherent confidence of the engineer to tame the wilderness, a mantra that continued to resonate with municipal authorities well into the twentieth century. In so doing, it contributes to research that has explored the hinterland exchange, as well as broader environmental histories of landscape development.[4] As with other themes explored here, this chapter shows differences of approach across place and time, but also highlights similarities that weave individual case studies into a national picture.

Mastery over nature?

Reservoir disasters were not particularly common in nineteenth-century Britain, but when they did occur they sparked understandable fears. By the mid-1860s two prominent disasters had occurred in Britain: the aforementioned collapse of Dale Dyke in 1864 and the collapse of Bilberry dam, near Huddersfield, in 1852. Both incidents became associated with national tragedy; at Holmfirth eighty-one people lost their lives, while between two hundred and fifty and three hundred people drowned in Sheffield. There was large-scale destruction to property, with hundreds of homes destroyed and thousands flooded. Both reservoirs were earthen embankment dams, the predominant method of reservoir construction well into the twentieth century, despite fears around safety. Remarkably, no tests were carried out at Bilberry before the reservoir was constructed. It is no surprise, then, that fault lines in the area had not been discovered. The reservoir was also not designed to anticipate extremely heavy rainfall, making it susceptible to flooding.[5]

As for Dale Dyke, environmental factors discovered after the disaster took the blame. Post-disaster excavations had revealed a landslip that was thought to have taken place over a hundred years previously, an issue previously unknown to the engineers as the reservoir foundation had not dug down far enough to discover it. Even though remedial work had been carried out on the reservoir after leaks were found, it was not enough to contend with the unpredictability of nature. This is, as Shane Ewen has highlighted, a salient point regarding all rural engineering: that 'the changeability of environmental conditions rendered it impossible to maintain complete control'.[6] And yet complete control was what water authorities yearned for and engineers promised.

Ewen has highlighted that both of these disasters stemmed from an evolving engineering knowledge that privileged previous experience over experimentation. It is for this reason that earthen embankment reservoirs remained the main design template into the twentieth century, at which point the masonry dam took precedence.[7] Nevertheless, the disasters at Bilberry and Dale Dyke remained in the collective memory and were invoked elsewhere. A case in point is Leeds's Washburn Valley scheme. While the borough surveyor for Leeds, Edward Filliter, had confidence in the integrity of the Washburn landscape when he proposed the scheme in 1866, not all were convinced. C. L. Dresser, a notable local figure and prominent opponent of the Washburn scheme, wrote a letter that was published in both the *Leeds Mercury* and the *Yorkshire Post*.[8] He wrote that he had examined the valley himself, using his experience as a surveyor to find that 'two, if not three, of the reservoirs are so placed that it is impossible for them, as at present planned, to be constructed with safety'.[9] He cited the prevalence of landslips that had taken place in the area and drew parallels with the dam disasters at Dale Dyke and Holmfirth, lambasting the council for taking the quicker and cheaper option of constructing reservoirs in the valley when other schemes were available, in particular a scheme to take water from the Lake District, which he favoured.[10] His arguments, very much a lone voice, were not enough to dissuade the Leeds Corporation.

As Dresser predicted, problems were encountered with the landscape during the construction of the reservoirs, further emphasising Ewen's argument that established engineering knowledge and precedent was privileged. A report presented to the waterworks committee by Filliter and Hawksley in 1873 outlined the difficulties that had been encountered at Lindley Wood and Swinsty. At Lindley Wood, the substrata on which the reservoir was being built had become 'upheaved, broken and pushed in a very unusual manner and to a very unusual depth'.[11] In addition, at Swinsty a large crack in the substrata had been discovered that 'descended to a great depth'.[12] Further issues were reported by the *Leeds Mercury*, including the weir at the foot of the River Washburn, where the Washburn meets the River Wharfe, which had been damaged by partial flooding, an incident that could have been avoided with 'but a little care and observation'.[13] The *Yorkshire Post* reported in 1874 that in addition to the issues with the substrata at Lindley Wood, labelling the judgement of the engineers as 'unsound', a landslip had occurred. In excavating the land for the reservoir by-wash, 'an immense quantity of earth descended from the hill-side'.[14] While the *Yorkshire Post* was mainly critical of the engineers from a fiscal point of view, it is clear that Dresser had forewarned of these issues.

Lessons were learnt during the construction of the Washburn reservoirs, again emphasising the evolving nature of engineering knowledge that Ewen highlighted.[15] When questioned on the suitability of the land at the proposed site of Fewston reservoir, Hawksley and Filliter argued that they were satisfied with the location, but modifications to the plans were necessary 'to suit the nature and the quality of the ground'.[16] In addition to this, the committee hired Professor David Ansted, a reputable geologist from Kings College, London, to survey the land.[17] Thus, the waterworks committee and the engineers were beginning to pay more attention to the intricacies of the landscape. This also shows that experience could and did help to develop engineering knowledge and practice. The issues with the Washburn landscape, though, would not finish with the completion of Fewston reservoir in 1879.

On 17 September 1880, less than a year after the opening of Fewston reservoir, an article published in the *Yorkshire Post*, reprinted from the *Wharfedale and Airedale Observer*, reported that an alarming subsidence of the land had taken place at Fewston village:

> [I]n some places the ground has sunk no less than two feet and large cracks in the soil, from six inches to a foot in width, may be seen in several places. Most of the buildings are cracking and shifting to an alarming extent.[18]

They described the condition of a house belonging to Mr Moon, a corn miller, noting that 'close observation shows that the movement is going on daily; in fact, the ground on which the house stands, and the garden in front, are gradually shifting toward the valley below'.[19] The *Leeds Mercury* published a further article, again reprinted from the *Observer*, outlining the amount of damage that had been inflicted on the village. Responding to criticism that the original reports had exaggerated the damage, a visit to the village found that 'the actual destruction to property is really greater than was originally represented'.[20] The report noted that cracks had appeared in land belonging to the diocese of Ripon, on which the vicar of Fewston lived, that were so large that cattle could not enter the field for fear of them falling and breaking their legs.[21] This painted a somewhat apocalyptic image of a formerly bucolic part of the area.

Tales of the sinking village brought spectators from near and far, so much so that local pubs did not have enough food to meet demand.[22] One local newspaper report estimated that up to five hundred people had visited the village, many of whom were reported to have been disappointed that the village was not in as bad a condition as they had expected.[23] One week later, it was reported that 'the subsidence seems to be getting more satisfactory to visitors than it was a few weeks ago, as very little was heard on Sunday about exaggerated reports'.[24] All the while, conditions for residents and the village more generally continued to worsen. Moon, whom the *Observer* referred to as a man of 'heroic fortitude, worthy of a British Admiral' as he went down with his ship, had measured his house sinking at the rate of half an inch a week.[25]

While the local press were quick to pick up and sensationalise the incident at Fewston, the Leeds waterworks committee moved more slowly. They had been alerted to the potential for subsidence as early as 10 September, a week before it was reported in the local newspapers. After pressure from Moon's solicitors to take responsibility for the subsidence and pay compensation, the committee sought independent expertise to strengthen their defence against claims that water from the reservoirs had seeped into the shale foundation of the village, removing that shale when the water pressure receded.[26] They commissioned Professor Henry Green, a geologist from Yorkshire College, to determine the cause of the subsidence. Green found in favour of the corporation, arguing that the geological nature of the land was prone to subside – weakening more general arguments about the safety of the reservoirs in that particular area – and that it was the area's geology, in addition to three exceptionally wet years that had been experienced, that explained why the subsidence occurred at that moment and on that scale.[27] This provided the corporation with the expert testimony needed to deny liability, leaving little recourse for the residents of Fewston.

Although Green's testimony provided the corporation with the legal protection they desired, it is difficult to reconcile the severity of the subsidence with the presence of the reservoirs. The fact that subsidence occurred on a greater level than experienced previously less than one year after reservoir construction was completed cannot have been coincidence. As Green acknowledged, the area was prone to subside, so it stands to reason that adding a greater volume of water pressure onto that landscape, locked into the parameters of the reservoir, would increase the potential for subsidence. If nothing else, it validated the criticisms of Dresser, who warned that the area was not fully suitable for reservoir construction. While no major disaster occurred, many local people lost their homes and subsidence still affects the area today. As with Dale Dyke and Bilberry, this episode highlights that, despite the belief of engineers to tame the wilderness, nature was never easily controlled.

Concerns around the structural integrity of reservoirs were not solely resigned to hindsight. The somewhat remarkable thing about the Fewston subsidence was that, despite concerns about reservoir safety, word of this incident does not seem to have travelled beyond Leeds and its hinterlands. This does not mean, though, that concerns about reservoirs were settled:

in some cases, councils and committees were more proactive. In the case of Liverpool's Vyrnwy scheme, which had been beset with issues among the lead engineers, the water committee launched an investigation into the reliability of the masonry dam that would form the main bulwark against the river. There were several potential reasons for this sudden interest in safety: aside from the aforementioned disasters that were still within living memory, Vyrnwy was one of the first masonry dams to be constructed in the United Kingdom. This was a new technology that engineers did not have decades of experience in utilising. Perhaps related to that was the acrimonious episode between the corporation and Thomas Hawksley, who left the project in 1885. While there was no suggestion that Hawksley attempted to sabotage the project, it is telling that the water committee instigated their investigation shortly after he left, perhaps feeling a lack of confidence more than anything.

The committee first approached an engineer familiar with the city and its waterworks, J. F. Bateman, to conduct an investigation into the safety of the designs for the masonry embankment and into the materials being used to construct it. Despite his previous work for the city on identifying new sources of water, Bateman declined, citing a busy schedule and 'much annoyance in the future, whichever way my report would be', perhaps a nod to the corporation's treatment of his learned colleague Hawksley.[28] After approaching several other engineers, the committee turned to Sir Andrew Clarke, a former colonial official turned consulting engineer, and Russel Aitken, a civil engineer. Neither of these figures were a part of the group of eminent water engineers that dominated the nineteenth century, perhaps evidence of the bridges burned while managing Hawksley.[29] Both were instructed to present independent reports and were able to request blocks of cement from the site to test structural integrity.[30]

Of the two, Aitken was the more communicative with the water committee. He sent a letter to the committee highlighting what he suggested was 'a disturbing element' in the designs of the reservoir, pertaining to the ability of compensation water to exit the work and the calculations related to the gravity of the dam.[31] He sent a further letter expressing concern about the implementation of the sluice valve, which appeared to have been designed to be removed but had been built into the body of the dam so could not be easily replaced. George Deacon replied that details regarding the valve had not been decided and was dismissive of concerns around gravity calculations. The water committee somewhat tersely resolved that 'as the questions as to the outlet valves [...] do not affect the stability of the embankment, this Committee are of the opinion that he [Aitken] should regard them as outside the scope of his inquiry'.[32]

Ultimately, both Aitken and Clarke were satisfied with the structural integrity of the dam wall. Worries over the masonry dam, however, did not go away following their reports. In questions to the president of the Board of Trade in the House of Commons in 1889, Stanley Leighton, the MP for Oswestry, expressed concerns over the dangers posed by the dam wall to residents in the area. He asked Sir Michael Hicks Beach whether the government could allay these fears with an independent investigation of the works. Given the localised nature of water supply and reservoir construction, which was administered by local authorities or private companies, not Parliament, this would have been a remarkable change in policy, one that Hicks Beach was not willing to pursue.[33] He responded that the government had no statutory authority over inspecting the works at Vyrnwy; it was up to the Liverpool Corporation to authorise such an inspection. He also noted that Liverpool had employed Andrew Clarke to inspect the works, returning a positive report. Leighton responded that there were large sections of the embankment that Clarke had not inspected, to which Hicks Beach reaffirmed the government's lack of statutory powers in this area.[34]

This exchange was reported in an article by the *Oswestry Advertiser*, a paper with an obvious stake in the topic. The article continued with a number of correspondences gleaned from other sources. Citing a letter to *The Times* from Russel Aitken, the paper brought attention to concerns he had with the use of clay for a portion of the masonry dam, which would be more susceptible to leaking. If exposed, it would be 'quite sufficient to cause considerable destruction in the upper part of the valley of the Vyrnwy'.[35] The *Liverpool Echo* responded to this letter by noting that Aitken had not previously expressed concern about the short clay section of the dam wall, and, as has been noted, that both he and Clarke had been satisfied with the quality of the work. A further correspondence from Thomas Hawksley was printed by the *Oswestry Advertiser* that attempted to ease concerns over the structural integrity of the masonry wall: 'I introduced into my calculations every element of danger and of counteracting stability which are known to exist in structures of this kind'.[36]

For Hawksley, the source of these fears was not the works at Vyrnwy itself, but a recent disaster that had taken place in America. Two weeks earlier, a severe storm over Johnstown, Pennsylvania resulted in between six and ten inches of rain falling in a twenty-four hour period, putting immense strain on the South Fork reservoir, which had dammed the Conemaugh River. Originally constructed to help facilitate the operation of Pennsylvania Canal during dry spells, ownership of the reservoir had passed to the South Fork Fishing and Hunting Club in 1879, who predominantly used the lake to fish.[37] The reservoir had not been properly maintained for some time, with straw and horse manure used to patch up weak sections of the structure, while the relief pipes used to help with overflows of water were sold as scrap metal. The lack of maintenance allied with the ferocity of the storm in May 1889 meant that once the dam broke, it took less than an hour for it to empty of water.[38] It was reported that 2,209 people lost their lives as the water rushed towards Johnstown, becoming the largest national disaster in the United States at the time.[39] While there were obvious differences between South Fork reservoir and Vyrnwy, particularly the lack of maintenance of the former, it is understandable that people would be concerned in the wake of another reservoir disaster. This was especially the case when worries over the integrity of the dam wall had been aired so publicly. It is also noteworthy that these concerns were becoming increasingly internationalised, led by a growth in the speed of transatlantic communication.[40]

Accidents abroad highlighted fears which carried into the twentieth century. The reports of engineers were ultimately statements of confidence in their ability to tame the wilderness, something that continued in the face of compelling evidence to the contrary, as seen in the Washburn Valley.[41] Despite fears around the integrity of the dam wall, it was accidents further down the supply line that demonstrated the lack of full control over nature. In February 1905, the *Weekly Dispatch* reported that the main water pipe carrying water from Vyrnwy to Liverpool had burst near Eaton Tarporley in Cheshire. The pipe burst with 'almost no warning', sending much of the 20 million gallons of water it was transporting across the Cheshire countryside and 'causing enormous damage', although fortunately there were no casualties.[42] A year later, during the construction of a second mains pipe from Vyrnwy to Liverpool, a mains pipe exploded under the bed of the River Elfe, a tributary of the River Dee on the England–Wales border. The *Wellington Journal* described it in dramatic fashion:

> Suddenly there was a loud explosion, and a huge column of water, as thick as a man's body, rushed a hundred feet in the air, carrying on its crest heavy masses of masonry and pieces of rock, while tons of earth and shingle were torn down from the hill side and filled up the river bed.[43]

Fortunately for the men working on the pipeline, the incident occurred at the weekend, so once again no one was injured or killed. Given the prominence of contemporaneous disasters that had caused deaths in other industries such as mining, incidents that did not result in death but nevertheless exhibited a lack of control over the wilderness are just as important to highlight.[44]

Additionally, the spectre of previous incidents continued to haunt accidents such as these. Reporting on the burst main in Cheshire, the *Weekly Dispatch* concluded by listing other instances where reservoirs had burst and led to deaths, including Dale Dyke in 1864, the collapse of a dam in the Mill River valley, Northampton, Massachusetts in 1874 that led to 144 deaths; and a reservoir failure in the French town of Vosges in 1895 that led to two villages being swept away and 110 deaths.[45] A burst pipe is not the same as a collapsed reservoir; however, the recurrence of these incidents shows how strongly they remained in the public imagination, as does the placing of minor incidents such as this among more tragic events. While events in the United States and France were more recent, Dale Dyke clearly continued to hold cultural currency. It also shows that, despite the claims of engineers to the contrary, complete control over nature had not been secured in England, Wales or elsewhere.

Although no reservoir disasters occurred in Britain after 1864, it is clear that the spectre of Dale Dyke and Bilberry loomed large over future projects. In the case of Leeds, it was individuals like Dresser and Moon who highlighted issues with the Washburn landscape, which was not as suitable for construction as Filliter and Hawksley believed. As for Liverpool, their uneasy relationship with Hawksley, as well as events in America, led them to question the suitability of the relatively new masonry technology, and even after concerns had been settled about the dam wall, there were issues further down the supply chain. Both of these case studies highlight that, despite the best efforts of engineers to tame the wilderness to better provide for urban populations, the natural environment could not be so easily tamed: at one point or another, it pushed back.

Dam building in the twentieth century

Disasters were not the only way that reservoirs altered their local environments – their very construction created socionatural environments, hybrid landscapes that were simultaneously social and natural. The construction of reservoirs also allowed engineers and those invested in the civic project, particularly newspaper correspondents, the opportunity to propagate humanity's ability to successfully tame nature. While this can be clearly seen in nineteenth-century waterworks touched on at the start of this chapter, the continuity of these narratives in the second half of the twentieth century is noteworthy.

The immediate post-Second World War period is also worth highlighting in this case because of another environmental factor: drought.

Drought had affected Britain periodically across the late nineteenth and early twentieth centuries. The droughts of the 1890s brought water politics to the fore in East London and Sheffield as consumers reacted to water restrictions, while the 1920s and 1930s were marked by three distinct periods of drought in 1921, 1929 and 1933–34.[46] Some cities suffered more than others from drought: Leeds and Manchester were badly affected by drought in 1929, while Leighton and Haweswater reservoirs were being constructed. The 1933–34 drought was linked to global meteorological patterns in the northern hemisphere that may have been caused by the Dust Bowl and contributed to drought as far as Asia.[47] However, the provision of new local water supplies meant that some English cities coped more comfortably in this period than others, as with Leeds. Similarly, Birmingham's great chain of waterworks in the Elan Valley drought-proofed the city for much of the interwar period.

Issues became apparent with Birmingham's water supply, though, in 1937. A lack of rain across Wales in that year prompted concerns about the resilience of the city's supply. Not only was drought affecting the availability of water, but water usage in the city had doubled between the opening of the Elan Valley works in 1904 and 1937, placing ever greater strain on the system.[48] Here we can see that drought was not just caused by meteorological conditions but was a sociotechnical event, shaped by ever increasing piped supply and water usage as well as a lack of rain.[49] Members of the Birmingham Corporation decided that it was time to enact the second part of James Mansergh's original plan: to build three reservoirs on the River Claerwen to link with those on the Elan. Due to engineering advancements, though, they were able to modify the plan: instead of three reservoirs, one enormous reservoir would be constructed instead.[50]

As with Leeds and Manchester twenty years earlier, war interrupted progress on Claerwen reservoir. Although royal assent was received in 1940, work on the scheme did not begin until 1946, and even then, construction was only allowed to begin because it was assigned as a high priority project by the government in the context of post-war austerity. The high priority status of Claerwen was undoubtedly approved because of the continuing water supply issues Birmingham faced during the 1940s. The water committee was clear that, given the corporation was intent on extensive housing development in the city after the war, the construction of Claerwen had to begin so that future water restrictions could be avoided, while the *Birmingham Daily Gazette* framed the reservoir as the remedy to 'drought fears'.[51]

From the start of construction in 1947, Claerwen reservoir was conceptualised within a nascent environmental framework, although not the same narratives that would later be associated with Cow Green and Kielder Water. The *Birmingham Daily Gazette* proclaimed that Birmingham was making a new, unofficial 'national park' in the Claerwen Valley that belonged 'exclusively to Birmingham'.[52] National parks were, of course, on the political agenda in the late 1940s; however, the rationale behind the national parks was, in theory if not in practice, about opening up and managing rural areas for all, not just for the residents of one city.[53] The *Daily Gazette*, then, was using contemporary vernacular to further strengthen the civic link between the city and its waterworks. Writing of the Elan Valley, the *Daily Gazette* went on to remark that 'great lakes were blasted out of the earth to become reservoirs of vital importance, but they were constructed with an eye on harmony, and the dams and control towers were built of rock which blended naturally with the existing surface. Indeed the valley is a beauty spot'.[54] Claerwen reservoir, and the wider Elan Valley, were conceptualised as improving the landscape. While there is an apparent contradiction between blasting the earth and structures blending naturally into the landscape, it seems that through the skill of the engineer, harmony with the environment had won out. The cultural aspects of this will be explored more fully in Chapter 4; however, these depictions play into progressive narratives of environmental change. As William Cronon has highlighted in the American context, some changes to the environment were seen in wholly positive terms, having little or no regard for what was lost or natural systems that were damaged by infrastructural development.[55] Humankind could conquer nature to provide for towns and cities, and Claerwen was just the latest example of that power.

Part of this illustration of humanity's ability to tame nature was depicting the scale of the project. A special correspondent of the *Daily Gazette* returned to Claerwen in 1948 to provide an update on the works. The normally peaceful and quiet valley was juxtaposed with the noise and chaos of a construction site: 'Tall Wellsian towers of steel reach towards the heavens. Across the river-bed is a network of cables along which giant steel cradles speed at 1,000 feet a minute'.[56] In contrast to reservoir construction in the nineteenth century, reports like this helped to convey a sense of urgency and grandeur – technology was helping engineers to build bigger and better. Among all this hustle and bustle were the workers themselves: 'tiny figures of men can be seen, ant-like, cutting jagged holes in the rocky banks and controlling the machine which crushes the rock'.[57] Again, a contrast was drawn between the magnitude of the project and those working on it to emphasise the ability to successfully tame nature. The workers, in both a literal and metaphorical sense, were dwarfed by the scale of the project, but they were succeeding in bending nature to their will, emphasising the Promethean scale of their work.[58]

It only took a further four years to successfully tame the Claerwen Valley, despite worries about faults found in parts of the rock foundation. On inspecting the state of the new works in 1951, a special correspondent for the *Birmingham Daily Post* noted the difficulties that had been encountered during construction: a severe winter in 1946 and heavy rains at the start of 1951, which suggests that nature was not letting engineers have it all their own way. Indeed, overcoming such obstacles made the feat even more impressive. The article also noted some of the technological advancements being used on the site, such as low-heat cement, which would stop the concrete heating and, therefore, prevent stress and cracks in the masonry. Technology, then, was at the heart of man's battle with nature, from the use of explosives and cable lifts to new cement mixtures.[59] This was a part of how reservoirs fitted into the discourse of rural modernity: the use of technology to remake the landscape into a new vision, one that could serve modern society into the future.[60]

Claerwen reservoir may have been one of the biggest waterworks projects of the post-war years, but it was not the only project. Several reservoirs were constructed during the 1950s and 1960s as towns and cities continued to struggle with periods of drought and increased demand from populations and industries. Leeds was one such city. As in Birmingham, the need for a new source of water became apparent quickly after the war. Despite issues with water supply in the early 1950s, the city did not take positive steps to remedy its shortage until the end of the decade. The city council decided to return to the Washburn Valley to complete the project that had been started almost one hundred years previously. The reservoir built at Thruscross in the 1960s, though, was very different to the one planned during the 1870s. Due to the aforementioned advances in technology, as well as greater engineering expertise, the new Thruscross was to be much larger than originally envisioned, holding a capacity of 1.7 billion gallons of water. This increased size meant that the original site of the reservoir had to be altered. The largest consequence of this was the subsequent flooding of West End village, one of a number of villages to be flooded in the name of urban water supply in the twentieth century.

A tender from Holland, Hannen and Cubitts Ltd. for £1,104,750 was accepted by the Leeds Corporation's waterworks committee in March 1961, the lowest of sixteen bids received according to *The Yorkshire Post*.[61] An article in *Water and Water Engineer* provided some detail as to how construction would progress, with the engineers proposing to install a ten tonne cableway and a two cubic yard concrete mixing plant that had been used in the construction of Clatworthy reservoir, West Somerset.[62]

Figure 2.1 Thruscross dam wall shortly after completion, c.1966, Washburn Heritage Centre

The experience of constructing Clatworthy, 'the largest concrete dam in the West Country', may have been a factor in the waterworks committee's decision, with 'key experienced personnel' from that project being brought to work on Thruscross – once more the privileging of existing expertise – with the remaining workforce locally sourced.[63] A dam face 123 feet high composed of over 200,000 cubic yards of mixed concrete resulted in a vastly different reservoir to those built lower down the valley in the 1870s.[64] As such, its impact on the landscape was more visible. Figure 2.1 highlights both the size and aesthetic of the dam face, making Thruscross a more striking feature on the landscape than the other three reservoirs, which have a more natural aesthetic.

Reports from the *Yorkshire Evening Post* written by Malcolm Barker provide an insight into how the construction affected the landscape, with striking similarities to the reporting of the Birmingham press on Claerwen fifteen years earlier. The first report from 1962 contrasts the usually quiet nature of the Washburn Valley with the nightmarish noises of construction. Once more this can be read within a framework of rural modernity. At the site of the dam wall, much of the rock was removed with 'scientifically placed blasts', suggesting a faith in the scientific proficiency of the engineers and navvies that was sometimes lacking in the nineteenth century. However, Barker's reporting also reflected the continued importance given to the need to tame the wilderness: 'down there in the great

Figure 2.2 Thruscross dam during construction, 1960s, Washburn Heritage Centre

gash is one of the few places where rock meets man on equal terms, the man armed only with pick and shovel and the rock with the thickness and stability of tens of thousands of centuries'.[65] Because the rock basin formed the foundation for the dam wall, it could not be removed with explosives as these may have destabilised the foundation. The construction of Thruscross reservoir, like Claerwen, was framed as a battle between nature and humankind, with humans seemingly outmatched by the obstinance of nature. This battle, termed 'the elemental struggle of the navvy', highlights the long-standing environmental attitude of the local press, that nature was there to be conquered by humankind. This struggle is encapsulated in Figures 2.2 and 2.3, which show a contrast between the size of the works and those struggling to conquer nature. This narrative was in the same vein as that expressed by Hawksley in 1869, that nature had to be conquered, and once again echoes the progressive narratives that Cronon has described.[66] A case in point is Barker's depiction of the navvies, armed with only a pick and a shovel against a rock formation that had stood for thousands of years. Figure 2.3 builds on this image, with the presence of everyday building equipment like ladders further emphasising the size of the task being undertaken. Barker's reporting paints changes to the landscape in a positive light, highlighting that nature must be conquered in order to gain a fresh supply of water, paying little attention to the negative effects of changing the landscape, such as ecological damage.

Figure 2.3 Cross-section of eastward dam with workers, 1960s, Washburn Heritage Centre

Barker's reporting serves to highlight the wider environmental attitudes of the *Evening Post*, as well as the continued prevalence of urban attitudes to the countryside that saw rural areas as wilderness to be tamed to better serve towns and cities.

A further report from 1964, entitled the 'half-term report', provided readers with an update on the progress that had been made at the construction site. Barker again remarked that it 'still resembles a raw gash in the valley [...] But it is a gash that is gradually being filled in and healed as the smooth white walls rise from the foundations'.[67] This gash and the subsequent white walls are evident in Figure 2.2, which again matches the literary flourish of Barker's writing. Once more, the building of the reservoir was framed as a narrative of improvement, with the navvy winning the elemental battle over nature and healing the landscape with technology. This is, perhaps, indicative of wider positive social attitudes to scientific experts and technology, epitomised by Harold Wilson's belief in the 'white heat' of scientific revolution that focused on civil rather than military research and development.[68] Importantly, the growth of technology during the Labour governments of the 1960s was linked to modernity.[69] As with Claerwen, technology was playing a key role in helping to tame nature, thereby linking environmental changes to narratives of modernity. While the engineers may have had a better understanding of the landscape, setbacks did occur, including a large rockfall and bad weather that halted work for three months in 1963.[70] Barker also referred to the vast amount of concrete being used in the construction of the dam wall, the purpose of which was to stop the River Washburn 'in its ancient track' and force it back up the valley, again emphasising that the building of Thruscross reservoir was an exercise in overcoming nature.[71] Figure 2.2 presents an image of this 'gash' on the landscape. While the surrounding land that would be submerged was yet to be affected, the trough created by the navvies is evident, as is the beginning of the dam wall that was starting to bridge the two sides of the valley.

The more visible intrusion of construction on the landscape as reservoirs became more technologically advanced highlights another environmental issue: their architecture. The nineteenth century saw a proliferation of earthen embankment reservoirs, which looked like natural lakes due to their sunken nature in the landscape. However, these building techniques also limited the size of the structures. It was not until masonry work and, later, cement was used in construction that reservoirs could be larger. In becoming larger, though, they became less hidden in the landscape. This is exemplified in the images above, particularly Figures 2.2 and 2.3, showing how visible the dam wall at Thruscross would become. This architectural style was indicative of rural modernism that Katrina Navikas and others have highlighted, embodied in reservoirs like Thruscross and Claerwen as well as power stations and electricity pylons.[72] These modern structures were not always subjected to criticism as progressives foresaw a role for this type of architecture in the countryside. The failures of sites of rural modernism to unite opinion in a progressive way was often due to the inability of authorities to cut through issues of class and regionalism.[73] Additionally, the increased size of these structures that new construction technologies enabled was driven by the demands of post-war life: greater living standards and the facilitation of a consumer culture.[74] Not only did this mean that more environmental resources were being extracted in a general sense, but the methods of doing so resulted in more obvious intrusions on the natural landscape. As some utilities were becoming increasingly hidden, water infrastructure in the countryside was becoming more visible.

The construction of Thruscross reservoir was completed in 1966. Barker once again returned to witness the damming of the River Washburn in order to begin filling the reservoir, commenting that the valley was to be transformed 'into a large and shimmering lake'.[75] Barker's reporting of the construction of Thruscross reservoir highlights a largely progressive narrative: humankind had won the battle with nature. While nature was seen as an obstacle to overcome, its agency was still felt by the engineers and workers at Thruscross reservoir. They could not use explosives to blast all the way down to what became the foundation of the dam wall, emphasising a greater understanding of what pressures the land could tolerate than in the 1870s. Although Barker portrayed the construction of Thruscross reservoir as a victory for humanity over nature, it was still constrained by natural limits, despite the implementation of a more sophisticated method than that used during construction in the 1870s.

Conclusion

It seems obvious to suggest that reservoir construction had an environmental impact. However, this chapter has highlighted the multifaceted and sometimes unintended environmental consequences of construction as well as the narratives that underpinned the quest for urban water. While looked at in isolation, the two themes are linked – the belief in the engineers' ability to tame the wilderness that continued well into the twentieth century made events like the subsidence of Fewston and accidents along the Vyrnwy supply line, as well as more prominent national and international cases, more notable. The narratives of the post-war period are important to stress as this was the period that environmental and ecological concerns around dam building were coming to the fore, as well as the growth of the wider environmental movement from the 1960s onwards.[76] While ecological concern was growing by the time Thruscross was constructed, it did not present much of a barrier to constructing the reservoir. This is perhaps due to the relatively unknown nature of the Washburn Valley, strengthening Katrina Navickas's argument about focusing on areas of 'non-outstanding natural beauty'.[77] This suggests that the unfettered belief in the engineer should have been tempered, however, as reporting from the construction of Claerwen and Thruscross in particular shows that belief remained as strong in the 1960s as it was in the 1860s.

As this chapter has shown, though, nature was never fully tamed. While concerns around reservoir safety diminished as accidents like those at Dale Dyke, Bilberry and Johnstown faded from living memory, signs of natural agency continued to be in evidence. The rocky relationship between authority and engineer led to Liverpool questioning the structural integrity of their own waterworks project. In the end, it was the supply line that would cause issues for the corporation. For Leeds, the unanticipated rate of subsidence caused by the construction of reservoirs left local residents without habitable homes. Subsidence continues to this day in the Washburn Valley, albeit on a smaller scale than that experienced in 1880. As projects became larger due to new technology and ever greater demand, their impact on the landscape became more visible; while the belief of the engineer to tame the wildness had not diminished, the handiwork was much more visible. All of these separate examples point to a unified approach to water supply and the environment during the nineteenth and twentieth centuries, bound up not just in a belief in technology but also in civic identity; by working on behalf of municipal authorities, engineers brought their skills and knowledge to bear on behalf of the city. It spoke well to the prestige of municipal governments that they could tap the bounty of the landscape by taming the wilderness. The incident in the Washburn Valley in the 1880s and along the Vyrnwy supply line in the 1900s, as well as more contemporary episodes like at Whaley Bridge in 2019, underline the importance of constant vigilance when it comes to reservoir safety, a reminder that despite the best efforts of engineers across the nineteenth and twentieth centuries, nature could never be fully tamed.

Notes

1. Shane Ewen, 'Sheffield's Great Flood of 1864: Engineering Failure and the Municipalisation of Water', *Environment and History* 20, no. 2 (2014), 178, https://doi.org/10.3197/096734014X13941952680954.

2. Caroline Lowbridge, 'Whaley Bridge Reservoir Collapse: Lack of Maintenance 'Exacerbated' Problem', BBC News, 16 March 2020, https://www.bbc.co.uk/news/uk-england-derbyshire-51912677.

3. Maria Kaika, 'Dams as Symbols of Modernization: The Urbanization of Nature Between Geographical Imagination and Materiality', *Annals of the Association of American Geographers* 96, no. 2 (2006), 276, https://doi.org/10.1111/j.1467-8306.2006.00478.x.

4. For key works see William Cronon, *Nature's Metropolis: Chicago and the Great West* (Norton, 1991); Tim Soens et al., eds., *Urbanising Nature: Actors and Agency (Dis)Connecting Cities and Natures Since 1500* (Routledge, 2019); Erik Swyngedouw, 'Modernity and Hybridity: Nature, *Regeneracionismo*, and the Production of the Spanish Waterscape, 1890–1930', *Annals of the Association of American Geographers* 89, no. 3 (1999), 443–65.

5. Shane Ewen, 'Socio-Technological Disasters and Engineering Expertise in Victorian Britain: The Holmfirth and Sheffield Floods of 1852 and 1864', *Journal of Historical Geography* 46 (2014): 15–20, https://doi.org/10.1016/j.jhg.2014.05.021.

6. Ewen, 'Socio-Technological Disasters', 20.

7. Ewen, 'Socio-Technological Disasters', 24.

8. Dresser was a member of prominent civic institutions in Leeds, such as the Leeds Philosophical and Literary Society and the Leeds Mechanics' Institute. He also gave research papers to the Leeds Philosophical and Literary Society, such as his presentation in 1850 on 'The Electric Light, with Experiments'. William White, *Directory of Leeds, Bradford, Huddersfield [...] Woolen and Worsted Manufactures* (William White, 1866), 62; 'Mechanics' Institution', *Leeds Intelligencer*, 2 April 1842, 4; 'Leeds Philosophical and Literary Society: Conversazione Last Evening', *Leeds Intelligencer*, 30 November 1850, 5; 'The Leeds Waterworks Reservoir at Eccup', *Leeds Times*, 26 October 1878, 2.

9. C. L. Dresser, 'Leeds Water Scheme', *Yorkshire Post*, 4 May 1867, 7 [also printed in *Leeds Mercury* on same date].

10. Dresser, 'Leeds Water Scheme'.

11. Leeds Corporation, 'Leeds Waterworks Committee Minutes, volume 3: 1870–1878', West Yorkshire Archive Service (WYAS), LLC22/1/3, 132–36.

12. Leeds Corporation, 'Waterworks Committee Minutes, volume 3'.

13. 'Leeds Water Supply', *Leeds Mercury*, 31 May 1873, 11.

14. 'The Washburn Reservoirs', *Yorkshire Post*, 2 July 1874, 6.

15. Ewen, 'Socio-Technological Disasters', 15–20.

16. Leeds Corporation, 'Waterworks Committee Minutes, volume 3', 214.

17. Leeds Corporation, 'Waterworks Committee Minutes, volume 3'.

18. 'Subsidence of Land at Fewston' [report from *Wharfedale and Airedale Observer*], *Yorkshire Post*, 17 September 1880, 2.

19. 'Subsidence of Land at Fewston', *Yorkshire Post*.

20. 'Subsidence of Land at Fewston' [report from *Wharfedale and Airedale Observer*], *Leeds Mercury*, 24 September 1880, 3.

21. 'Subsidence of Land at Fewston: Threatened Destruction of the Village', *Yorkshire Post*, 24 September 1880, 5.

22. 'Fewston', *Wharfedale and Airedale Observer*, 8 October 1880, 3.

23. 'Fewston', *Wharfedale and Airedale Observer*, 1 October 1880, 3.

24. 'Fewston', *Wharfedale and Airedale Observer*, 8 October 1880, 3.

25. 'Fewston', *Wharfedale and Airedale Observer*, 17 December 1880, 5; 'Fewston', *Wharfedale and Airedale Observer*, 19 November 1880, 4.

26. Expert witnesses were increasingly utilised in legal matters from the nineteenth century onwards. While presenting the air of objectivity, many witnesses tended to argue for their employer rather than scientific reason. See Roy MacLeod, 'Introduction', in *Government and Expertise: Specialists, Administrators and*

Professionals, 1860–1919, ed. Roy MacLeod (Cambridge University Press, 1988), 3. 'Subsidence of Land at Fewston', *Leeds Mercury*, 24 September 1880, 3.

27. Leeds Corporation, 'Leeds Waterworks Committee Minutes, volume 4: 1878–1885', WYAS, LLC22/1/4, 138–41.

28. Liverpool Corporation, 'Liverpool Water Committee Minutes, 1885', Liverpool Record Office (LRO), 352 MIN/WTR 1/21, 417.

29. G. M. Binnie, *Early Victorian Water Engineers* (Thomas Telford, 1981).

30. Binnie, *Early Victorian Water Engineers*, 435.

31. Liverpool Corporation, 'Liverpool Water Committee Minutes, 1886', LRO, 352 MIN/WTR 1/22, 17.

32. Liverpool Corporation, 'Water Committee Minutes, 1886', 40.

33. John Hassan, *A History of Water in Modern England and Wales* (Manchester University Press, 1998).

34. 'The Oswestry and Vyrnwy Embankments: Questions and Replies in the House of Commons Last Night', *Oswestry Advertiser*, 19 June 1889, 5.

35. 'Oswestry and Vyrnwy Embankments', *Oswestry Advertiser.*

36. 'Oswestry and Vyrnwy Embankments', Oswestry Advertiser.

37. Patty Wharton-Michael, 'The Johnstown Flood of 1889: The *Johnstown Tribune*'s Commonsense Coverage vs. Common-Practice Sensationalism', *Journalism History* 38, no. 1 (2012): 23, https://doi.org/10.1080/00947679.2012.12062869.

38. Emily Godbey, 'Disaster Tourism and the Melodrama of Authenticity: Revisiting the 1889 Johnstown Flood', *Pennsylvania History* 73, no. 3 (2006), 275.

39. Wharton-Michael, 'Johnstown Flood of 1889', 23.

40. Bob Nicholson, 'Transatlantic Connections', in *The Routledge Handbook to Nineteenth-Century British Periodicals and Newspapers*, ed. Andrew King et al. (Routledge, 2016), 167.

41. Ewen, 'Socio-Technological Disasters', 14.

42. 'Main Bursts: Cheshire Swept by 20,000,000 Gallons of Water', *Weekly Dispatch*, 5 February 1905, 1.

43. 'The Vyrnwy Main Bursts', *Wellington Journal*, 1 September 1906, 7.

44. See Ann-Marie Foster, 'The Barry Urban District Council, Disaster Relief Funds and Civic Society, 1913–1934', *Urban History*, 48, no. 4 (2021): 685–700, https://doi.org/10.1017/S0963926820000577.

45. 'Main Bursts', *Weekly Dispatch.*

46. Vanessa Taylor et al., 'Drought Is Normal: The Socio-Technical Evolution of Drought and Water Demand in England and Wales, 1893–2006', *Journal of Historical Geography* 35, no. 3 (2009): 568–91, https://doi.org/10.1016/j.jhg.2008.09.004.

47. Gerald A. Meehl et al., 'How the Great Plains Dust Bowl Drought Spread Heat Extremes Around the Northern Hemisphere', *Scientific Reports* 12, article 17380 (2022), https://doi.org/10.1038/s41598-022-22262-5.

48. Birmingham Corporation, *City of Birmingham Waterworks* (James Upton Ltd, 1967), 15.

49. Taylor et al., 'Drought Is Normal'.

50. Birmingham Corporation, *City of Birmingham Waterworks*, 15.

51. 'Plans to Remove Drought Fears: Birmingham's Proposed New £1,700,000 Dam in Wales', *Birmingham Daily Gazette*, 1 February 1946, 3.

52. 'Vast New Dam Seen in the Making: Birmingham's Own "National Park"', *Birmingham Daily Gazette*, 21 July 1947, 3.

53. David Evans, *A History of Nature Conservation in Britain*, 2nd ed. (Routledge, 1997).

54. 'Vast New Dam', *Birmingham Daily Gazette.*

55. William Cronon, 'A Place for Stories: Nature, History, and Narrative', *The Journal of American History* 78, no. 4 (1992): 1356, https://doi.org/10.2307/2079346.

56. Special correspondent, 'Rapid Progress Made on Great New Dam Project', *Birmingham Daily Gazette*, 27 August 1948, 1.

57. Special correspondent, 'Rapid Progress Made'.

58. Kaika, 'Dams as Symbols of Modernization', 276.

59. Special correspondent, 'Birmingham's New Dam', *Birmingham Daily Post*, 1 May 1951, 2.

60. Linda M. Ross, et al., 'Introduction', in *New Lives, New Landscapes Revisited: Rural Modernity in Britain*, ed. Linda M. Ross et al. (British Academy, Oxford University Press, 2023), 8.

61. Leeds municipal correspondent, '£1m Contract for Reservoir: Work on Biggest Leeds Project May Start Soon', *Yorkshire Post*, 24 March 1961, 15.

62. 'Leeds Corporation's Thruscross Reservoir', *Water and Water Engineer*, May 1961, extract from 'Leeds CB Thruscross Reservoir', National Archives, HLG 127/29.

63. 'Leeds Corporation's Thruscross Reservoir', *Water and Water Engineer*; Ewen, 'Socio-Technological Disasters'.

64. Leeds municipal correspondent, 'Work on New Dam Starts in Spring', *Yorkshire Post*, 9 December 1960, 13.

65. Malcolm Barker, 'The Birth of a Reservoir ... A Nightmare of Sound in the Quiet Valley', *Yorkshire Evening Post*, 24 August 1962, 10.

66. Cronon, 'A Place for Stories', 1356.

67. Malcolm Barker, 'Thruscross Half-Term Report', *Yorkshire Evening Post*, 15 September 1964, 6.

68. David Edgerton, 'The "White Heat" Revisited: The British Government and Technology in the 1960s', *Modern British History* 7, no. 1 (1996): 58, https://doi.org/10.1093/tcbh/7.1.53.

69. Peter Jones, 'Posting the Future: British Stamp Design and the "White Heat" of a Technological Revolution', *Journal of Design History* 17, no. 2 (2004): 163–176, https://doi.org/10.1093/jdh/17.2.163.

70. Barker, 'Thruscross Half-Term Report', 6.

71. Barker, 'Thruscross Half-Term Report'.

72. Katrina Navickas, 'Building Amenity in Areas of Non-Outstanding Natural Beauty in the Southern Pennines', in *New Lives, New Landscapes Revisited: Rural Modernity in* Britain, ed. Linda M. Ross et al. (British Academy, Oxford University Press, 2023), 96.

73. Katrina Navickas, 'Conflicts of Power, Landscape and Amenity in Debates over the British Super Grid in the 1950s', *Rural History* 30, no. 1 (2019): 100, https://doi.org/10.1017/S0956793319000013.

74. Matthew Kelly, 'The Politics of the British Environment Since 1945', *The Political Quarterly* 94, no. 2 (2023): 210, https://doi.org/10.1111/1467-923X.13275.

75. Malcolm Barker, 'First Cup from the New Reservoir', *Yorkshire Evening Post*, 5 January 1966, 10.

76. Christine S. McCulloch, 'Political Ecology of Dams in Teesdale', in *Long-Term Benefits and Performance of Dams*, ed. Henry Hewlett (Thomas Telford, 2004), 49–58; John McNeil, *Something New Under the Sun: An Environmental History of the Twentieth Century* (Penguin, 2001), 339.

77. Navickas, 'Building Amenity', 96.

Chapter 3

Seeing the wood for the trees: afforestation and managing water supply

The 1918 meeting of the British Waterworks Association (BWA), a body comprising waterworks managers from municipal and private waterworks across the country, heard a paper from Joseph Parry on afforestation.[1] On the face of it, planting trees has little to do with building reservoirs or managing municipal water pipes. The topic, though, was apt for a number of reasons. First, trees could be enormously beneficial in maintaining a pure water supply, while also protecting the banks of reservoirs from erosion. Second, the space around reservoirs was, in the first instance, not especially useful – planting trees had ecological benefits and could provide authorities with a source of income from timber. Third, 1918 was the point at which British authorities were starting to tackle the country's sparse timber stock. The blockades of British ports during the First World War had brought home the reality that the majority of Britain's timber stock was imported, and that action needed to be taken to make the country more self-reliant.

It was apt, too, that the person speaking to the BWA was Parry, the forestry manager of Liverpool's Vyrnwy estate. While national authorities had been slow to take afforestation in Britain seriously, Liverpool Corporation began to afforest Lake Vyrnwy as early as 1897.[2] A number of other local authorities, including Birmingham and Leeds, followed suit in the early years of the twentieth century, recognising that afforesting reservoirs could have practical and financial benefits. While this was good waterworks management, looking at cases of municipal afforestation can illuminate on a number of other themes. Like other chapters in this book, the theme of civic pride is closely associated with activities on the urban periphery – afforestation was certainly a part of the growing civic project undertaken in rural areas like Vyrnwy or Washburn. There are other themes, though – ecology, governing the urban periphery and, in the case of Leeds, the politics of unemployment – that all intersect with waterworks management and afforestation. This chapter will highlight these themes, showing first, that civic pride was at the heart of the actions of water authorities regarding afforestation throughout the period examined here, and second, that waterworks management could and did impact on other areas of urban governing. While a number of municipal authorities engaged in afforestation – and reference will be made to several of them – two main case studies will be examined here: Leeds's Washburn Valley scheme in the early years of the twentieth century, and Liverpool's Vyrnwy scheme after the First World War. This will demonstrate how afforestation became a vital part of waterworks management, as well as how managing the urban periphery became important to these towns and cities in a wider sense: as a way to draw a link between the city and the country, or as an arena for urban political narratives to play out upon. As such, the reciprocal nature of the urban–rural relationship is stressed here, going beyond older environmental histories which have seen this relationship as one solely of urban extraction.[3]

Focusing on afforestation helps to highlight the wider metabolic function of urban waterscapes, contributing to a neglected aspect of histories of afforestation that have focused on centralised efforts, particularly from the Forestry Commission after 1918.[4] Ostensibly a process to help protect waters from pollution, there were wider social and cultural impacts that will be explored in this chapter. The first half of the chapter will focus on early municipal programmes at the turn of the twentieth century. Focusing on Leeds, one of the pioneers in mass tree planting around reservoirs, this section will show how afforestation became intertwined with the politics of unemployment. This will also provide context on a period of forestry history in Britain that has often been characterised by inaction. The second half of the chapter will focus on municipal efforts after the First World War. While national forestry schemes have been examined elsewhere, this chapter will highlight continuity in local efforts, emphasising the importance of reservoir afforestation to the civic project. The focus here will be on Liverpool's Vyrnwy scheme, the progenitor of efforts before the war and the most well-developed municipal reservoir in terms of forestry in the interwar years.

Early afforestation schemes and the politics of unemployment

It is worth briefly focusing on why afforestation was taken up by municipal authorities in the early twentieth century. Although authorities would not have used the word, they recognised the 'ecological' benefits trees could bring to the watershed of reservoirs. The primary benefit was in creating a barrier between the edge of the watershed and the land, so that residents or visitors would find it harder to pollute the water. Trees helped to reduce the potential for bank and soil erosion, which would lead to silt and other detritus entering the water supply, thereby making the edges of reservoirs more secure. Trees also helped to mitigate the damage of flooding while also contributing to the hydrological cycle – the leaves of trees return moisture to the atmosphere through evapotranspiration. While this did not help to combat drought to the extent believed by contemporaries, they were right to recognise the link between trees and moisture.[5] There was also a financial imperative – the planting of trees to sell in years to come was seen as prudent forward planning even before the issues encountered with timber imports during the First World War. The prioritisation of these two primary reasons for afforestation – pollution and income – were flipped during the interwar years, when the financial imperative became more important, and the benefits to combating pollution an added bonus.

While the ecological benefits of afforestation have long been recognised in an international historiographical context, work on tree planting in Britain has treated the subject somewhat unevenly.[6] Research on afforestation before the First World War has predominantly focused on the efforts of private landowners afforesting estates, more for aesthetic than ecological reasons.[7] In the twentieth century, historians such as John Sheail focused on the approach of central government to forestry, concentrating on the results of the Acland Report in 1917 and the subsequent establishment and work of the Forestry Commission in 1919.[8] While an important development, the broader historiography has neglected two key issues: the efforts of municipal authorities like Liverpool and Leeds before the First World War, and the continued success of municipal tree planting initiatives after the war, key contributions of this chapter.

Afforestation became a priority for Liverpool Corporation, with work starting on the scheme in 1897. Five years later, twelve years after construction on the waterworks had been completed, 162,000 trees had been planted on the Vyrnwy estate over an area of 470 acres. The scheme was hailed as a success even at this early stage, with Parry's expertise sought for Royal Commissions on tree planting, as well as in helping to push the schemes of other cities, such as Leeds.[9] Afforestation also began at Birmingham's Elan Valley scheme in 1902, with between eight hundred and nine hundred acres planted by 1916.[10] It was not just municipal authorities that engaged with afforestation, with the Derwent Valley Water Board beginning planting around Derwent reservoir in 1908.[11]

Within this context, it is no surprise that Leeds Corporation began to think seriously about an afforestation project of their own in the Washburn Valley. A suggestion by Arthur Currer Briggs, the Lord Mayor of Leeds, marked the scheme as unique: that the work should be carried out by the unemployed in order to help 'alleviate distress' during the winter months.[12] Unemployment had become a major issue in Britain during the 1880s, with the effects of cyclical employment resulting in the growth of trade unions and the labour movement. The first decade of the twentieth century saw the first attempts from municipal and central governments to tackle the issue, most notably David Lloyd George's policy of unemployment insurance.[13] Although Currer Briggs was nominally a Liberal Unionist, the desire for unemployment relief is evidence of the pressure being exerted on the corporation by the newly influential labour movement in Leeds, which wanted increased municipal expenditure on social reform.[14] Moreover, as has been noted more widely of labour colonies, some Liberal and socialist reformers believed rural camps were an adequate antidote to urban unemployment.[15] Even at this early stage, the politics of unemployment was becoming entwined with managing water supply. Support was offered by the Independent Labour Party for afforestation schemes organised by Liverpool and Manchester during this period, as well as the support of the politically radical John Burns MP, president of the Local Government Board from 1905 to 1914.[16]

The success of cities like Liverpool undoubtedly helped the afforestation cause. From 1897 until 1914, Liverpool successfully planted two and a half million trees across 884 acres.[17] In 1914, Liverpool entered into an agreement with the British government to plant four thousand acres of land around Vyrnwy with the help of centralised funding, a vast scaling up of their operations that spoke to the success the corporation had experienced over the previous seventeen years.[18] In contrast to Leeds, the Liverpool Corporation utilised local labour rather than the unemployed. The greater distance between Liverpool and Vyrnwy is certainly one explanation for this; however, tree planting at the waterworks was also seen as a remedy for rural depopulation. Across the Irish Sea, the editor of the *Newry Reporter* looked on the efforts of cities like Liverpool favourably, remarking that afforestation presented an opportunity in Ireland to stop the rural exodus and subsequent urban congestion.[19] Similarly, reports on the 1909 Royal Commission into forestry noted that nearly all of the twenty-three men local to Vyrnwy working on the scheme would have 'drifted into our large towns' if not for the scheme.[20]

Afforestation, then, was becoming increasingly popular with municipal authorities and commentators, and Leeds set about finalising its own scheme. The scheme would, of course, further alter the landscape, as Maps 3.1 and 3.2 highlight. Map 3.2, an Ordnance Survey map from 1910 of the area around Swinsty reservoir, shows a plantation on the banks of the reservoir, called Swinsty Moor Plantation, which is not present in Map 3.1, an Ordnance Survey map from 1893. Like other aspects of waterworks management in the Washburn Valley, the afforestation scheme was possible due to a series of compulsory land purchases that had taken place in the 1890s and early 1900s, ostensibly under the guise of pollution control.

By November 1904, the waterworks committee was putting arrangements into place to accommodate unemployed workers in the Washburn Valley. The men would be paid £1 a week, with the men themselves given one shilling, ten shillings deducted for catering, and the remaining nine shillings sent to the families of the men to be collected at the Unemployed Bureau. Accommodation for the workers was provided at a structure known as 'the bungalow'.[21] There was also provision for additional activities, with books available at the bungalow, accessible at a rate of two shillings per week, and piece work preparing holes for the seeds was also available at a rate of two shillings and three pence per hundred holes bored. While it was envisioned that men would stay at the bungalow for a set period of time, provision was made to allow workers to travel from Leeds via train, so long as they completed the three-hour walk to the work site from nearby Otley each Monday morning by 10.30 a.m.[22]

A resolution from 1905, at the start of the scheme, noted that the men would be paid for time worked at a rate of five and a half pence per hour. If the working day described by one former worker was accurate, this would amount to four shillings a day, and therefore twenty shillings per week. The important distinction is that the men did not get paid for time they did not work, with bad weather accounting for much of this broken time. At times, then, nine shillings would not have been enough to send back to be collected by families. In the same year, the subcommittee enlisted Professor William Fisher of the University of Oxford, a leading authority on forestry, to advise on the scheme.[23] He produced a detailed report in 1905 that outlined the benefits of afforestation, particularly in helping to stop pollution of the watershed and in providing valuable timber, which he argued was 'the duty of every Municipality'.[24] The planting of trees around the reservoirs, he argued, would have no deleterious effects on the water supply themselves, while they would help to reduce

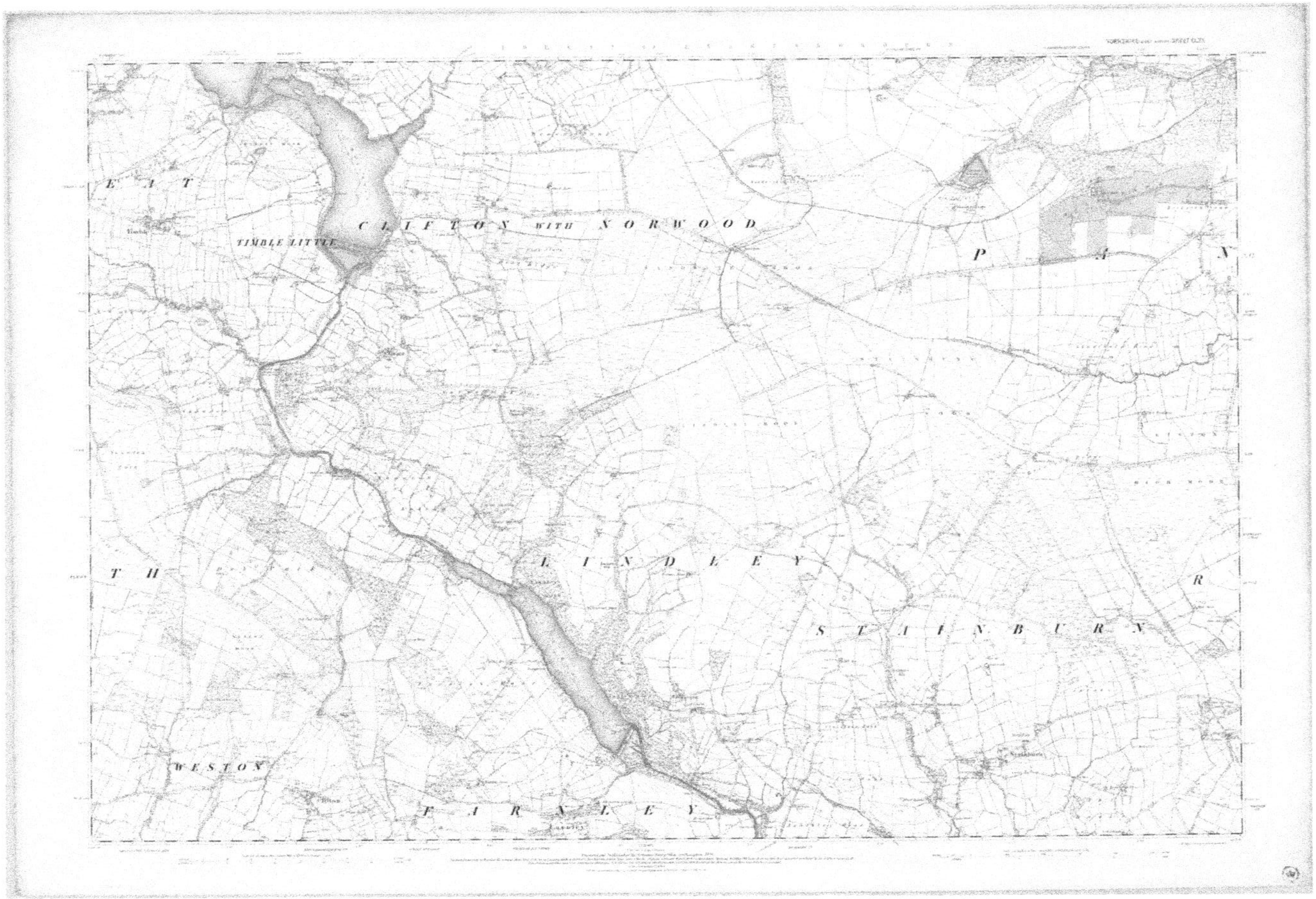

Map 3.1 Ordnance Survey map showing Swinsty reservoir, 1893. Reproduced with permission of the National Library of Scotland.

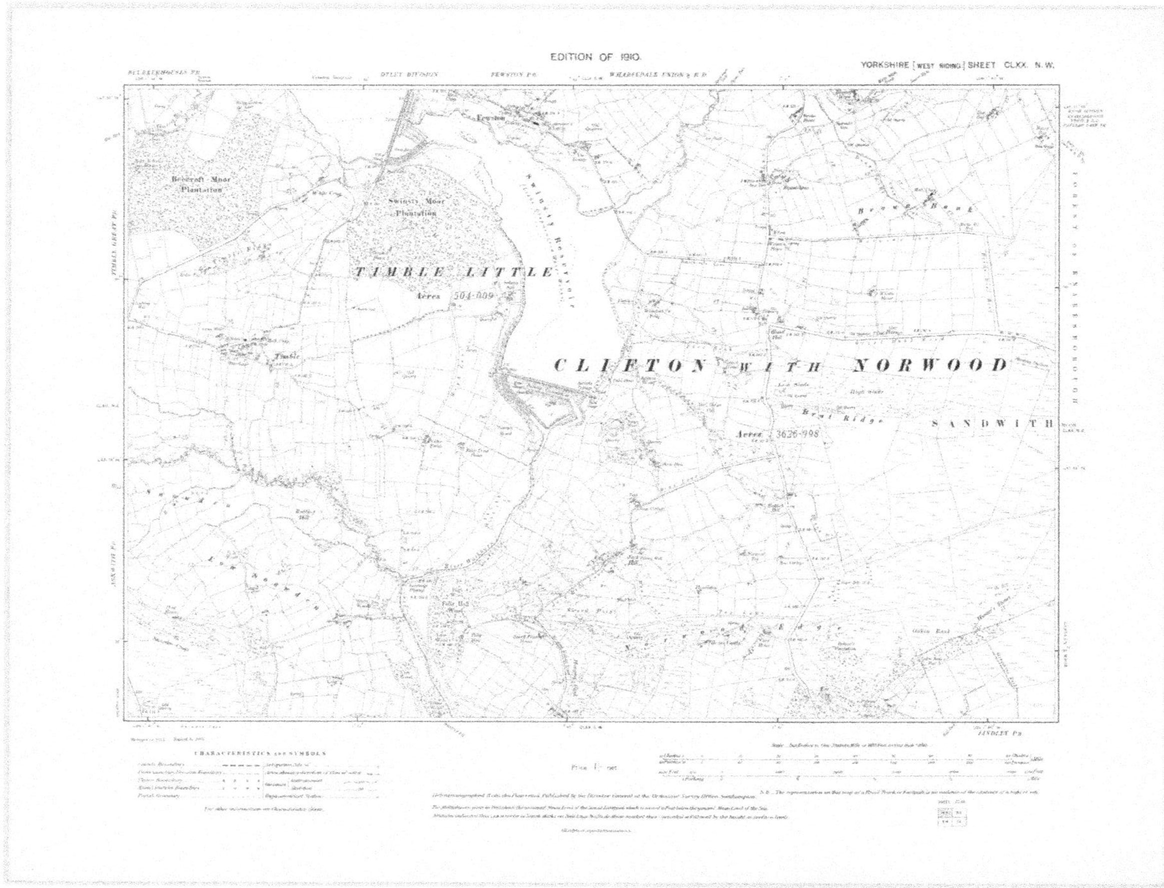

Map 3.2 Ordnance Survey map showing Swinsty reservoir, 1910. Reproduced with permission of the National Library of Scotland. Creative Commons Attribution 4.0 International (CC BY 4.0)

the evaporation of water from the reservoirs and the ground. The trees would also encourage ground percolation, which would lead to a reduction in the surface flow of rain and help to prevent the build-up of silt.[25] The concluding comments of the report regarded the hard nature of the labour, with Fisher warning that 'it would not be profitable to employ any but those who are willing to face the conditions of country employment, and able to *really* work properly and thoroughly'.[26] This warning, though, was not heeded.

The subcommittee approved his plans and ordered Douglas fir, Scots pine and Corsican pine seeds. It is important to note that two of these types of trees, Douglas fir and Corsican pine, were not native to Britain. Although they were deemed to be good species for water management, this is another example of a municipal authority altering the ecology of rural areas for urban gain. The first year of the scheme, starting in the winter of 1905, passed without complaint, beginning with forty men from the Unemployed Bureau being employed in December. The subcommittee minutes, however, reveal that problems were starting to surface that hinted at the political difficulties of managing the rural landscape in such a way. In February 1906, it was reported to the subcommittee that the North Eastern Railway company was not able or willing to provide reduced rail fares for workers on the scheme travelling home from Otley to Leeds. In addition to transport issues, the subcommittee resolved that the head forester should exercise greater control on both expenditure and 'the amount of work done by the men', suggesting that work was not progressing as well as expected.[27]

However, the following year the Local Government Board gave the Leeds distress committee £1,000 to assist the scheme, indicating that the scheme was seen favourably by those in Westminster.[28] This grant, though, brought the scheme under greater scrutiny than the previous year, with the distress committee later expressing disappointment 'with the general character of the unemployed who have been given the opportunity of earning wages [...] and the extent of their work'.[29] The *Yorkshire Post* reported that of the 203 unemployed men who had been offered the work, 139 accepted, 102 actually went, and no more than twenty or thirty worked on the scheme at any given time.[30] It seems that Fisher's warning was coming to pass. The *Yorkshire Evening Post* covered the subject extensively: they published a special report on the scheme, with a correspondent travelling to the valley to inspect the conditions.[31] One interviewee described the valley as 'British Siberia', adding that

> apart from the hardships of working in so barren and bleak a locality at this season of the year, there are so many deductions of lodgings, pocket-money, and broken time, owing to the bad weather, that at the

> week-end there is very little, if anything, left for the wife, children, or other dependents left in Leeds.[32]

The bleak conditions and lack of pay were major issues for the unemployed men, particularly given the distance between the valley and Leeds. While the corporation had built living quarters for the men, it was, according to a correspondent calling himself 'Disgusted', a 'four-mile tramp' to the work site.[33] Despite the claims of the labourers, the *Evening Post* continued to attack. One article quoted the chairman of the distress committee, Herbert Brown, as saying, 'There is nothing in the nature of the work in the Washburn Valley that genuine, honest, pecunious citizens would not do. The few who have stuck to it are better in health themselves than when they went'.[34] Not only was their character brought into question by Brown, but the scheme was also portrayed as being able to improve these apparent deficiencies in the physical, and by extension moral, health of the unemployed men.

Criticism was not just consigned to figures of authority. In an article entitled 'The "Work-Shy" Brigade: More replies to charges of laziness', the secretary of the Leeds Trades and Labour Council, Councillor Owen Connellan, argued that 'Many of these [workers ...] are nothing but parasites on the community, and their conduct seriously prejudices the chances of the honest, but impecunious workers'.[35] The language used by Connellan, a prominent local trade unionist, was incendiary, labelling those that could not bear the harsh working conditions as parasites, once more harnessing an 'us and them' narrative. It also called into question the masculine identities of the unemployed men, particularly at a time when 'national efficiency' and urban degeneration were lingering issues. Although fears of degeneration among the urban poor were most keenly expressed in London, as Bill Luckin has highlighted, similar narratives appeared in provincial areas that castigated the urban poor for supposedly lacking the moral or intellectual tools for self-improvement.[36] This is an example of what has been termed 'honest poverty', which consisted of two factors: the willingness of men to work, and the want to responsibly provide for the family.[37] Both were called into question by the *Evening Post*, thereby questioning the masculine identities of the unemployed men, whom they saw as being neither fit nor willing to fulfil the breadwinner role.

Although some had previously sought to defend them, the criticism levelled by Brown and Connellan prompted a reaction from those who had experienced the works. Many wrote under pseudonyms that simultaneously highlighted their experience of working in the valley and their anger at the *Evening Post*. A letter from 'One Who Has Tried It' condemned the work, labelling it as 'a form of exile and white slavery'. He concluded that if the work continued, fewer men would sign up to the Unemployed Bureau in order to avoid the afforestation scheme.[38] Another writer stressed the respectable nature of the men who worked on the scheme, urging readers to look not to the men's presumed laziness but to other factors, citing the example of one man he knew who had walked all the way from Leeds because he could not afford to take public transport: 'A lazy man would not walk 17 miles to work, and then leave, unless there were [...] reasons for doing so'.[39]

All correspondences highlighted the poor working conditions and the fact that many were inadequately prepared for such demanding labour. 'Disgusted' pointed to the poor weather as a reason why many left the works: 'I am not so silly as to blame the authorities for the weather, but when the weather is bad and the men cannot work, the wives and dependents of the men in Leeds get little or nothing'.[40] A correspondent commenting on the plight of the labourers suggested that the treatment of dependents in Leeds was to blame:

> In one case I know of, a wife with three children received one week, 9d., and the week following, 1s. 4d. The husband, after these two weeks, returned to Leeds. And who blames him? How could any honest man stay away from his wife and children under such conditions? Living well himself, miles away from home, those whom he hoped to benefit are left pining.[41]

He concluded by arguing that those men who remained at the works were to blame for reinforcing the poor treatment of dependents by the corporation, somewhat generously characterising the living arrangements for the men in the valley.[42] The letters all pointed to the lack of provision provided, either within the valley or in terms of financial remuneration. They demonstrate a tension between the corporation providing some unemployment relief for residents of the city and not properly equipping the men to succeed.

While figures such as Connellan did not shy away from criticising the calibre of the unemployed men sent to the Washburn Valley, other parts of the labour movement sought to defend the character and integrity of the men. William Morby, the president of the Leeds Trades and Labour Council, condemned their treatment in a meeting of the distress committee in 1907, highlighting several of the issues that the unemployed men had complained about to the *Evening Post*, such as the long journey to the work site and the prohibitive cost of lodging and food.[43] Similar criticisms of the scheme were issued by trade unions in meetings of the Trades and Labour Council in 1907 and branches of the Labour party, particularly in

South Leeds.[44] The issues raised by the unemployed men in the *Evening Post* and Morby were also raised in the House of Commons by James O'Grady, Labour MP for Leeds East in questions to John Burns. As with the distress committee, Burns dismissed concerns over pay, deductions, board, travel and the isolated nature of the area, and defended the actions of the corporation and the distress committee.[45]

The *Evening Post* was also not swayed by the defence of the unemployed men. A special correspondent of the newspaper visited the works and delivered a damning report: 'Not fifty per cent., but fully eighty per cent. of the men sent out to Fewston this year have been absolute wasters', a figure apparently corroborated by the forester, Alexander Pope, and the lodging keeper, Mrs. Hodgson.[46] What constituted an 'absolute waster' in this context was not specified. The report focused on the living conditions at Fewston, dismissing the complaints of correspondents as having not 'a tittle of foundation', highlighting the selfish nature of the men themselves, who were portrayed as happy to take the food of the corporation as their dependents starved in Leeds.[47] The editor of the *Evening Post* further underlined this criticism, arguing that although the work was admittedly hard, many of the men who had undertaken it had little room to complain and were part of the 'work-shy brigade', and urged the public not to waste their sympathy on these 'wasters'.[48] These narratives continued into the winter of 1907, with an *Evening Post* article drawing attention to the 'weary willies – men whose one great aversion in life is work of any kind' that were expected on the works, with some men having already left.[49] The second visit to the valley of John Burns underlined the failure of the scheme, which he felt did not solve the unemployment issue and had a pauperising effect.[50] Despite the efforts of former workers to more accurately portray the works in the Washburn Valley to improve conditions, the scheme was condemned by both the *Evening Post* and by important figures such as Burns as a failure.

Funding for the scheme supplied by the Local Government Board was withdrawn in light of this perceived failure. The scheme to utilise the unemployed men of Leeds ended in 1909, with the corporation employing workmen who were physically able to carry out the work. A special correspondent for the *Yorkshire Post* in 1913 wrote that more than sixty per cent of the trees planted by the unemployed failed, with ten skilled staff working to rectify the damage.[51] There was progress after 1909, though, as the head forester Alexander Pope outlined in 1914. In describing the past troubles with the scheme, Pope took a more conciliatory tone, noting somewhat generously that although 'the Waterworks Committee were forced to the conclusion that many did not want regular work', he highlighted that the majority of the unemployed men who joined the works were 'physically incapable' of the tough manual work that was asked of them:

> The class sent out may be taken as a fair sample of the 'Unemployed' in our large towns, and were of all trades, painters, bakers, clerks, iron-workers, bootmakers etc., and general labourers. Very few were accustomed to outdoor work, and numbers had never previously handled a spade or any tool used in planting.[52]

In listing their former professions, Pope wrote of the unemployed men as respectable individuals, rather than an amorphous group with little to no moral character, finally providing some context to the debate. He continued to list the problems that had been encountered with the scheme, mainly owing 'to the character of the land'.[53] He also noted the dangers posed by fire, particularly during hot, dry summers, as the trees were not yet large enough to act as fire breaks.[54]

It is clear from the report, though, that progress was finally being made on the scheme. By 1917, the *Evening Post* praised the foresight of Currer Briggs, suggesting that the scheme was finally coming to fruition.[55] An *Evening Post* report from 1943 commenting on the British government's plan to invest £40 million into afforestation at the end of the Second World War praised the Leeds Corporation for enacting this process forty years previously.[56] The scheme, therefore, became a success in the long term. It was, in some ways, a positive step in the development of unemployment relief; indeed, the failure of the scheme did not deter wider calls for the use of unemployed men on afforestation schemes, nor the publication of a Fabian tract on the same issue in 1912.[57] It both provided valuable timber for the corporation and added to the natural aesthetic of the valley, signalling the importance of amenity to these landscapes.

However, the valley became a stage for the relations between the municipal authority and its unemployed men to be played out, far enough away geographically from Leeds to be out of the public gaze. The landscape of the valley, largely controlled by a local authority, was shaped, in part, by the exercise of municipal power, reinforced by the city's newspapers. In using unemployed men to manage the landscape, residents of Leeds were employed that were not prepared or trained to complete the necessary work. Ultimately, this lack of training allowed the blame to be passed onto the unemployed men, readily taken up by the city's newspapers, instead of the corporation that had failed to properly provide for their workers. This highlights an aspect of the Promethean project that was noted in the previous chapter: successfully taming and utilising rural landscapes was harder and more labour intensive than realised by engineers and planners. It also helps to complicate narratives of civic pride that became associated with the valley: the valley was not just a space for positive civic engagement but also a space where urban politics failed. While afforestation was, on the surface, an exercise in landscape management, it is possible to see how power was exercised by the corporation, not just through managing its water supply but also its provision of unemployment relief and the reinforcement of social stigma by the provincial press.

Forestry in the interwar years

Leeds struggled to link its afforestation scheme to the wider civic project, largely because of how municipal authorities treated their unemployed citizens. Liverpool, on the other hand, was much more adept in this regard. Wider fears around the condition of British forestry predated the First World War, if not by much. A departmental committee appointed by the Board of Agriculture warned of wastage amid a global decline of forestry stock in 1903, while in 1909 a Royal Commission on afforestation and coastal erosion urged for government intervention in planting more trees to abate the deterioration of the nation's stocks.[58] The war, though, brought the nation's dependence on global stocks into sharp focus. Blockades on imports highlighted that Britain relied on other nations for ninety per cent of their timber stock.[59] This realisation prompted the government to set up a forestry subcommittee, part of a wider reconstruction committee, in 1916 under the auspices of Sir Francis Acland. A year later, Acland produced a report advocating for the government to take an active role in stimulating the country's timber stocks. Much of the report provided the basis for the Forestry bill, 1919, which committed the government to afforest 1.7 million acres by the end of the twentieth century. To help reach this target, the government established the Forestry Commission in the same year. Despite the economic pressures of the 1920s and threat of the Geddes Axe, the commission went on to become the largest landowner in Britain, helping to replenish the country with home-grown timber.

As the first part of this chapter showed, though, municipal government had already taken steps, albeit somewhat unevenly, to help facilitate the afforestation of rural areas under their control. While they did not have the resources of the centrally funded Forestry Commission, they continued to play a positive role after the First World War – sometimes in conjunction with the commission, and sometimes on their own. Cities that had been at the forefront of afforestation before the war, most notably Liverpool, maintained their efforts, protecting their water supplies and helping to provide much-needed timber for the country. For Liverpool in particular, these efforts became intertwined with the civic project; the boons of municipal afforestation were used to promote the ability of the city to positively affect the rural hinterland, thereby strengthening the idea of the Promethean project.

The success of afforestation at Liverpool Corporation's Lake Vyrnwy during the last years of the nineteenth century was underlined by the corporation's commitment to further tree planting in the twentieth century. Plans to expand the project were put in place before the First World War, with 4,680 acres marked as suitable for tree planting at Vyrnwy.[60] Despite the lack of a central forestry body in 1913, the government had committed to advance £5 per acre planted up to £25,090 to help finance a scheme that would not turn a profit for decades.[61] Work began during the war, with 416 acres planted by 1916. The work undertaken at Vyrnwy during the war, as the need for domestic timber supply became ever more apparent, was an important factor in the scheme's success. Throughout the interwar period, the scheme was praised for leading the way by local newspapers within and outside of Liverpool.[62]

The project was not without controversy, though. The initial reporting of the scheme in 1913 noted that it would involve the termination of several tenancies held by farmers in the area, a fate postponed due to the war. This was nothing new: towns and cities were able to gain powers of compulsory purchase from Parliament to tackle pollution and protect their watersheds, as occurred in the Washburn Valley in the late nineteenth and early twentieth century.[63] The postponement in terminations lasted until 1923, when the *Western Mail* reported that the Llanfyllin Rural Council (LRC) had objected to a proposal to evict six farmers to make way for afforestation. While the human element was highlighted, the main objection of some critics, including the chairman of the LRC and a correspondent for the centre-right periodical *Truth*, was the loss of good farming land. Representation was made in Parliament by Ellis Davies, the MP for Denbigh, who questioned Acland on the legitimacy of the Liverpool Corporation's actions given that the land claimed lay outside the watershed of Lake Vyrnwy. Acland argued that the afforestation of Vyrnwy predated the Forestry Commission, their role in the matter being to carry out the responsibilities agreed to by the Treasury in 1913.[64] Ultimately, the scheme continued unabated, a reminder of the power of municipal and central government over small rural communities, and the social impact that could be wrought by waterworks management on those communities.

The expansion of works at Vyrnwy typified approaches to afforestation around reservoirs in the interwar period. Liverpool, of course, was not the only authority to expand its tree planting efforts. In 1918, Birmingham Corporation undertook to plant 760 acres of land in the Elan Valley, in addition to the 560 acres planted since 1902.[65] The success that Liverpool and Birmingham had both before and after the First World War saw them held up as examples to follow. Reporting on the near completion of the Corby (Northants) and District Water Board's Eye Brook dam, the *Northants Evening Telegraph* remarked that the planting of trees around the waterworks would follow the examples of Vyrnwy and Elan.[66] Other projects, such as Plymouth's Burrator reservoir on Dartmoor, engaged in afforestation without the aid of the Forestry Commission, although the commission took management of the project after the Second World War.[67]

Like all forestry schemes, the success of the Vyrnwy project was assessed in time. This point came in 1952 when it was announced that new roads, paid for jointly by the Liverpool Corporation and the Forestry Commission, would be constructed at the Vyrnwy plantations. These were primarily to facilitate the transport of thinnings for sale, which would help to produce a surplus profit of £7,000. On news of this profit, the *Liverpool Echo* praised the long work of the water committee, noting that the nation, in need of timber, would be grateful for their efforts.[68] Elsewhere, thinning began at Burrator reservoir in the 1960s, although this was firmly under the auspices of the Forestry Commission and not Plymouth Corporation. Not all schemes turned a profit, though. A. E. Fordham, the general manager and secretary of the Birmingham Water Department, noted that there was a deficit of £1,070 for the Elan Valley afforestation project by 1950, although this did not affect further plans to afforest the area due to the national need for timber.[69] Despite this, Elan continued to be held up with Vyrnwy as a success story for other towns and cities to emulate.[70] It is clear, then, that not all schemes were rampantly successful financially, but the success that Liverpool Corporation encountered before the First World War continued well into the twentieth century.

The success of the Vyrnwy scheme was not just measured in acres planted, timber produced or income generated, but in cultural capital in the form of civic identity. As has been noted, despite a perceived decline in expressions of civic identity by 1914, historians have recently pointed to the continuity of civic pride, albeit in a form adapted to time and place.[71] Civic festivals held during the interwar period, such as the Civic Weeks in Manchester, helped to promote a sense of urban belonging through entertainment and education.[72] Given the continued success of afforestation at Lake Vyrnwy, celebrated within and outside the city itself, it is no surprise that Liverpool Corporation sought to strengthen the link between the city and the waterworks through education at such events. At the 1938 Royal Lancashire Agricultural Show, Liverpool Corporation ran a stall demonstrating the uses of timber from Vyrnwy. A correspondent for the *Liverpool Echo* wrote:

> If the average Liverpool man or woman were asked what Lake Vyrnwy is famous for he would, of course, reply 'water,' but if a Midlands coalminer were asked the same question he would say without hesitation 'Why, pit props, of course.' Few of Liverpool's citizens can be aware of what a flourishing business the city has in its timber estate at Vyrnwy.[73]

The purpose of the stall was to educate visitors to the show, predominantly drawn from Liverpool given that the show took place in Wavertree, East Liverpool, on the successful ways in which the corporation governed the city's watershed. Not only did the stall seek to demonstrate the economic success of the afforestation programme but it also tied the successful management of waterworks to the economic and cultural success of Liverpool. Through careful management, the trees planted protected the water supply and provided the city with a source of income that was helping to benefit industry elsewhere. This was supported by evidence; one of the facts put forward by the corporation at the stall was that one million linear feet of timber had been supplied to Midlands collieries in the preceding twelve months.

Even around reservoirs, though, approaches to afforestation were not uniform. At the meeting of the British Waterworks Association in 1918 that started this chapter, a number of councillors and engineers expressed doubts as to the viability of afforestation. Three main criticisms were noted: first, the practicality of planting trees when most corporations did not own the land surrounding their waterworks; second, the cost of planting with no government help, thereby having to rely on the rates to fund projects; and third, the removal of potential agricultural land, particularly for sheep grazing. Indeed, the representative of Birmingham, a city largely supportive of afforestation, stated that 'It requires a very patriotic Corporation to start and to maintain a large system of planting at the heavy cost which does at the present time fall upon them', once again situating afforestation within a wider civic drive.[74] Although the Forestry Commission and some municipal authorities tried to boost their efforts, issues remained after the Second World War. R. M. Prothero, a geographer from the University of Edinburgh, noted in 1950 that only one authority had twenty per cent of its land afforested, and thirteen authorities had no afforested land at all. In mitigation, he pointed to issues around the cost of such schemes and land ownership that had previously been highlighted in 1918, showing that there had been little progress on this particular issue.[75]

A case in point was Manchester's efforts around Thirlmere and Haweswater reservoirs. Afforestation around Thirlmere began in 1907 and finished in 1926, with the Manchester Corporation arguing that there was little to no land around Thirlmere that could be economically afforested. This attitude extended to Haweswater, where no afforestation would take place as much of the land was owned by farms or classified as common land.[76] These were practical reasons for ceasing operations. However, it is noteworthy that the Liverpool Corporation and others, such as the Derwent Valley Water Board and the Forestry Commission on Dartmoor, were expanding their efforts at this time. Geography was an important issue here too: the Lake District was a key battleground for preservationists during the interwar period. Although the work of the Manchester Corporation around Thirlmere was pointed to by advocates of municipal afforestation, they did not seem as committed to this issue as other large cities during the 1920s.

Another key issue in debates around afforestation was amenity: in short, the idea that afforestation would damage the aesthetic of rural areas. This was due predominantly to the use of non-native monocultures, as noted earlier in the chapter in the Washburn Valley, which, it was deemed, would look unnatural. Preservationist battles took place across the country. However, the most notable was, unsurprisingly, in the Lake District. The Forestry Commission's purchase of seven thousand acres of land in Eskdale, five thousand of which were unsuitable for silviculture, prompted opposition from the Friends of the Lake District preservationist group. After political wrangling in Westminster, which also involved representation from the Council for the Preservation of Rural England, Eskdale was classified as a 'special area', which meant that consultation would be required before afforestation.[77] Worries about the damage to the aesthetic of rural areas were also evoked during discussions on Haweswater. A correspondent of the *Western Chronicle* conjured romantic imagery in his description of Haweswater as one of the most lovely of lakes: 'There is something primitive in it, a native wildness as a scene untouched by man's aid, for afforestation has wrought big changes around other lakes'.[78] In planting non-native trees, the primitive wilderness of Haweswater, an area in the process of being modified by urban engineering, would be further damaged, a fate that had befallen other rural areas.

As set out in the opening chapter, amenity was an amorphous concept that could also be utilised by those in favour of afforestation. Early proponents of afforestation before the First World War cited its beautifying effects on rural areas as a reason municipal governments should plant trees around their reservoirs. While the *Western Chronicle* may have lamented the impact of afforestation in the interwar period, the chairman of the Manchester waterworks committee, Sir Edward Holt, claimed that, without trees, Haweswater was 'much over-rated as a beauty spot'.[79] There is clear political motivation to this statement, but it highlights how amenity could be utilised to support tree planting. Even some preservationists were in favour of afforestation. In a discussion of the impeding construction of Ladybower reservoir, Victor Pochin, the vice-chairman of Leicestershire County Council and chairman of a Leicestershire preservationist body, stated that he had been deeply impressed by the afforestation of other areas of the Derwent Valley, despite opposition from the Council for the Preservation of Rural England. He was particularly impressed with how the cottages, made of local stone, did not clash with the newly planted trees.[80] In much the same way as reservoirs came to be seen as a feature of the romantic idyll, afforestation could positively affect the cultural landscape, the focus of the following chapter.

This conceptualisation continued after the Second World War, as rural modernism helped to link large-scale projects like afforestation to how the landscape was seen. During the second reading of the National Parks and Access to the Countryside bill in the House of Lords in 1949, the Conservative peer Lord Harlech praised the afforestation of the Elan Valley for improving the beauty of the countryside.[81] Similarly, the *Birmingham Gazette* claimed in 1953 that the 'Elan Valley will be beautiful again' as afforestation sought to repopulate an area that had been stripped for mine props during the Second World War.[82] While urban demand stripped rural areas of their aesthetic appearance, afforestation by municipal government could re-beautify the countryside, continuing the trend of urban authorities positively re-engineering the landscape. The concept of amenity was not just the preserve of the preservationists.

Like with amenity, afforestation continued to be linked with civic education after the Second World War. An afforestation display, brought from Lake Vyrnwy, was a regular feature of the Liverpool Show during the early 1950s. The 1953 show featured a warning to visitors on the potential of forest fires, with the slogan 'One match can damage a million trees. One tree can make a million matches' prominently displayed.[83] This slogan sought to educate on the uses of the city's timber supply and reinforce the need to properly manage the area to protect Liverpool's economic fortunes. Bringing features from Lake Vyrnwy again provided the residents of Liverpool with a tangible link to an important civic area outside the city that would, otherwise, have been out of reach for many. In providing these stalls, the Liverpool Corporation sought to educate its citizens on the use of rural space the city owned and managed around their watershed, thereby creating a tangible civic link between the city and its far-off hinterland. As seen in the discussions of civic education and amenity, the cultural aspects of afforestation were as important to maintaining a sense of civic identity as the strict management of the waterworks.

Conclusion

British forestry developed greatly over the course of the twentieth century, and this chapter has shown that waterworks management was a prominent element of that development, a factor that has been neglected in previous histories of forestry. It has also shown that tree planting, an activity somewhat removed from the provision of water to towns and cities, was deeply connected to waterworks management, as well as politics and civic identity. It is important to stress local efforts here: Liverpool very much led the way, being the first to afforest its reservoirs in a meaningful way. That success continued well into the post-Second World War period, with the product of the Vyrnwy plantations used to show citizens of Liverpool what their city could provide. Afforestation efforts, though, were not always as straightforward or successful, demonstrating the need to highlight efforts even when they went wrong. Leeds and its experiment with unemployed people was a case in point. Despite the benefits of afforestation, and the progressive nature of the city's plans, the scheme actually revealed tensions between work, unemployment and masculinity. In not providing training, the unemployed men were set up to fail, allowing the city's newspaper press to use divisive rhetoric that belied unease with unemployment, far from the initial intentions to protect Washburn waterworks from pollution. Analysing the responses of the unemployed men to their treatment, and taking a history-from-below approach, helps to illuminate how waterworks management shaped not only the municipally owned landscape but also the treatment of central actors employed to protect the city's water supply. While the scheme was a failure, it brought the idea of unemployment relief to national significance, even if that history has been forgotten. Similarly, after the First World War, despite the success of Liverpool and Birmingham Corporations in afforesting Vyrnwy and Elan, their success was not replicated uniformly, as municipal authorities had to contend with the financial costs of such schemes, issues around land ownership and the potential of costly land purchases, and debates around preservation and amenity.

This chapter, then, has shown that engaging in the more environmental aspects of reservoir development beyond landscape change provides more nuance to ideas around waterworks management, as well as how, in some cases, reservoirs became sites of tension as well as sites of civic pride. Highlighting the cultural aspects of afforestation – how it was presented to urban residents – is important in showing how these rural areas continued to be linked to the city: in other words, how civic identity was reinforced beyond the construction of reservoirs and the supply of water itself. It highlights and develops the dynamic between local and national stories. It has also shown the benefits of examining municipal efforts at afforestation, an understudied aspect of forestry historiography. Not only were municipal authorities like Liverpool, Birmingham and Leeds key players in efforts to plant trees in Britain, especially before the centralised efforts of the Forestry Commission, their involvement belied a wider web of issues including politics, economics and civic identity, showing that there was much more to planting trees than putting saplings in the ground.

Notes

1. Joseph Parry, 'Afforestation', *British Waterworks Association: Proceedings 1918–1920, volume 2* (British Waterworks Association, 1920), 121–7.

2. John Sheail, *An Environmental History of Twentieth-Century Britain* (Palgrave, 2002).

3. The most prominent example of this is William Cronon, *Nature's Metropolis: Chicago and the Great West* (Norton, 1991).

4. Historians who have looked at forestry pre-1918 have mainly focused on efforts by the landed gentry to afforest estates. See James Winter, *Secure from Rash Assault: Sustaining the Victorian Environment* (University of California Press, 1999), 83–103. For key texts on post-1918 forestry, see Sheail, *Environmental History*; Matthew Kelly, *Quartz and Feldspar: Dartmoor – A British Landscape in Modern Times* (Vintage, 2016).

5. Stephen Mosley, *The Environment in World History* (Routledge, 2010), 34–5.

6. Richard H. Grove, *Green Imperialism: Colonial Expansion, Tropical Island Edens and the Origins of Environmentalism, 1600–1860* (Cambridge University Press, 1995).

7. Winter, *Secure from Rash Assault*, 83–103.

8. Sheail, *Environmental History*; Kelly, *Quartz and Feldspar.*

9. 'Editorial', *Yorkshire Post*, 26 October 1904, 6.

10. Robin Goodfellow, 'Birmingham Timber Growing', *Birmingham Mail*, 7 October 1916, 6.

11. 'To Be Opened by H. M. The King: Full Description of the Ladybower Reservoir', *Derbyshire Times*, 21 Sept 1945, 7.

12. 'Summary of the News', *Yorkshire Post*, Editorial, 26 October 1904, 6.

13. John Field, *Learning through Labour: Training, Unemployment and the State 1890–1939* (University of Leeds, 1992), 6.

14. Raymond David Dalton, 'Labour and the Municipality: Labour Politics in Leeds 1900–1914' (unpublished doctoral thesis, University of Huddersfield, 2000), 117.

15. Field, *Learning through Labour*, 18–19.

16. Winter, *Secure from Rash Assault*, 99.

17. Parry, 'Afforestation', 122–3.

18. Parry, 'Afforestation', 122–3.

19. 'Editorial', *Newry Reporter*, 17 October 1905, 3.

20. 'Afforestation: Mistakes in Our System', *Buckinghamshire Examiner*, 22 June 1909, 3.

21. The precise location of the bungalow is not stated in contemporary sources, and there is no other information to inform where the structure was constructed.

22. Leeds Corporation, 'Leeds Waterworks Sub-Committee Minutes, volume 3: 1900–1906', West Yorkshire Archive Service (WYAS), LCC22/2/3, 117–18.

23. Leeds Corporation, 'Leeds Waterworks Sub-Committee Minutes, volume 3: 1900–1906', WYAS, LCC22/2/3, 105–14.

24. W. R. Fisher and Samuel Margerison, 'Reports on the Afforestation of the Washburn Valley Estate', City of Leeds Waterworks (1905), held at Special Collections, Brotherton Library, University of Leeds, Sheppard Pamphlets FIS, 6–7.

25. Fisher and Margerison, 'Reports on the Afforestation of the Washburn Valley Estate', 44.

26. Fisher and Margerison, 'Reports on the Afforestation of the Washburn Valley Estate', 115.

27. Leeds Corporation, 'Leeds Waterworks Sub-Committee Minutes, volume 3: 1900–1906', WYAS, LCC22/2/3, 124–25.

28. 'Untitled', *Yorkshire Post*, 3 December 1906, 8.

29. 'Leeds Unemployed on Public Works', *Yorkshire Post*, 20 February 1907, 9.

30. 'Leeds Unemployed on Public Works', *Yorkshire Post*.

31. Stephen Caunce, 'Yorkshire Post Newspapers Ltd: Perseverance Rewarded', in *Leeds City Business 1893–1993: Essays Marking the Centenary of the Incorporation*, ed. John Chartres and Katrina Honeyman (Leeds University Press, 1993), 30.

32. 'Making the Leeds Forest: Lot of the Labourers in the Washburn Valley', *Yorkshire Evening Post*, 17 January 1907, 4.

33. Disgusted, 'Neither Idle Nor Work-Shy', *Yorkshire Evening Post*, 22 February 1907, 4.

34. 'Too Lazy to Work: Washburn Experiment a Complete Failure', *Yorkshire Evening Post*, 20 February 1907, 4.

35. Anon, 'The "Work-Shy" Brigade: More Replies to Charges of Laziness', *Yorkshire Evening Post*, 23 February 1907, 7.

36. Bill Luckin, 'Revisiting the Idea of Degeneration in Urban Britain, 1830–1900', *Urban History* 33, no. 2 (2006): 234–52, https://doi.org/10.1017/S0963926805003275.

37. Marjorie Levine-Clark, *Unemployment, Welfare, and Masculine Citizenship: 'So Much Honest Poverty' in Britain, 1870–1930* (Palgrave Macmillan, 2015), 2.

38. One Who Has Tried It, 'The "Work-Shy" Brigade', *Yorkshire Evening Post*, 22 February 1907, 4.

39. S. G. Macbeth, 'Asked to Suspend Judgement', *Yorkshire Evening Post*, 22 February 1907, 4.

40. Disgusted, 'Neither Idle Nor Work-Shy', *Yorkshire Evening Post*, 22 February 1907, 4.

41. W. J. M., 'A Critic Who Thinks They Expect Too Much', *Yorkshire Evening Post*, 23 February 1907, 7.

42. W. J. M., 'Critic Who Thinks'.

43. Dalton, 'Labour and the Municipality', 136.

44. Dalton, 'Labour and the Municipality', 136–37.

45. HC Deb (4th series) 19 March 1907 vol. 171, c.662.

46. Special correspondent, 'At "Work-Shy" Colony: A Day with the "Wasters" at Fewston', *Yorkshire Evening Post*, 26 February 1907, 4.

47. Special correspondent, 'At "Work-Shy" Colony'.

48. 'The Ethics of Unemployment', *Yorkshire Evening Post*, 7 March 1907, 4.

49. 'Tales from Washburn Valley: The Tree-Planters at Work Again', *Yorkshire Evening Post*, 14 October 1907, 5.

50. 'The Unemployed Problem', *Yorkshire Evening Post*, 11 December 1907, 3.

51. Special correspondent, 'Leeds Afforestation: Its Bearing on the Water Supply', *Yorkshire Post*, 11 January 1913, 10.

52. Alexander Pope, 'The Washburn Valley Afforestation Scheme of the Leeds City Council' (reprinted from the *Quarterly Journal of Forestry*) (Laughton and Company, 1914), 4.

53. Pope, 'Washburn Valley Afforestation Scheme', 5.

54. Pope, 'Washburn Valley Afforestation Scheme', 7.

55. 'Leeds City's Millions of Trees: The Scheme That Angered the Economists', *Yorkshire Evening Post*, 21 September 1917, 3.

56. 'Diary of a Yorkshireman', *Yorkshire Evening Post*, 27 February 1943, 4.

57. Sheail, *Environmental History*, 89; Arthur P. Grenfell, 'Afforestation and Unemployment', *Fabian Society Tracts, nos. 134–166* (Fabian Society, 1912).

58. Sheail, *Environmental History*, 82; Winter, *Secure from Rash Assault*, 99.

59. Sheail, *Environmental History*, 82.

60. 'Liverpool's Water Catchment Areas: Great Afforestation Scheme for Vyrnwy', *The Scotsman*, 6 May 1913, 8.

61. 'Afforestation at Lake Vyrnwy', *Northern Whig*, 9 May 1913, 2.

62. 'More Forests Wanted: Means of Assisting Water Storage', *Sunderland Daily Echo*, 16 August 1934, 5; '"Witchcraft" Fodder in Trays for Cattle at Show', *Liverpool Echo*, 29 July 1938, 5.

63. Leeds Corporation, 'Leeds Waterworks Committee Minutes, volume 7: 1896–1903', WYAS, LLC22/1/7, 79–165; Leeds Corporation, 'Leeds Corporation Waterworks Plans and Sections of Proposed Additional Works, November 1866', WYAS, QE20/1/1866/6.

64. 'Farmers' Notice to Quit: Afforestation Schemes at Lake Vyrnwy', *Liverpool Echo*, 19 May 1924, 12.

65. 'Birmingham City Council: Revision of Tramway Fares', *Birmingham Daily Post*, 10 April 1918, 3.

66. 'Eye Brook Dam Nears Completion', *Northants Evening Telegraph*, 21 August 1939, 6.

67. Kelly, *Quartz and Feldspar*, 172.

68. Listener, 'Talk of the Town: Liverpool's Trees Are Doing Nicely', *Liverpool Echo*, 4 November 1952, 4.

69. 'Elan Valley Forestry Plan May Not Pay', *Birmingham Gazette*, 1 September 1950, 5.

70. 'Great Easton Dam Nearing Completion', *Market Harborough Advertiser and Midland Mail*, 25 August 1939, 2; G. B. R., 'Down in the Forest: Drink to the Trees', *Western Mail*, 2 April 1948, 2.

71. Ben Roberts, 'Entertaining the Community: The Evolution of Civic Ritual and Public Celebration, 1860–1953', *Urban History* 44, no. 3 (2017), 444–63, https://doi.org/10.1017/S0963926816000511.

72. Tom Hulme, *After the Shock City: Urban Culture and the Making of Modern Citizenship* (Boydell Press, 2019), 73.

73. '"Witchcraft" Fodder', *Liverpool Echo*, 29 July 1938, 5.

74. Parry, 'Afforestation', 183–92.

75. 'The Elan Valley Plantations: Not Yet a Commercial Proposition', *Birmingham Daily Post*, 1 September 1950, 2.

76. 'Tree Planting at Thirlmere and Haweswater', *Penrith Observer*, 13 July 1926, 8.

77. Sheail, *Environmental History*, 95–7.

78. 'A Gigantic Water Scheme: How Manchester Is to Meet Its Needs', *Western Chronicle*, 27 February 1925, 2.

79. 'Haweswater Scheme', *Lancashire Evening Post*, 18 July 1925, 3.

80. 'A Visit to Derwent Valley: Water for Leicester Will Submerge Two Villages', *Leicester Mercury*, 21 July 1939, 10.

81. HL Deb (5th series) 19 October 1949 vol. 164 cc.949–1010.

82. 'Elan Valley Will Be Beautiful Again', *Birmingham Gazette*, 5 June 1953, 3.

83. 'Liverpool Show is Getting Better and Better: Entries Up by 1,000', *Liverpool Echo*, 16 July 1953, 5.

Chapter 4

Romantic waterscapes: the development of cultural landscapes

> *And then, the great dams they're building all over the world ... Yes, water's the wildest thing of all, and the chap who can master it's the greatest. Think of what it can give you when once it's tamed. At Niagara there's four million horse-power running to waste at this moment. By the Nile and Euphrates there are thousands upon thousands of square miles of swamp and desert, only waiting for drainage and irrigation to feed half the world. Even here, water's running to waste under our very eyes. In fifty years' time, unless something's done to conserve it, all the cities of the Midlands – to say nothing of London – will be dying of thirst. That's why I've been bicycling into Wales – just looking for water. They've got to look westward. Liverpool's done so already. They'll be filling the lake they've made at Vyrnwy next year. I rode up there last week. The valves are still open, of course, and the river's trickling away; it doesn't know yet that it's been mastered; but when once they're closed ... Imagine what it means. Twelve thousand million gallons – the actual weight of it! That's pressure of fifty tons to every square foot of masonry. If you make the least error in calculating the factors of safety and your dam gives way you'll kill every living thing in the Severn valley. That's where* we *come in. The dams I build won't give way. They'll last for ever. You see!*[1]

The reader could be forgiven for thinking that this is the pitch that a young Thomas Hawksley or J. F. Bateman gave to an unsuspecting municipal authority. The quote is from Francis Brett Young's 1932 novel *The House Under the Water*, a novel that tells the story of a lower gentry family living in the fictitious Dol Escob, Wales, an area that eventually becomes a reservoir.

Young took his inspiration from the flooding of Nantgwyllt to build Caban Coch Reservoir in the Elan Valley. Fittingly for a house that was once home to Percy Shelley, the novel employs ideas of Romanticism and nostalgia, both in its narrative and its descriptions of Dol Escob and Forest Fawr. *The House Under the Water* presents an interesting counterbalance to many of the cultural narratives that surrounded reservoir construction. One might expect contemporaries of the Romantic persuasion to be concerned about urban engineering ruining the aesthetic of the rural idyll, and indeed some in the nineteenth century were. However, the majority of narratives propagated by those who wrote most often about these areas, notably local newspapers and guidebook writers, saw the imposition of urban engineering as helping to make the landscape more beautiful, rather than more industrial and mechanistic.

This novel, as well as other media like newspapers and poetry, forms the basis for this chapter, which looks at how the building of reservoirs affected the cultural landscape of rural areas. Literary depictions of landscapes altered by the construction of reservoirs helped urban residents to see these areas in different ways, thereby helping to develop these areas as sites of leisure, the focus of the following chapter. Focusing on the different ways that the cultural landscape was changed as a consequence of reservoir construction helps to broaden the ideas of amenity that were highlighted in the previous chapter, as well as show the different influences and lineage of writing about reservoirs, from Romanticism through to rural modernism in the mid-twentieth century. It also helps to augment ideas around civic pride and linking these waterscapes with the city, deepening the historiography of civic identity.[2] In short, writers helped not only to promote these rural areas as improved by urban engineering, but placed the city at the heart of this change, thereby further cementing the link between parts of the countryside and the city.

Before the reservoirs: the countryside and the Romantics

The relationship between rural areas and Romanticism has been the subject of in-depth studies for some time, most notably by Jonathan Bate, James Winter and, more recently, Fiona Sampson.[3] Much of this work has focused on the Lake District, one of the first areas of the United Kingdom to be associated with Romanticism due to the writings of William Wordsworth, Samuel Taylor Coleridge and others. It was through their writings, as well as the drawings of William Gilpin and artists such as J. M. W. Turner that depictions of the rural landscape as idyllic and picturesque

Figure 4.1: J. M. W. Turner, *The Valley of the Washburn, Otley Chevin in the distance* (1818), Leeds Museums and Galleries (Leeds Art Gallery) UK© Leeds Museums and Galleries, UK/Bridgeman Images

were constructed. While the reservoirs would not be built for a number of years, these figures helped to project an image of areas like the Lake District or the Washburn Valley that would have an impact in later years. While situated in the Lake District, Thirlmere was an interesting counterpoint to many of the other Cumbrian lakes, such as Windermere, which were more aesthetically Romantic. Lying in a narrow valley with high crags on either side, overshadowed by the imposing peak of Helvellyn, Thirlmere was, as Harriet Ritvo has noted, an 'aesthetic litmus test'. Many were perturbed by Thirlmere from an aesthetic perspective, but those who were not demonstrated an inclination for the sublime. As time went by, many were enchanted rather than intimidated by Thirlmere's beauty, aided by the writings of Coleridge in particular.[4]

Perceptions of the Washburn Valley were brought to wider audiences by the art of J. M. W. Turner, who became friends with Walter Fawkes and stayed at Farnley Hall in the lower valley annually between 1811 and 1824.[5] It was from the steps of Farnley Hall that he painted *Snow Storm: Hannibal and His Army Crossing the Alps* (1812), inspired by a lightning storm over Otley Chevin. Although they are less well known, Turner also painted a number of scenes from the Washburn Valley, many of which are still held in the private collections of Farnley Hall. One such example, currently held by Leeds Museums and Galleries, is Turner's 1818 *Valley of the Washburn* (Figure 4.1), which focuses on a section of the Farnley Hall estate. The painting is indicative of the picturesque and Romantic styles in conveying an irregular, hilly scene, but one that idealises the rural environment. It depicts the lower valley from a high vantage point, the foreground showing the River Washburn as a gentle stream flowing down the valley towards the wide vista of Wharfedale in the background. It constructs the valley as an area of quiet serenity, the sparseness of the riverbanks juxtaposed with the green fields and wooded areas in the distance. It provides an image of the rural idyll comparable to other examples during the early nineteenth century, such as the artistic work of John Constable or the aforementioned works of Wordsworth.

The Elan and Claerwen valleys became associated with Romanticism due to the brief presence of Percy Shelley. Unlike Turner, who sought to construct a Romantic image of the Washburn, Shelley had yet to fully develop his literary skills before spending time with his uncle at Cwm Elan, the largest house in the Elan Valley. Shelley went to Cwm Elan following his expulsion from the University of Oxford in 1811 for espousing atheism. With his new wife, Harriet Grove, Shelley attempted to purchase Nantgwyllt, the largest house in the Claerwen Valley, staying there for a short time before having to leave due to lack of funds. While the rivers Elan and Claerwen are never mentioned by Shelley, his attitudes to the area more generally are conveyed in snapshots in letters sent to family and friends. In letters written from Cwm Elan, Shelley wrote that: 'This country is highly romantic; here are rocks of uncommon height and picturesque waterfalls. I am more astonished at the grandeur of the scenery than I expected.'[6]

While this type of description corresponds to Romantic understandings of wild and natural countryside in the early nineteenth century, it is a little misleading. As Sampson has noted, the landscape that Shelley found so enchanting had been framed to look as such; Shelley's uncle had converted much of his ten thousand acres of land in accordance with the ideas of the picturesque two decades earlier.[7] Despite the lack of urban engineering, which would come nearly one hundred years later, the Romantic constructions of areas like the Elan Valley, and the Washburn Valley in Yorkshire as depicted by Turner, were just that – constructions framed according to particular aesthetic ideals.

Focusing on aesthetic ideals can demonstrate how these landscapes, rural areas that were essentially urban liminal spaces, were thought of as a consequence of the reservoirs. It would be reasonable to assume that reservoirs and dams would have ruined the Romantic associations these areas had. In many cases, however, reservoirs, particularly those built in the nineteenth century, sunk into the ground to appear as natural lakes, were often deemed to make these areas more beautiful and help them further conform to Romantic ideals. Focusing on these areas shows the benefits of focusing on less well-regarded landscapes or, as Katrina Navickas has termed them, areas of non-outstanding natural beauty.[8] Matthew Kelly has noted that Romantic poets in Dartmoor wrote about the passage of water across the landscape in almost mythical terms, yet areas of Devon had been drawing water from the area for centuries, while Plymouth Corporation would complete a major waterworks project in Burrator reservoir in 1898. Dartmoor was, as Kelly has termed it, an anthropic landscape, made not just by the direct actions of human and non-human actors but also by how human actors perceived and depicted the landscape culturally.[9] This term could be applied to all of the landscapes looked at here, and many that are not.

Waterworks and the rural idyll

Many of the rural areas looked at here, then, were already strongly associated with Romanticism. The construction of the reservoirs, though, transformed these areas, both physically and culturally. During the construction of Leeds's Washburn Valley scheme, newspaper correspondents sporadically commented on the aesthetic of the valley during the period of construction itself. Articles in Leeds newspapers regarding the valley during the 1870s typically covered three aspects: engineering, economics and romantic description. Of the seventeen articles published by the *Yorkshire Post*, *Leeds Mercury* and *Leeds Times* during the decade, seven fell into the first two categories, while ten fell into the latter category. While the articles that covered the engineering or economic aspects of the reservoirs stressed the dimensions, construction issues and increasing financial expense, articles in the latter category stressed the picturesque nature of the valley, in some cases in spite of the effects of construction.[10] Articles from 1869 remarked on the isolated nature of the valley as well as its natural beauty, 'as point after point in it is turned, the eye rests on scenery which awakens the highest admiration'.[11] The lack of images in newspapers during this period gave greater importance to the written word, as authors had to convey the Romantic nature of the valley through language. Additionally, newspaper correspondents did not overtly encourage the residents of Leeds to visit the valley, perhaps conscious of the lack of access, with the closest railway stations in Otley and Pool-in-Wharfedale some miles away.[12]

The completion of waterworks schemes brought different dimensions to the cultural landscape. These dimensions were overwhelmingly viewed in positive terms, with the reservoirs adding to the natural aesthetic of these areas. In heightening the beauty of areas like the Washburn Valley or the Elan Valley, the reservoirs made them more attractive places in the eyes of many commentators, who engaged in promoting these spaces as improved by urban engineering. Towns and cities often marketed and sold themselves through the selective use of place that purposefully ignored problems or issues, such as crime.[13] This is indicative of how place was marketed and sold in a literal sense through commercial products, which did not occur in places like the Washburn Valley or Vyrnwy. However, there was drive from local newspapers and locally produced guidebooks to promote these areas according to Romantic ideals. This engaged with what Peter Larkham and Keith Lilley have referred to as 'subverse place promotion': documents that were not created to commodify an area, but that did rely on the rhetoric used in place promotion and civic boosterism.[14] The improvement of rural landscapes by urban engineering, in addition to further changes that contributed to an idealised rurality such as afforestation schemes, linked cultural landscapes with the city. The influence of the city was aided by how the rural landscape was conceived in the late nineteenth century as a place distanced from urban life, which enhanced myths of rurality within the popular imagination.[15] This is what Maria Kaika has termed the urban–rural dialectic, the idea that the city and the countryside held antithetical definitions of each other. The city was seen as either dirty and industrial in contrast to the pristine and pure countryside, or as a place of technological modernity set against rural backwards tradition.[16] Reservoirs, then, acted as cultural capital for cities like Leeds, Liverpool and others that helped to link the landscape to the civic project, a theme that was underscored by the city's newspapers and guidebooks.[17]

In the case of Leeds's Washburn Valley scheme, this process began as early as 1879, shortly after the completion of Fewston reservoir, in the *Leeds Mercury*: 'These great reservoirs, so far from defacing the valley, have added fresh beauty to a place that was previously so pleasing in scenery that it was thought it could not be improved'.[18] There is a recognition that the valley was a site of beauty prior to the construction of the reservoirs before remarking on how the reservoirs had further added to this beauty. The timing of articles like this is significant given that the scars of construction must have remained in certain places not long after the completion of Fewston reservoir. The *Yorkshire Post*, opposed to the building of the reservoirs during the 1860s and 1870s, took a more positive tone in 1882 in describing the waterworks as a 'magnificent chain of reservoirs'.[19] Instead of lauding the aesthetic appeal of the valley, the *Yorkshire Post* instead argued that the reservoirs would bring attention to a previously unknown part of Yorkshire, such as the home of the Thackerays to whom William Makepeace belonged.[20] Even if the reservoirs did not inspire Romantic thoughts, literary associations could fill that role.

The *Leeds Times*, which supported the Washburn scheme from its inception, was keen to emphasise the positive impact the reservoirs would bring to the landscape. In particular, it sought to draw comparisons between the reservoirs and the Lake District, employing the term 'The Leeds Lake District'. Although Matthew Kelly has argued that, before the formation of the Lake District as a national park in 1950, there was no distinct cultural idea of the Lakes, contemporaries did draw parallels between the lakes of Cumbria and their reservoirs.[21] One correspondent named 'A Son of the Times' did just that in 1897:

> I see that a confrere is dragging our readers right away to the other side of England to see some lakes for a 'Holiday Tour'; there is no necessity to go a quarter of the distance, the lakes of Leeds are within 20 miles, and will in beauty compare with those of a distance. They lie amid beautiful scenery, and for size will more than equal Rydal Water or Grasmere, high sounding names though they be.[22]

The development of tourism in the area, alluded to here, will have aided writers local to Leeds in making connections between Cumbria and their own Lakeland. Between the completion of the reservoirs in 1879 and the closure of the *Leeds Times* in 1900, the term was used thirteen times. Although various schemes had sought to dam lakes by 1880, such as Glasgow's Loch Katrine waterworks, as well as a short-lived proposal from Leeds to take water from the Lake District, the 1870s and 1880s was the period that several cities, including Liverpool with Lake Vyrnwy and Manchester with Thirlmere, utilised lakes in order to supply large amounts of water.[23] It was during this period that lakes, in particular the Lake District, were associated with a more utilitarian purpose as well as being areas of natural beauty. This term, then, not only evoked the Cumbrian Lake District, which was undergoing its own experiences of urban engineering, but sought to place the waterworks scheme in comparison with other industrial towns and cities, tacitly inducing civic rivalry.

In 1880, a correspondent named 'The Rambler' invoked this language as he sought to emphasise how engineering prowess and nature could combine to produce a visually pleasing end product:

> The Leeds Corporation have demonstrated that it does not follow because waterworks are formed in a beautiful valley – like the Washburn for instance – that the charms of the scenery are to be destroyed. With

> an engineer like Mr. Filliter, who has an eye to picturesqueness combined with utility, the lake district of Leeds, in the valley of the Washburn is every year becoming more charming.[24]

The celebration of engineering skill in these publications was not uncommon or just consigned to the United Kingdom, as Kaika and Matthew Gandy have highlighted in their studies of Athens and New York respectively.[25] Indeed, the borough surveyor Edward Filliter's aesthetic appreciation was later commented on by a correspondent of the *Wharfedale and Airedale Observer*, who remarked, 'in the contour lines of the reservoirs [...] and in the judicious planting of trees and shrubs on the borders of the lakes, evidences of the true instincts of the landscape gardener are visible in every direction'.[26] This, once again, emphasised a progressive environmental narrative that was noted in Chapter 2, as well as offering a riposte to those that were concerned about the effects of urban industrialisation on the countryside.[27] The reservoirs, because of their earthen embankment design, blended in with the natural appearance of the valley, a feature that the *Leeds Times* credited to Filliter. Thus, the reservoirs not only fulfilled their purpose in providing a pure supply of water to Leeds, but did so while heightening the natural beauty of the valley.

It was not enough, then, for engineers to design waterworks that functioned correctly: they also had to have an eye for the aesthetic. The skill of the engineer in remaking the rural landscape was commented on in an article in the *Morning Post* regarding Lake Vyrnwy. The writer noted the loss of a picturesque village under the waters of Vyrnwy; however, 'it is much to the credit of those who designed the work that [...] it has been successfully carried out with a view to beauty as well as utility'.[28] In Leeds, John Lee, a regular contributor to the *Leeds Times* who wrote under the pseudonym 'The Owl', often commented on the Washburn Valley as a site of beauty that had been improved by the addition of the reservoirs, praising Filliter's design prowess in combining strength and beauty.[29] Lee was particularly keen on drawing the comparison to the Lake District. In an obituary to the former waterworks committee chairman, Alderman Samuel Croft, who presided over the construction of the reservoirs, 'The Owl' noted:

> Guided by the skill and taste of Mr Filliter, waterworks engineer to the Leeds Corporation, the deceased alderman and the committee over which he presided for many years had the good sense to combine the useful with the beautiful, and the 'Lake District' of the Leeds Corporation will compare for utility and picturesqueness with any town in the kingdom.[30]

While the *Leeds Times* often focused on the picturesque and Romantic elements of the reservoirs, it continued to be married to a sense of utility and nature. The reservoirs heightened the beauty of the valley, but their purpose in providing water for Leeds was also important to recognise. Unlike the Lake District of Cumbria, these lakes were man-made, and therefore humanity had tamed the wilderness and improved it, while also providing an important utility. One newspaper that might have been expected to carry negative opinions towards the reservoirs was the *Wharfedale and Airedale Observer*; however, even it praised the impact of the engineering works on the valley's aesthetic. One article argued that the decline of industry, impact of construction and rural depopulation were positives, as the waters would be less threatened from pollution, and the picturesque beauty of the valley would be preserved intact as a consequence.[31]

Reservoirs also became associated with another type of utility: fishing. The importance of fishing to these waterscapes is discussed in more detail in the following chapter; however, it is worth noting that it was often fishing correspondents who wrote effusively about these rural areas. An article in the *Montgomeryshire Express* extolled the virtues of these newly made fishing spots in Wales: 'Lake Vyrnwy is beautiful and majestic in its wild loneliness; the lakes of the Elan Valley are greatly to be admired for their charming situation and lovely views'.[32] Despite being tamed by humankind, to this writer Vyrnwy continued to encapsulate a sense of wildness that enticed visitors, while the Elan Valley reservoirs were praised for views which were, ultimately, unnatural. This was pointedly referred to by a correspondent of the *Illustrated Sporting and Dramatic News* in 1894, when they noted that 'next to Loch Katrine, Lake Vyrnwy is admitted to be the most beautiful lake in the United Kingdom, and this in spite of it being artificial'.[33]

A trend across the case studies looked at here is the continued emphasis placed on the role of local government in making these spaces. A correspondent to the *Yorkshire Post* in 1910 sought to do just that when writing about the Washburn Valley. After noting that the area had not been recorded in the Domesday Book because of its remoteness, he argued:

> It is this remoteness and miniature charm which have environed it at last with fame, art and science having combined to secure it for human use in a distant city [...] But [for] the colossal earthworks buttressing the dams, these lakes are perfectly natural, washing on shingly margins in miniature coves and headlands, under hill and wood and island.[34]

This framed the reservoirs not only as improving the area as feats of urban engineering, but simultaneously natural in composition due to their integration into the landscape. It is clear from this correspondence that not only did the reservoirs heighten the beauty of the valley, but it was because they were man-made that this was possible. Given the commonality of language used by newspaper writers across the country, this could easily be describing Vyrnwy or the Elan Valley. The engineers and navvies had rescued these areas from remoteness and had constructed a second nature, a conscious, 'pride-inducing' remaking of the natural landscape that improved on its former appearance, which had simultaneously made the wilderness serviceable and positioned the city apart from nature as an area engineered to be distinct from the urban.[35] It further emphasises the centrality of urban engineering to the remaking of the cultural landscape, and the sense of civic pride that it evoked. This construction of nature was somewhat pointedly remarked on by a correspondent of the *Yorkshire Evening Post* who, on a walk in the valley, came across three men, described as being of 'the artisan class', arguing over why the banks of the reservoirs were white. On telling the men that this was because of the amount of flowers at the sides of the reservoirs, one replied, 'Ah, say maister, theer's no wonder ert t' rates going up when t' Corporation plants t' reservoir sides wi' flowers ter mak t'watter look nice'.[36]

Guidebooks also offer an insight into how rural areas like the Washburn Valley were conceptualised externally. Guidebooks became increasingly popular during the nineteenth century as middle-class urbanites began to explore the countryside, as well as other countries, with guides by John Murray and Karl Baedeker particularly popular. Guidebooks that covered small areas of the country, like those examined here, conditioned readers to think within smaller geographical frameworks, thereby helping to establish areas like the Washburn Valley or Wharfedale as distinct.[37] One such guidebook was Tom Bradley's *The Washburn*, published in 1895. Bradley wrote a series of articles for the *Yorkshire Post*'s 'Weekly Post' supplement on the rivers of Yorkshire, such as the Nidd, the Wharfe and the Derwent, among others, which were later published as pocket-sized books. Once again, the river was the main focus of the guide, which opens:

> The River Washburn is one of the very few of the Yorkshire rivers which enjoy distinction of retaining their natural beauty and peaceful rest unsullied and undisturbed by the noisy rush of the railway engine, the scream of its frantic whistle, and the settling pall of grime that follows in its wake.[38]

Although the valley was missed by the expanding railway network, Bradley's account neglects the industrial history of the area. This had declined by 1895, but there was a pre-existing relationship with the Washburn Valley and the flax-spinning industry, which is ignored by

Bradley in his depiction of the valley as a place of timeless peace. He also ignored the ways in which the valley had been previously engineered, such as the creation of small reservoirs at Blubberhouses for West House Mill.[39] He did acknowledge the presence of engineering in the valley, particularly the reservoirs; however, he argued 'it [engineering] has tended rather to heighten its beauties than depress them, and the reservoirs with their broad spreading surfaces and luxuriant margins have all the appearance of natural lakes'.[40] Once more, the natural aesthetic of the valley was improved by technology.

Although technology had improved the appearance of the valley, Bradley lamented the lack of tourist activity in the area. In describing the beauties of Lindley Wood, he remarked that the reservoir would make a 'magnificent yachting and boating resort' for 'the toilers in our busy hives'.[41] This activity would not have been permitted on Lindley Wood as the sporting rights to the reservoir had been secured by the Fawkes family. Indeed, boating was not an activity undertaken on the reservoirs until the late twentieth century, when Thruscross was used by the Leeds Sailing Club from shortly after its completion in 1966 until 1995.[42]

Bradley's guide was followed by another prominent writer on Yorkshire, Harry Speight. Speight also came from a journalistic background, writing articles for the *Bradford Observer*, among other newspapers. Whereas Bradley used the rivers of Yorkshire as his primary focus, Speight wrote about more specific areas of North and West Yorkshire, such as lower Wharfedale, Nidderdale and Craven. Like many guidebooks, Speight's account of the Washburn Valley, published in 1900, started in Leathley, in the south of the valley, which he described as having 'too tempting a *bonne bouche* to be omitted from the rambler's holiday *menu*'.[43] From here, one could follow the Washburn to reach 'the Leeds "Lake District"' where 'the long bright expanses that supply that famous city with pure water may be viewed, gleaming in the distance, lake-like for many miles'.[44] The reservoirs were presented by Speight and others as grand landmarks, both in terms of size and aesthetic. This was further emphasised by Edmund Bogg in his guide *Two Thousand Miles in Wharfedale*, in which he lauded the engineering skill of the reservoir's engineers while simultaneously reinforcing the link between the valley and 'the Cumberland lakes'.[45] Speight further remarked: '[h]ow the mind of the poet and antiquity fondly turns to scenes such as these, recalling the many changes of the place and of faces and forms that have vanished, and of the fleeting works of man, while Nature alone is ever young and fair'.[46] There is a misrepresentation of the past in this quote; as has been established, the natural landscape was vastly altered as a result of the reservoirs. Speight also emphasised less positive aspects of the valley's representation, on this occasion damage from floods that had destroyed bridges at Lindley Wood and Dob Park.[47] However, like Bradley, Speight sought to elicit a sense of timeless peace in his description of the valley, a sense that was more fiction than fact.

Despite the similarities between how the reservoirs of Leeds, Liverpool and Birmingham were culturally depicted, it is interesting that those writing on Vyrnwy and Elan never directly compared those lakes to the Lake District as with Leeds. That did not mean that the civic links between Vyrnwy and Liverpool or Elan and Birmingham were any less strong. The *Liverpool Echo* pointedly referred to this civic link in 1930 in an article about Central Wales, arguing that 'Liverpool people can claim to have created in Vyrnwy the most beautiful lake in Wales'.[48] Just as with afforestation, the civic link between Liverpool and Vyrnwy is cemented here; not only is the emphasis placed on the people of Liverpool rather than the corporation or the engineers, but the use of 'created' also speaks to the socionatural hybridity of Vyrnwy. In effect, this was a space that the people of Liverpool, through their city council, had made, and in so doing had made that area more beautiful, a tribute to the city and its denizens.

It was not just proponents of the cities themselves that celebrated these waterworks. H. V. Morton took in the Elan Valley while searching for Wales in the 1930s. After providing contextual information on the reservoirs, he detailed his journey around the valley. In keeping with the Romantic context, Morton was especially interested in learning more about Nantgwyllt, providing some colourful detail on Shelley and his time in Wales. He then went on a tour of the dams themselves, describing the thunderous sound of the water disappearing down dark iron tubes, once again invoking ideas of rural modernism that became prevalent during this period. Unlike J. B. Priestley, who paid little attention to the Washburn Valley reservoirs on his *English Journey*, Morton was taken by the Elan Valley reservoirs, writing that 'The Elan Valley is, to my mind, more beautiful than any lake scenery in the Principality'.[49] Additionally, Morton was clear on who was responsible for creating this idyllic scenery; on returning to the surface following his tour of the dam, he 'looked out at the placid lake where a man in a boat was trying to catch trout in the bath water of Birmingham'.[50]

The defence of the rural idyll

Not all depictions of these rural areas were positively influenced by the reservoirs. Although few in number, they are nonetheless informative when looking at notions of place and how attitudes towards the cultural landscape were shaped by broader literary ideals. A letter to the *Manchester Guardian* was quick to bemoan the changes occurring at Thirlmere in 1880: 'the beauty of the little lake – let what may be said, one of the wildest and most romantic of them all – is gone'. As the paper was quick to point out, though, construction work had hardly begun on the reservoir, suggesting that even impending engineering works affected the cultural landscape for some.[51] In the case of the Washburn Valley, this narrative, somewhat unsurprisingly, mainly originated within the valley through the work of Reverend Thomas Parkinson. Parkinson, a resident of Crag Hall near Fewston village, but vicar to the parish of North Otterington, North Yorkshire, wrote a number of books on the area, including an account of folklore in Yorkshire and a collection of writings relating to the Forest of Knaresborough.[52] His collection *An Idyll and Ballads of Washburndale* offers an insight into his perceptions of the changing valley. The poem 'A Dirge for the Vale' provides a eulogy to the valley before the coming of the reservoirs:

> Brother, dost thou remember,
> The valley bright and fair,
> Where ran the sparkling river,
> And breath of peace was there [...]
>
> But, ah! the village changeth!
> The villagers are fled;
> No sound of mirth ariseth –
> All rural life is dead.[53]

Whereas the extracts examined so far have sought to emphasise how the reservoirs heightened the beauty of the valley, Parkinson highlighted the idyllic past, showing what had been lost to urban engineering. The final verse presented a sterile vision of rural life that was somewhat hyperbolic, as rural life continued long after the construction of the reservoirs. However, it does highlight a sense of loss. Predicting that the reservoirs – 'this new thing in our vale' – would bring the people of Leeds to the valley, he concluded:

> In us who knew the 'older';
> This new thing cannot wake;
> The old associations;
> Now buried 'neath this lake.[54]

For Parkinson, the reservoirs symbolised the end of a way of life for many, signs of a better time lost beneath the waters. In some ways this undoubtedly happened, with the reservoirs negatively impacting on population decline generally and Fewston village specifically following the subsidence. This is evidence from a more declensionist perspective of the anthropic landscape that Kelly refers to.[55] The demolition of Fewston Mill, the ruins of which now lie under the waters of Swinsty Reservoir, encapsulated a loss of employment and population. For Parkinson, the reservoirs were visible signs of urban expansion into the countryside and rural depopulation that signalled the end of a way of life for many in the valley.

Parkinson was not the only resident of the valley to express dismay at the decline of rural life. A letter to the *Yorkshire Post* in 1903 from 'A Native' further underlined the transformative effects of the reservoirs and how they had impacted on meanings of place:

> It is probably unknown to nine-tenths of the inhabitants of Leeds how greatly the appropriation of the once remote, peaceful, and prosperous valley of the Washburn to the purposes of the Leeds water supply, has had the effect of desolating and materially and socially altering this retired spot, not only by substituting large lake-like reservoirs for its purling river and attractive river scenery, but also by sweeping away historical and other landmarks, disinheriting its old yeoman families, and removing or alienating their ancestral homes.[56]

The correspondent employed the same techniques as Parkinson in portraying the valley as a more idyllic place before the coming of the reservoirs. Although industry was, for a time, relatively successful in the valley, its decline was precipitated by factors other than the reservoirs. The correspondent further sought to contrast the Washburn Valley of the past, the 'purling river' and historic landmarks, with what remained, echoing Parkinson's narrative that the past was lost under the waters of the reservoirs. 'A Native' claimed that he was not complaining about these losses, but was informing those who were less informed in Leeds. However, both Parkinson and 'A Native' imbued the Washburn Valley with a meaning that was not reciprocated by wider narratives, that the construction of the reservoirs had not added to the valley but had removed its history and heritage.

It is also worth dwelling briefly on one of the main waterworks projects that was not the focus of writers, particularly guidebook writers. Accounts of Thirlmere from guides to the Lake District sought to portray the reservoir in scientific terms, perhaps because the Lake District as an area was already heavily associated with Romanticism. A guidebook from 1895 did not comment on the aesthetic merits of Thirlmere but concentrated more on its engineering qualities.[57] Another from 1905 further detailed the ways in which Thirlmere had been engineered, although it did comment that a dam on the north 'enhanced its beauty'.[58] However, as Ritvo has noted, Thirlmere was considered by guidebook writers as a secondary attraction that writers included by default due to its location next to the A591. Additionally, it was an area that, above all else, was difficult to enjoy owing to restrictions on access imposed around the reservoir and surrounding land by the Manchester Corporation, to a much greater extent than imposed by other municipal authorities.[59] In what was perhaps the first cultural landscape to be associated with Romanticism, it is understandable that those seeking aesthetic delights would be less inclined to visit Thirlmere over Windermere.

There were, then, some negative portrayals of reservoirs to go with the large number of positive representations. Francis Brett Young's 1932 novel *The House Under the Water* offers an interesting counterbalance to the constructions presented thus far. Young specialised in the regional novel, focusing on the Black Country in a period of transition from the late nineteenth to the mid-twentieth century. However, like Birmingham Corporation, his interests extended beyond Warwickshire to encompass the borders of Radnorshire.[60] The novel follows the fortunes of Griffith Tregaron, a tenant farmer who married into minor Italian aristocracy following his time fighting for Garibaldi during Italian unification. Tregaron is summoned by his uncle to Nant Escob, a large house in Forest Fawr, Wales, where he bequeaths his home to his nephew before shortly dying. The story then charts the travails of Tregaron, who goes through periods of boom and bust with various enterprises, and his family, in particular his youngest daughter Phillipa (Phil) who becomes one of the point of view characters.

Published in 1932, the novel sits at a nexus point. Young's construction of Forest Fawr is undoubtedly inspired by the picturesque and Romantic movements. Influenced by the time the novel was set in the late nineteenth century, Phil's first impressions of Forest Fawr are not to be overawed by its intimidating nature but to fall in love with it, much like the early Romantic aesthetes approaching Thirlmere. Later in the novel, when Phil realises that the engineer Charles Lingen, the object of her romantic desires and whose monologue opened this chapter, has returned to Forest Fawr in order to dam the valley and flood the house, it breaks her heart. Furthermore, it is not so subtly implied that ill fortune will follow anyone who betrays Nant Escob. Shortly after selling the house to the North Bromwich Corporation – a thinly veiled pseudonym for the city of Birmingham – Tregaron suffers from various economic setbacks: the death of his second son fighting in South Africa, ill health, losing almost all the money he made selling the house, and eventually succumbing to a brain aneurism. Young implies that there is a cost to modernity, then, for both the central protagonists.

David Cannedine has noted the close relationship between Brett Young and the Conservative politician Stanley Baldwin during the interwar years, arguing that Young's novels spoke to the same notions of wholesome rural traditions that Baldwin advocated during his time as prime minister in the 1920s.[61] The novel, though, is not anti-modern by any means, and as such corresponds to broader historiographical arguments about rurality during the interwar period put forward by Peter Mandler and David Matless.[62] Indeed, Kristin Bluemel has argued that the novel, written for a middle-class audience well versed in Brett Young's linguistic style, urged readers to reject the idea that rural places were victims of modernity but could respond to social and economic changes with resilience.[63] Tregaron's eldest son, Rob, treated as the black sheep of the family due to being born out of wedlock to another woman, is a case in point. When he leaves Nant Escob following a confrontation with Tregaron, he travels to North Bromwich to design first bikes and then motor cars, making a small fortune in the process. Rob, presented as a good and honest character alongside Phil, is shown to be rewarded for his hard work and good nature in comparison to other characters who are often punished for their vanity. Furthermore, rurality is not necessarily held up as a perfect way of life. Of the family, only Phil fully enjoys her time at Nant Escob, with other characters, such as Tregaron's Italian wife, Lucrezia, depicted as lonely and isolated from the life they once knew. Tregaron also initially struggles to adapt to life in Forest Fawr, struggling to make a living from sheep farming and resorting to selling timber from the estate.

In some ways, *The House Under the Water* points backwards to Romantic traditions, to a way of seeing and engaging with the rural landscape that valorises untouched nature. However, in other ways the influences of the 1930s come to bear; as novels such as *Brave New World* pointed to the social dangers of trusting to science, Young's novel is not so black and white. Through the character of Phil, it comes to terms with change – while Phil's heart is broken by Lingen's dream to flood the valley, when she returns years later she sets out to see her former home:

> Yes, Nant Escob was gone, and Barradale had done his worst, yet the spirit of Forest Fawr, resurgent, inviolable, had perfected, out of man's disfigurement, a new loveliness surpassing any that conscious man could achieve. Phil dismounted, trembling. The pony wandered away. As she sat on the escarpment, still gazing, tears started to her eyes so that she could not see: tears of thankfulness, tears of joy, and others, inexplicable tears.[64]

'Man's disfigurement' here can be juxtaposed with Lingen's narrative of mastery that opened this chapter, highlighting the scale of the Promethean project. In some ways, this is the perfect description of the socionatural hybridity of these cultural landscapes, altered by humans but still shaped by nature, becoming an entanglement of the intentions and actions of both. It also symbolises that change in these rural areas, often characterised negatively, could be seen as a positive, thereby producing a more nuanced understanding of the relationship between social actors and modern society.[65]

The perspective put forward by Young is interesting for a number of reasons. First, while literary, Nant Escob and the subsequent reservoirs are thinly veiled descriptions of Nantgwyllt, the one-time home of Percy Shelley, and the Elan Valley reservoirs. Indeed, one of the nearby homes in the novel is called Glen Elan. The meanings put forward in his novel, then, can be taken to be representative of the Elan Valley itself, seen through fictional eyes but processing real emotions. Second, the perspective is more nuanced than any other looked at in this chapter. Rather than being the product of longer-standing Romantic traditions, the novel is emblematic of a rural modernism that conceptualised the landscape in a more complex way. As Bluemel has highlighted, the ending provides a happy ending for both Phil and the reader, but not necessarily in preservationist terms. Brett Young's engagement with nostalgia for a landscape lost results in a more complicated resolution for the heroine, showing that rural people and rural places could face modern changes with resilience.[66]

Conclusion

Newspapers and guidebooks had definitively moved away from describing waterworks in rural areas in Romantic terms after the Second World War. There were instances where the civic link between the city and the countryside was stressed; however, in line with the wider social trends of the post-war period that emphasised the white heat of scientific revolution, there was little place or appetite for writers to remark on how these rural areas had been altered by urban engineering. This was especially the case with guidebooks, which became much more utilitarian in purpose, providing clear instructions on how to get from one location to another. The lack of description left it up to the walker to determine meaning, but this does mean that the continuity of meaning between the city and the country weakened.

A related factor was the decline of local government in the post-war years, with power increasingly centralised in Westminster. Water governance remained in local control longer than other utilities, but the industry was pseudo-centralised during the 1970s with the creation of the regional water boards, before being privatised in the 1980s. This removal of power from local government meant that there was little reason to stress the link between urban engineering and the rural countryside to the residents of cities like Leeds or Liverpool, especially when some of the waterworks projects had been built over one hundred years previously. While private water companies such as Yorkshire Water have engaged with the history and heritage of these sites, they ultimately remain privatised structures serving interconnected regions rather than individual cities.

In this context, then, the return of narrative walking books in the twenty-first century is worth noting. A number of books have been published that provide commentary on the process of walking in nature that pays attention not just to idealised landscapes but also to areas that would have previously been dismissed, such as peat bogs or former industrial sites, perhaps reflecting a greater public interest in the environment. As Matless has noted, this combination of nature writing and memoir, propagated by writers like Robert MacFarlane and Helen Macdonald, has become increasingly popular and has revived what was deemed to be a lost form of writing that highlights the impact of the non-human as well as the human.[67] Matless argues that these works are part of a broader cultural geography that links the landscape with Englishness, an observation that ties into how waterworks like Rutland Water were conceptualised from the 1970s onwards.[68] Reservoirs such as those in the Elan Valley or at Vyrnwy have yet to be re-evaluated by what might be called public walking histories or narratives. Despite Sampson's recent dismissal of the Elan reservoirs, which she argues are a 'huge simplification' of the landscape, there remains a cultural fascination with these waterworks, as seen in novels such as Sarah Hall's *Haweswater* among others.[69] The interpretation of these waterworks by contemporary writers would add a fascinating layer to an already rich history of their cultural landscapes.

This chapter has shown that newspapers and guidebooks were heavily invested in reinforcing this civic link. Writers clearly attributed meaning to reservoirs, structures implemented by urban authorities that remade the countryside. Writers depicted these areas as being improved and made more beautiful by urban engineering, a conclusion that people like Ruskin would have most likely bristled against given his opposition to Thirlmere. The presence of similar tropes to describe these areas across newspapers and guidebooks speaks to their cultural currency in lieu of statistics on readership, which are hard to ascertain for local publications. As with other means of altering these waterscapes, like afforestation, the centrality of the city was key. As such, the city was not seen in opposition to the countryside but as an active agent in making the countryside more idyllic. This conclusion, as with other aspects of reservoir management highlighted in other chapters, helps to move beyond the culture/nature binary, or indeed the city/country dialectic identified by Kaika – the construction of reservoirs helped to facilitate a reciprocal hinterland relationship between the city and the country, and the cultural landscape was an important part of that relationship. Charting the development of literary writing from Romanticism to rural modernism in the twentieth century helps to show how attitudes to the cultural landscape were more complex than can first appear. There are, once again, differences across the individual case studies, but the similarities help to draw a national picture of how reservoirs were largely conceived within the popular imagination. It also underscores the importance of rural modernism as a theme of this book, showing that there was more to understanding landscape than feelings of nostalgia. The development of writings about the cultural landscape encouraged urban citizens to see places like the 'Leeds Lake District' for themselves, facilitating a growth in leisure that is explored in the following chapter.

Notes

1. Francis Brett Young, *The House Under the Water* (Heinemann, 1932), 88–9.

2. See Simon Gunn, *The Public Culture of the Victorian Middle Class: Ritual and Authority in the English Industrial City 1840–1914* (Manchester University Press, 2000), 163–82; Tom Hulme, *After the Shock City: Urban Culture and the Making of Modern Citizenship* (Boydell Press, 2019).

3. Jonathan Bate, *The Song of the Earth* (Harvard University Press, 2000); James Winter, *Secure from Rash Assault: Sustaining the Victorian Environment* (University of California Press, 1999); Fiona Sampson, *Starlight Wood: Walking Back to the Romantic Countryside* (Corsair, 2022).

4. Harriet Ritvo, *The Dawn of Green: Manchester, Thirlmere, and Modern Environmentalism* (University of Chicago Press, 2009), 13–14.

5. David Hill, *In Turner's Footsteps: Through the Hills and Dales of Northern England* (John Murray Ltd, 1984), 22; M. Sharples, 'The Fawkes-Turner Connection and the Art Collection at Farnley Hall, Otley, 1792–1937: A Great Estate Enhanced and Supported', *Northern History* 26, no. 1 (1990): 142, https://doi.org/10.1179/007817290790175935.

6. Percy Shelley, 'Letter to Elizabeth Hitchner' (1811), quoted in Sampson, *Starlight Wood*, 73.

7. Sampson, *Starlight Wood*, 73.

8. Katrina Navickas, 'Building Amenity in Areas of Non-Outstanding Natural Beauty in the Southern Pennines', in *New Lives, New Landscapes Revisited: Rural Modernity in Britain*, ed. Linda M. Ross et al. (British Academy, Oxford University Press, 2023), 96.

9. Matthew Kelly, *Quartz and Feldspar: Dartmoor – A British Landscape in Modern Times* (Vintage, 2016), 121.

10. This was particularly true of articles in the *Leeds Times*, which firmly supported the construction of reservoirs for both utilitarian and tourist purposes. See 'Local news', *Leeds Times*, 28 August 1869, 3.

11. 'The Future Water Supply of Leeds', *Yorkshire Post*, 24 August 1869, 3.

12. According to guidebook writer Tom Bradley, Otley was 2.5 miles away from Leathley in the south valley, whereas Pool-in-Wharfedale was 1.75 miles. Tom Bradley, *The Washburn* (Old Hall Press, 1988 [first published 1895]), 33.

13. Stephen Ward, *Selling Places: The Marketing and Promotion of Towns and Cities 1850–2000* (E. & F. N. Spon, 1998), 1.

14. Peter J. Larkham and Keith D. Lilley, 'Plans, Planners and City Images: Place Promotion and Civic Boosterism in British Reconstruction Planning', *Urban History* 30, no. 2 (2003): 197, https://doi.org/10.1017/S0963926803001123.

15. Pyrs Gruffudd, 'Selling the Countryside: Representations of Rural Britain' in *Place Promotion: The Use of Publicity and Marketing to Sell Towns and Regions*, ed. John R. Gold and Stephen V. Ward (Wiley, 1994), 261; Jeffrey Hopkins, 'Signs of the Post-Rural: Marketing Myths of a Symbolic Countryside', *Geografiska Annaler: Series B, Human Geography* 80, no. 2 (1998): 65, https://doi.org/10.1111/j.0435-3684.1998.00030.x.

16. Maria Kaika, *City of Flows: Modernity, Nature, and the City* (Routledge, 2005), 14.

17. Jon Stobart, 'Identity, Competition and Place Promotion in the Five Towns', *Urban History* 30, no. 2 (2003): 167, https://doi.org/10.1017/S0963926803001111.

18. Special correspondent, 'Agriculture in Yorkshire', *Leeds Mercury*, 19 November 1879, 8.

19. 'Local and Other News', *Yorkshire Post*, 24 February 1882, 3.

20. William Makepeace Thackeray was a prominent British novelist during the nineteenth century, most notably the author of *Vanity Fair* (1848); 'Local and Other News', *Yorkshire Post*.

21. Matthew Kelly, *The Women Who Saved the English Countryside* (Yale University Press, 2022), 95.

22. A Son of the Times, 'Leeds Water Supply: The Inspection by the City Council', *Leeds Times*, 24 July 1897, 5.

23. Ritvo, *Dawn of Green*, 109; Owen Roberts, 'The Politics of Health and the Origins of Liverpool's Lake Vyrnwy Water Scheme, 1871–92', *Welsh History Review* 20, no. 2 (2000): 320.

24. The Rambler, 'The Leeds Lake District', *Leeds Times*, 25 September 1880, 2.

25. Kaika, *City of Flows*; Matthew Gandy, *Concrete and Clay: Reworking Nature in New York City* (MIT Press, 2003).

26. 'Spring in the Washburn Valley', *Wharfedale and Airedale Observer*, 15 June 1888, 2.

27. Vicky Albritton and Fredrik Albritton Jonsson, *Green Victorians: The Simple Life in John Ruskin's Lake District* (University of Chicago Press, 2016), 12–13.

28. 'The Magazines for March', *Morning Post*, 5 March 1890, 2.

29. The Owl, 'Notes by the Owl', *Leeds Times*, 3 December 1881, 5.

30. The Owl, 'Notes by the Owl', *Leeds Times*, 24 November 1883, 4–5.

31. 'Spring in the Washburn Valley', *Wharfedale and Airedale Observer*, 2.

32. 'Mochdre Reservoir', *Montgomeryshire Express*, 28 August 1906, 4.

33. 'Trout-Fishing on Lake Vyrnwy', *Illustrated Sporting and Dramatic News*, 14 April 1894, 21.

34. Correspondent, 'The Washburn Valley', *Yorkshire Post*, 24 November 1910, 4.

35. Kaika, *City of Flows*, 107; Kaika, 'Dams as Symbols of Modernization: The Urbanization of Nature Between Geographical Imagination and Materiality', *Annals of the Association of American Geographers* 96, no. 2 (2006): 295, https://doi.org/10.1111/j.1467-8306.2006.00478.x.

36. 'Making "T'Watter" Look Nice', *Yorkshire Evening Post*, 12 September 1913, 4.

37. Gráinne Goodwin and Gordon Johnston, 'Guidebook Publishing in the Nineteenth Century: John Murray's *Handbooks for Travellers*', *Studies in Travel Writing* 17, no. 1 (2013): 43–61, https://doi.org/10.1080/13645145.2012.747791; Marjorie Morgan, *National Identities and Travel in Victorian Britain* (Palgrave, 2001).

38. Bradley, *The Washburn*, 3.

39. Diana Parsons, *The Book of the Washburn Valley: Yorkshire's Forgotten Dale* (Halsgrove, 2014), 44–5.

40. Bradley, *The Washburn*, 3.

41. Bradley, *The Washburn*, 7.

42. Yorkshire Dales Sailing Club, 'History of YDSC', accessed 30 January 2018, http://yorkshiredales.sc/history-of-ydsc/.

43. Harry Speight, *Upper Wharfedale* (Elliot Stock, 1900), 107.

44. Speight, *Upper Wharfedale.*

45. Edmund Bogg, *Two Thousand Miles in Wharfedale* (James Miles, 1904), 344–5.

46. Speight, *Upper Wharfedale*, 126.

47. Speight, *Upper Wharfedale*, 107.

48. 'The Wonderland of Central Wales', *Liverpool Echo*, 7 July 1930, 6.

49. J. B. Priestley, *English Journey* (Heinemann, 1934), 178; H. V. Morton, *In Search of Wales* (Methuen, 1932), 190.

50. Morton, *In Search of Wales*, 192.

51. *Manchester Guardian*, quoted in 'Untitled', *Crewe Chronicle*, 18 September 1880, 5.

52. Parkinson was instituted to North Otterington, which lies to the south of Northallerton, by the Archbishop of York in 1871. It is somewhat ironic that Parkinson was so moved by the construction of the reservoirs when he would have been one of the few whose employment was not directly affected. Anon., 'Local and General', *Leeds Mercury*, 9 December 1871, 8; Parsons, *Book of the Washburn Valley*, 57.

53. Thomas Parkinson, *An Idyll and Ballads of Washburn-dale* (East Kent Works, n/d), 45, 52, edition held by Leeds Library.

54. Parkinson, *Idyll and Ballads*, 53–4.

55. Kelly, *Quartz and Feldspar*, 121.

56. A Native, 'The Leeds Corporation and the Washburn Valley: A Wail', *Yorkshire Post*, 3 November 1903, 4

57. *The English Lake District, Including Furness Abbey, Shap Spa, Seascale, etc., etc.* (George Philip and Son, 1895), 77–8.

58. *The English Lake District; Being the fourth edition of 'Morecambe and the Lake District Illustrated'* (William Mate and Sons, 1905).

59. Ritvo, *Dawn of Green*, 174.

60. L. J. Jay, 'The Black Country of Francis Brett Young', *Transactions of the Institute of British Geographers* 66 (1975): 62, https://doi.org/10.2307/621621.

61. David Cannedine, *In Churchill's Shadow: Confronting the Past in Modern Britain* (Penguin, 2003), 161

62. Peter Mandler, 'Against "Englishness": English Culture and the Limits to Rural Nostalgia, 1850–1940', *Transactions of the Royal Historical Society* 7 (1997): 155–75, https://doi.org/10.2307/3679274; David Matless, *Landscape and Englishness*, 2nd ed. (Reaktion Books, 2016).

63. Kristin Bluemel, 'Rural Modernity in Britain: Landscape, Literature, Nostalgia' in *New Lives, New Landscapes Revisited: Rural Modernity in Britain*, ed. by Linda M. Ross et al. (British Academy, Oxford University Press, 2023), 58.

64. Young, *House Under the Water*, 680.

65. Jeffrey Mathes McCarthy, *Green Modernism: Nature and the English Novel, 1900 to 1930* (Palgrave, 2015), 9.

66. Bluemel, 'Rural Modernity in Britain', 57.

67. Matless, *Landscape and Englishness*, 22.

68. Matless, *Landscape and Englishness*; Dennis Cosgrove et al., 'Landscape and Identity at Ladybower Reservoir and Rutland Water', *Transactions of the Institute of British Geographers* 21, no. 3 (1996); 534–51. https://doi.org/10.2307/622595.

69. Sampson, *Starlight Wood*, 76; Eileen Pollard, '"When the Reservoir Comes": Drowned Villages, Community and Nostalgia in Contemporary British Fiction', *C21 Literature: Journal of 21st-Century Writings* 5, no. 3 (2017), 1–21, https://doi.org/10.16995/c21.9.

Chapter 5

All play and no fun: waterworks and the pursuit of leisure

Given the propensity of water authorities to accentuate the 'natural' appearance of their artificial reservoirs, aided by local newspapers and guidebooks, it is not surprising that these areas became popular sites of leisure. The pursuit of leisure has often been described as a product of nineteenth-century industrialisation and the growth of individual liberties, although more recent histories of leisure have underlined a longer lineage.[1] The development of modern leisure pursuits, if not the product of industrialisation, was certainly affected by the growth of an industrial society.[2] Angling, for example, had been engaged in for decades, but fly fishing increased in popularity with the middle classes during the nineteenth century, as did coarse fishing with the working classes.[3] As leisure pursuits such as fishing and rambling increased in popularity, the contemporaneous construction of waterworks schemes in the countryside made these areas desirable to visit and enjoy. In most cases, leisure was not at the forefront of engineers' or water authorities' plans; however, municipal governments in Birmingham, Liverpool and Leeds, to name a few, soon recognised the benefits that incorporating leisure into the management of the waterworks could bring in strengthening the civic link between the city and the country, as well as the value to amenity recognised in the previous chapter.

The increased use of these rural areas, though, was not necessarily plain sailing. As authorities managed this increase, the feasibility and desirability of fishing in municipal reservoirs was questioned, while authorities closely guarded the edges of reservoirs from walkers and ramblers as battles for access to the countryside ensued. The purpose of this chapter, then, is to examine how the use of waterworks schemes for leisure purposes developed, focusing primarily on angling and rambling during the late nineteenth and early twentieth centuries. Leisure is vital for understanding how marginalised landscapes came to be valued beyond their utility, a consequence of how cultural landscapes were remade following the construction of reservoirs. Not only does this show how leisure pursuits became intertwined with civic identity, but it also recognises the cultural value of the hinterland exchange, thereby becoming a part of the wider Promethean project to remake the countryside for urban need. Although leisure may have been considered as an afterthought, it became a key element in strengthening the civic ties between waterworks projects that cost hundreds of thousands of pounds and the urban residents who relied on them. The use of these areas for leisure was a celebration of civic achievement and, in the case of fishing, allowed urban residents to perform their civic duty in maintaining a healthy water supply, thereby adding to our historiographical understandings of leisure and citizenship.[4] Barriers to leisure did remain, though. There remained unease with the increased use of rural areas by the working classes, while women did not become properly involved in leisure pursuits until mass participation in rambling took place in the twentieth century.[5]

The development of leisure

Areas of the countryside had long been associated with leisure pursuits, predominantly for the upper classes. The main leisure activity undertaken in these rural areas was, historically, shooting. Hunting rights were apportioned to areas such as the Forest of Knaresborough in North Yorkshire or the New Forest in Hampshire, where hunting was permitted with permission from the Crown. It is unsurprising, then, that the hunting of game, particularly grouse, developed and became a carefully managed pastime of the rural gentry. Grouse shooting was not consigned to one area of the country, as a variety of landed estates was utilised for upper-class recreation. The development of the sport in rural areas such as the Washburn Valley or Lake Vyrnwy had much to do with wider changes to rural social life; the Enclosure Acts, the undercutting of British agriculture with foreign imports, and the development of the railways were just a few factors in the weakening of rural economic and social life in Britain during the nineteenth century. As rural populations and communal rights declined, the upper classes were well placed to cultivate areas of the countryside for the pursuit of game. Country estates started to engage in landscape management, not only in cultivating heather for grouse to feed off and live among, but in building shooting lodges and butts across the uplands.[6]

The social and economic upheaval that affected the development of shooting was further exacerbated by the construction of waterworks schemes. Waterworks schemes across the country greatly affected the sanctity of long-held sporting rights, as municipal government and private water authorities began to dictate how small pockets of the countryside should be used for leisure. Sporting rights often featured as a part of negotiations with local landowners when authorities tried to gain parliamentary approval for waterworks schemes: F. H. Fawkes negotiated the sole sporting rights around Lindley Wood reservoir in the Washburn Valley as part of his settlement with Leeds Corporation in 1867 that allowed the passing of the Leeds Waterworks Act of that year.[7] The ownership of sporting rights on municipally owned land became entwined in the rent of certain properties, such as Swinsty Hall in the Washburn Valley. The rental of other, smaller properties in the valley provided the opportunity for members of the middle class to participate in shooting.[8] The provision of these shooting rights, and the subsequent engagement of members of middle classes, contributed to a trend of middle-class participation that became increasingly common across the country prior to the First World War.[9] The lease for the newly constructed Vyrnwy Hotel in 1890 came with fishing and shooting rights, thereby doubling the appeal of the area to those interested in leisure.[10] While shooting had previously been the preserve of the upper classes, the gaining of sporting rights through land purchases provided water authorities with the opportunity to offer access to those aspiring to an upper-class lifestyle.

The *Yorkshire Post* regularly provided readers with updates on how the sport fared during the shooting season from across the country, reflecting the newspaper's desire to be read nationally. Areas covered by their regular round-ups included prominent sporting areas of Yorkshire such as Bolton Abbey and the South Yorkshire uplands, as well as the Peak District, Derbyshire, Cumberland, Cleveland and Northumberland, Lancashire, and areas of Scotland and North Wales.[11] As such, grouse shooting was undoubtedly popular in areas of the country targeted for municipal gathering grounds. The otherwise little-known Washburn Valley was propelled into the spotlight in 1888 after Lord Walsingham, the owner of Blubberhouses Hall, set out to challenge talk about the poor quality of his shooting stock. He embarked on twenty drives, purportedly shooting a record 1,070 birds in one day.[12] This largesse, though, was a large factor in the decline of the sport among the upper classes. While great prestige could be bestowed, it was an expensive pursuit that brought little to no income for landowners. Walsingham is a case in point: driven to bankruptcy by his love of shooting, he sold Blubberhouses Hall to Leeds Corporation in 1901 as part of the authority's programme of compulsory purchases, as well as his London mansion, now the Ritz hotel.[13] Links between these waterscapes and leisure, then, predated the coming of the reservoirs; however, reservoirs accelerated the development of activities in rural areas.

Angling

Bodies of water owned by water authorities presented a commercial leisure opportunity: angling. It is a contradiction of sorts that angling was, at one time, one of the most popular sports in Britain, and yet has received relatively little attention from historians.[14] One reason for this may be the relative lack of sources around fishing. It is difficult to provide national or local participation figures; however, it is possible to gain an insight into the number of people, mainly men, who participated in the sport. During the nineteenth century, anglers across the country were increasingly taking advantage of rural and urban rivers, canals and lakes. For example, in 1900 one and half thousand members of Birmingham Anglers Association, the largest angling club in the world in the early twentieth century, travelled to Abingdon, Oxfordshire to fish in the Thames.[15] Participation in Leeds was similarly high: the Leeds and District Amalgamated Society of Anglers claimed in 1902 that the society had two thousand members from Leeds.[16] Most fishing activity initially took place on rivers, which had been used for sport from the early modern period.[17] The impact of industrialisation on rivers, though, gave rise to concerns about the state of fishing stocks, leading to a level of state intervention with the 1865 Salmon Fishery Act.[18] Angling was often framed as an escape from the industrial town to engage with and enjoy the picturesque.[19] The construction of reservoirs, whose waters would be protected from pollution, therefore provided an opportunity for anglers and water authorities alike. Access to the reservoirs to fish, though, was not a straightforward decision as leisure became intertwined with the management of urban water supply and the civic project.

Despite the opportunity that reservoirs presented to municipal authorities and urban, predominantly middle-class, leisure seekers, fishing was often not permitted in the first instance. In some cases, this was because of pre-existing sporting rights that corporations had established or agreed to honour when trying to defeat opposition to waterworks bills in Parliament. In the case of Leeds's Washburn Valley reservoirs, the sporting rights to Lindley Wood reservoir had been secured by the local landowner F. H. Fawkes, which prohibited any use by members of the public. In the case of Liverpool's Rivington reservoir, land was purchased in the area by Liverpool Corporation in 1895 to facilitate fishing, some thirty-eight years after construction had been completed.[20] For some reservoirs that predated the great expansion of reservoir construction from the 1860s onwards, such as Manchester's Gorton reservoir, built in the 1820s, fishing provision was only granted in the late nineteenth century.[21]

A similar process took place in the Washburn Valley. However, the initial proposal came not from a fishing association or municipal authority, but from a resident of the valley. In 1879, Thomas Priestly, the master of Board School at Norwood, asked the Leeds waterworks committee for permission to fish in Swinsty and Fewston reservoirs. The committee agreed to this request, although fishing would only be permitted by ticket. The committee also forbade boating on the reservoirs, an attitude that persisted into the twentieth century.[22] While this position, also adopted at Thirlmere, may have been to prevent pollution, it was not an approach adopted universally, with boating offered at Lake Vyrnwy and in the Elan Valley.[23] The decision-making process around fishing, seen as an afterthought in the first instance, shows that the recreational use of reservoirs was not necessarily included in the plans of authorities or engineers. Although the impact to the health of fish was a part of the Thirlmere Defence Association's parliamentary battle against the Manchester Corporation, as well as the subsequent transportation of char to Thirlmere in 1879 and 1886, angling did not become a major use of the reservoir, which remained off limits to anglers despite the corporation holding the sporting rights.[24] This is perhaps due to the uniqueness of Thirlmere, inaccessible to many until the coming of the motor car, while questions were posed over the ability of fish to thrive in the reservoir.[25] Fishing in reservoirs, then, was often an afterthought, but an afterthought that was of enormous benefit to authorities in terms of providing leisure avenues for urban residents and in terms of managing the quality of the water supply. One reservoir in which this was not the case was Caban Coch Reservoir, the third reservoir of the Elan Valley scheme, which was planned to be stocked with fish as construction was still underway.[26] Finished in the first years of the twentieth century, this decision was, no doubt, linked to the success of angling in Craig Goch and Pen y Garreg reservoirs, as well as other municipal reservoirs in Wales like Lake Vyrnwy.

Levels of participation are hard to gauge, given that municipalities rarely if ever recorded and published the number of anglers that visited waterworks, despite the use of tickets at many sites. The feats of anglers, though, were publicised in local newspapers and specialist journals like

Table 5.1 Number of fish caught in Elan Valley reservoirs, 1905–1913[27]

Year	Fish caught	Cumulative weight
1905	2,476	1,106 lb. 4oz.
1906	-	-
1907	5,523	2,757lb. 12 oz.
1908	6,169	2,967lb. 14 oz.
1909	5,574	2,887 lb.
1910	5,723	2,241 lb.
1911	2,473	994 lb. 8 oz.
1912	Over 4,000	-
1913	4,134	1,087 lb. 12 oz.

the *Fishing Gazette* and *The Field*, which provide an insight into how popular these sites were for fishing. Angling at Lake Vyrnwy began in 1891 and was immediately popular, with 4,143 fish caught that year.[28] The city that took the most pride in the success of angling in their reservoirs was Birmingham. Between 1905 and 1913, Birmingham Corporation published figures, widely circulated by local newspapers, detailing the fish caught in the Elan Valley reservoirs and their cumulative weight. As seen in Table 5.1, the figures undulate, peaking at over six thousand fish caught in 1908. This undulation can be linked to a series of factors, most notably climate and weather. When compared to Lake Vyrnwy, the Elan Valley reservoirs were marginally more popular; over the same period covered in Table 5.1, an annual average of 4,502 fish were caught in the Elan reservoirs compared with an average of 3,382 at Vyrnwy.[29] In some ways it is not surprising that Birmingham Corporation published these figures, or that they were more popular with anglers than other municipal reservoirs, given the prevalence of the civic gospel that had created links between the city and its utilities.[30] The Elan Valley may have been seventy-three miles away from the city, but it was clearly a source of pride to highlight so widely the popularity of fishing in Birmingham's grand reservoirs.

Liverpool Corporation took the somewhat unique step of constructing a municipal hotel on the banks of Lake Vyrnwy. The proposition was contentious when first suggested in 1888, seen by some as more expense off the back of a scheme that had become embroiled in controversy with the main engineer Thomas Hawksley. Editorials in the *Liverpool Echo* denounced the proposal as little more than a hotel for councilmen to retire to, an 'aldermanic booze den'.[31] These concerns were heightened in 1890 when it was announced that the hotel would cost over double the initial projection of £5,000, with work needed to make the building habitable for its first tenant.[32] While controversial, the hotel offered additional opportunities for leisure seekers. It not only provided the means for urban residents to extend their stay many miles from Liverpool or other towns and cities, but it cemented a further civic link between the city and its premiere watershed. This was evident in an advert from 1933 that claimed the hotel offered the opportunity for an ideal fishing holiday, 'the most productive Hotel fishing in Wales for consistent and abundant sport'. The advert claimed the hotel offered 'country house comfort', with tennis, golf and shooting all available to take advantage of in the surrounding area.[33] Despite the expansion of working-class leisure during the interwar period, the advert clearly targeted middle-class leisure seekers, while taking a subtle dig at other municipal leisure provision, principally Birmingham's Elan reservoirs. Initially built to house dignitaries and councilmen, the expansion of leisure meant that the hotel and fishing became entwined with the management of the Vyrnwy watershed and provided a further civic link to Liverpool.

The types of fish stocked by water authorities was also an important factor. The principal fish used for angling in reservoirs across England and Wales was brown trout, the primary fish along with salmon sought after by game anglers, who were mainly drawn from the upper and middle classes.[34] There were some variations, particularly in the Washburn Valley, which was provided with an order of golden tench in 1880 by the local landowner Lord Walsingham.[35] In order to help increase the number of fish in their reservoirs and, therefore, the quality of the sport, the Birmingham waterworks committee took the decision in 1913 to build small fish hatcheries at each of the Elan Valley lakes, contributing an extra twenty thousand brown trout ova that had been obtained from a fishery in Dumfries.[36] Care was taken to provide good quality fishing once authorities embraced fishing in the reservoirs, again suggesting that water authorities were taking the pursuit seriously.

Fully embracing angling in municipal reservoirs, though, was not a straightforward process, particularly in Leeds, which points to the wider difficulties that councillors had in managing watersheds. In 1896, a story in the local newspapers was brought to the attention of the Leeds waterworks committee, centring on a speech made by George Hodges, the vice president of the Leeds and District Amalgamated Society of Anglers, who argued that several corporations in the country had allowed angling societies to control fish stocks in reservoirs in order to improve the purity of the water supply. This was a concession that they had been seeking from the Leeds Corporation without success, an assertion that came as a surprise to members of the committee. Despite this, they sought to gain information on the feasibility of allowing angling societies to stock the reservoirs.[37] A month later, it was reported that the town clerk had corresponded with the town clerks of Manchester, Huddersfield and Hull

Corporations, informing the committee that it was not the practice of those towns and cities to allow angling societies to manage fishing in their reservoirs, information that contradicted that provided by Hodges. It was resolved that the waterworks committee would not transfer the fishing and stocking rights of the reservoirs to any society, but would continue to grant the usual facilities for fishing.[38]

One benefit for anglers in Leeds was the price of admission, or lack thereof, as the waterworks committee decided to provide free fishing permits for ratepayers. The cost of renting good fishing water rose greatly during the nineteenth century, so the provision of free fishing to the ratepayers of Leeds was a boon.[39] This was not the case with other reservoirs. An advert for Vyrnwy Hotel from 1895 offered fishing day tickets for two shillings and sixpence, and week tickets for twelve shillings and sixpence. Fishing was offered in the Elan Valley at the slightly more favourable weekly rate of ten shillings and sixpence, a rate that nevertheless priced out the 'respectable workingman'.[40] The various ways in which fishing was priced, be it free access for ratepayers in Leeds or charged elsewhere, in conjunction with the stocking of trout, marked the reservoirs out as the province of the middle-class angler. This demarcation was further heightened by the accessibility of places like the Washburn Valley or Lake Vyrnwy that lay several miles away from the city. The Washburn Valley was an isolated area with no railway to link it to nearby urban centres, while Lake Vyrnwy and the Elan Valley were accessible by train but still tucked in the heart of the Welsh countryside. Accessibility for the working class was, therefore, restricted.

Despite seemingly putting the case to bed in 1896, questions over the management of fishing in the Leeds reservoirs continued to rumble, with some asking whether it was a good idea to stock fish in the water supply at all. The question of allowing the Leeds and District Amalgamated Society of Anglers to stock the reservoirs was once again raised in July 1902. The honorary secretary of the society, J. N. Green, presented an offer, initially to the waterworks committee, to pay twenty-five pounds per year for the sole right to fish in Swinsty and Fewston reservoirs. The society planned to charge its members and the ratepayers of Leeds sixpence a day, and others two shillings and sixpence, with the profits used to restock the reservoirs. This deal had formally been agreed to by the waterworks committee; however, by August the resolution had been rescinded, and in September Councillor Nichols, as chairman of the waterworks committee, forwarded a motion to the full corporation to rescind the offer, a motion that Nichols himself disagreed with.[41]

Nichols's issues stemmed mainly from the issue of trespassing; he reported that in the previous month four hundred people had fished without permission, 'and when accused had not only used abusive language but threatened to throw the officials into the reservoir'.[42] This incident was not the behaviour of the respectable middle classes, suggesting that working-class anglers were present in the valley. As Jeff Hill has noted, the majority of those who participated in leisure activities, regardless of class or gender, did not conform to this type of behaviour, yet the actions of the minority acting in unrespectable ways were highlighted above others.[43] It also stressed fears of delinquency that had become heightened during the late nineteenth century as the effects of urbanisation, increase in leisure and perceived imperial decline created social panic, an issue also present in depictions of working-class ramblers in the twentieth century.[44] By transferring powers to the Leeds and District Amalgamated Society of Anglers, they would charge the residents of Leeds a nominal cost, and employees of the corporation would not have to deal with the more violent instances of trespassing cited; they would, however, be ceding the management of the landscape to the society. Nichols also noted that fishing rights had been leased to angling societies in Sheffield, Bradford, Wakefield, Halifax and Huddersfield, which established a local precedent. The society argued that it had successfully managed the Roundhay Park fishery and, containing nearly two thousand members from Leeds, it was in their members' best interests to help maintain the purity of the water supply with fish. This assertion was called into question by Dr Arthur Hawkyard, a family physician and Liberal councillor, who argued that pollution could be caused by dead fish and excrement, and therefore called for fishing in the reservoirs to cease entirely.[45]

Despite the contradictory information received by the waterworks committee, similar discussions were happening in other towns and cities regarding the use of their reservoirs for fishing. A meeting of Liverpool Corporation in 1889 discussed a proposal to stock Lake Vyrnwy with trout fry, primarily in order to protect the purity of the water. In response to objections over the cost of the proposal, Councillor J. B. Smith responded that if fish were not present in the water to consume vegetable matter the water would be unwholesome, 'they had spent two millions on the scheme, and it would be rendered useless unless they spent £150 on this object'.[46] This is a slight exaggeration, but it shows that there was clearly a developing ecological dimension to the debate around fishing, something that would extend beyond the council chamber.

The motion of the Leeds waterworks committee to reject the society's offer was passed; however, the discussion that had taken place within the corporation reflected a tension between embracing the economic benefits of leisure, the role of the civic authority in protecting the waters of the reservoir, and unrespectable behaviour, concerns that would emerge again during the interwar period with regards to working-class ramblers. The deliberations of the corporation prompted debate from correspondents to the *Yorkshire Post*, all of whom took issue with the suggestion that fishing in the reservoirs should cease. The first correspondent, E. G. Arnold, claimed that he had fished in the reservoirs for twenty years and had seen little evidence of poaching or trespassing, pointedly remarking 'to-day, I think, there is no fisherman in the Council'.[47] As to the suggestion that the fish may be deleterious to the quality of the water supply, he argued that fish ate insects and other aquatic life and therefore had a cleansing effect. He also pointed out that it would be difficult, without engineering work, to stop fish from entering the reservoirs, as both Fewston and Swinsty reservoirs had natural inlets. To ban fishing in the reservoirs, therefore, would result in an overabundance of fish in the water supply.[48] This sentiment was echoed by W. Richardson, who argued that: 'It is a matter of common knowledge among the owners of fisheries that unless a reasonable amount of fair fishing be permitted, the number of fish increase more rapidly than the food supply'.[49]

H. Knight Horsfield argued that, in light of the increasing monopolisation of fishing sites by angling societies, the Washburn Valley reservoirs provided an opportunity for ratepayers to fish free of charge, highlighting a civic benefit that the corporation was looking to take away for seemingly frivolous reasons: 'The matter of pollution would be more serious if it were true that trout pollute the water; but precisely the opposite is known to be the fact'.[50] This point was reiterated by Edmund Barker, a member of the River Coquet Salmon Fisheries Conservancy Board, who noted that not only did trout eat frog spawn, tadpoles and other microscopic organisms, but the presence of trout thriving in water was a positive sign of purity.[51] A further correspondent, W. C. Dawson, who had been a member of the Yorkshire Fishery Board, argued that while the corporation was wrong to question the positive effect of trout on water purity, the trout that he had previously fished in the reservoirs had been of poor stock, and he had given up 'in disgust'. He pointed to the work done by Liverpool Corporation at Lake Vyrnwy as a positive example for the Leeds Corporation to follow:

> Eleven years ago Lake Vyrnwy was practically virgin water. It was then stocked with fish suitable to the place under the direction of an expert pisciculturalist, and is to-day a sporting and a prosperous fishery, and a valuable asset to the Liverpool City Council.[52]

He concluded by arguing that to neglect fishing, as was being proposed, 'would be both from a utilitarian and sporting point of view a very great mistake'.[53] All the letters concluded that fishing was not just a leisure pursuit, but helped to fulfil civic duty in maintaining an ecological balance in the water supply. Additionally, the link between fishing in the reservoirs and civic identity was underscored, particularly in pointing to other municipalities such as Liverpool, which had succeeded in offering good quality sport in its reservoirs.

Ultimately, control over fishing remained with the waterworks committee, and angling continued to be enjoyed in Fewston and Swinsty reservoirs. Although the corporation decided to embrace the economic and civic benefits of angling in the reservoirs, the Leeds and District anglers continued to play a role in the governance of fishing. In 1917 they successfully pressured the waterworks committee to reinstate fishing in Fewston reservoir after suspension due to the First World War.[54] However, the debate over the positives and negatives of fishing in the reservoirs highlights both the potential benefits that fishing brought to Leeds's water supply and the battle that had to be fought inside and outside the corporation for access to angling, battles that did not have to be fought in other towns and cities. In examining the use of reservoirs for fishing, it is clear that the sport was popular in municipal reservoirs, particularly when considering that there were many rivers and fisheries that could have been visited instead. A seemingly frivolous pastime, it helped to create a further link between the reservoirs and the city, as seen in the level of discourse in the *Yorkshire Post* defending the presence of fish in the reservoirs. As such, fishing in municipal reservoirs became an expression of civic pride. An important element of this link was the free access for the ratepayers of Leeds that helped to link this particular leisure activity with civic identity, as did the attention to good quality stock in reservoirs of Birmingham and Liverpool. The reservoirs did not solely supply water but also healthy recreation to urban residents, and, as seen in the correspondences above in Leeds, responsible management of the natural fish stock helped to manage the city's water supply. This free access continued in Leeds into the post-war period, described by one correspondent as 'a rare privilege', further cementing utility and pleasure, although complaints around the stock of some reservoirs also continued.[55]

However, the debate over access to reservoirs to fish was revisited on several occasions, and the reporting of unrespectable behaviour reveals an unease with the widening of access to the working classes. There is also little, if any, evidence to suggest that women participated in angling in the reservoirs examined here. Although female anglers increased in number and visibility during the early years of the twentieth century, many of the women's groups reported in local newspapers took to sea fishing. Additionally, in a move that somewhat mirrored developments in women's football, women were banned from participating in matches of the National Angling Clubs' Association in 1934.[56] The link between fishing and civic pride, then, was as exclusionary in gender terms as it was in class terms. Those that took advantage of municipal angling were overwhelmingly middle-class, due to factors such as distance and lack of transport to these areas, and male. Additionally, concerns were raised about unrespectable behaviour, which sought to frame angling as a pursuit of the middle-class leisure seeker. Corporations were able to utilise their waterworks to great effect, creating a link between the activity and the civic project. However, this link was felt by some more than others.

Rambling

While fishing was undoubtedly popular, particularly among the middle classes, it did not become a mainstream activity in the way that walking has. In 2018, the Lake District alone received 19.38 million tourists, emphasising the continued popularity of walking that owes much to the battles fought in the early twentieth century over access to the countryside.[57] The most famous battle was that fought in the Peak District, which culminated in the mass trespass of Kinder Scout in 1932. Battles for access with local landowners were fought all over the country, particularly in water catchment areas. Although historians such as Jeremy Burchardt have pointed to conflict between walking groups and water authorities, there has been no in-depth examination of these issues. This section unravels the growth of rambling around reservoirs and waterworks, the issues that arose due to this growth, and the class tensions that continued to be expressed as these areas of the countryside were slowly made more available for urban leisure seekers.

Rambling as a leisure activity became increasingly common during the late nineteenth century as a pursuit of the middle classes, reflected in travel literature that sought to construct areas of natural beauty as enrichening places to visit, before becoming popular with working-class ramblers into the twentieth century.[58] Burchardt has pointed to three reasons for the uptake in rambling among the middle classes: the influence of the Romantic movement, urbanisation, and a rising interest in the natural sciences.[59] The previous chapter highlighted the influence of the Romantic movement on depictions of waterworks, and an interest in the natural sciences is evident in several of the rambling accounts published by the local newspapers. This was often expressed by showing an appreciation for the various plants and wildlife encountered by correspondents. One writer on a winter ramble in the Washburn Valley in 1893 noted:

> True, Nature may be dead, but she is magnificently embalmed [...] Look yonder in that clump of trees. What can be more beautiful than the reddish hue of the Scottish fir mingled in delicate harmony with the silvery birch? See where the ivy has hung itself in graceful festoons upon the bared limbs of the gnarled oak.[60]

Although Burchardt has argued that this interest in the natural sciences diminished among ramblers during the late nineteenth and early twentieth centuries with the development of professional science and the decline of the Romantic movement, there remained an amateur scientific interest in these rural areas.[61] One correspondent, writing in 1905, commented on the botanical range that the Washburn Valley offered throughout the year: 'whether in spring under the spell of the wood anemone and the nodding daffodil, or later [...] when the autumn flames in the tree tops or winter robes the land in chastest white, it is a thing of beauty'.[62] On a ramble to Lake Vyrnwy in 1895, a correspondent of the *Coventry Herald* remarked on the 'soft green pastures alternating with oak and larch woods, varied here and there by silver birch trees'.[63] While there was an element of romantic place-making to these descriptions, the identification of various trees implies an interest in botany and silviculture in their readers. Though these areas offered aesthetic beauties, ramblers were also encouraged by newspaper correspondents to enjoy their walks on a more scientific level.

Waterworks that lay in relative isolation made them prime destinations for ramblers, who would sometimes look to walk in excess of twenty miles from their designated starting point. Even though rambling did not become a mass activity until the twentieth century, it is clear from a report in the *Wharfedale and Airedale Observer* that the Washburn Valley was popular with day trippers as early as 1894, with visitors travelling on foot or by bicycle, carriage or wagonette.[64] While many ramblers in the twentieth century would travel by bus or car to Lawnswood, north of Headingley, and ramble some ten miles from there, train stations at Pool-in-Wharfedale and Otley provided a closer starting point, albeit still requiring a walk of several miles to reach the valley. Changes in transport also helped to reach waterworks in more remote areas of the country. The opening of Bala Junction railway station in 1882 provided access to areas of Wales, including Lake Vyrnwy, which lay roughly nine miles from the station, while the Elan Valley was accessible by coach or rail.[65] Further into the twentieth century, companies such as Midland Red offered day trips from cities like Birmingham to the Elan Valley and Lake Vyrnwy.[66] The Washburn Valley was well placed for ramblers coming from Leeds; however, changes in transportation made waterworks in more remote areas of the country more accessible as well.

Although some rural areas utilised for waterworks were celebrated by walkers, rambling was discouraged in others. A case in point was Thirlmere, lying at the heart of the Lake District. This was an area that had grown in popularity with visitors following the effusive descriptions of Romantic poets like Wordsworth, as well as the development of the Furness railway. Like fishing, rambling remained at the bottom of the list of priorities of the Manchester Corporation, despite notions during the parliamentary battle that pedestrian access to the surrounding areas would be guaranteed. After the construction of the reservoir, signs prohibiting access were placed around the area, although ramblers could walk along the western edge to the top of Helvellyn.[67] This was reflected in how Thirlmere was discussed in guidebooks of the Lake District, which sought to extol its engineering rather than aesthetic qualities.[68] While Thirlmere was an impressive example of engineering prowess, guidebook writers did not write about it in a way that would entice walkers and ramblers to visit, no doubt to the pleasure of members of the Manchester Corporation.

It was not until the twentieth century that the working classes, aided by the establishment of rambling clubs as well as better and cheaper transport links, began to traverse the countryside for leisure. Rambling became particularly popular as a working-class activity during the interwar period, as mass unemployment and low transport fares provided time for and accessibility to the countryside.[69] Additionally, rambling became, to some, a political act. This was a way of challenging a lack of access to the countryside in the face of upper-class land ownership, which culminated in the mass trespass of Kinder Scout, Derbyshire in 1932.[70] For many, though, rambling presented an opportunity for rational recreation, to leave the industrial city and enjoy the bucolic countryside. Newspaper articles during the summer months or public holidays commented on large crowds of people in Otley, West Yorkshire, en route to the Washburn Valley. One article in the *Leeds Mercury* on Good Friday, 1929, commented:

> At Otley, the traffic was heavier than last year, and a feature of the invasion was the number of trampers who passed through the town. Clad in flannels, with shirts open at the neck, they penetrated to all parts of Wharfedale, a large number of them bent on exploring the natural delights of the Washburn Valley.[71]

This popularity was further outlined by the listing of rambling events by local newspapers during the 1920s and 1930s, many of which were undertaken by voluntary organisations that increasingly participated in outdoor recreation after the First World War.[72] To take Leeds as an example, rambles were organised to the Washburn Valley by Leeds Rambling Club, Leeds All-Weather Rambling Club, Leeds Co-operative Holiday

Association (CHA), Leeds Ruc-Sac Club, Leeds College of Commerce, Leeds and District Health and Strength Rambling Club, and Headingley Road Club.[73] Importantly, the valley was not just popular with rambling clubs from Leeds, with members of Huddersfield Rucksack Club rambling from Bradford. The area was also popular with Pudsey and District Rambling Club, Huddersfield Healthy Life Ramblers' Club, and Seacroft and Cross Gates Cycling Club, who organised a ramble to the valley in order to promote their cycling cause.[74]

It is not necessarily surprising that most of the clubs that visited the Washburn Valley were from the surrounding area, given the relative obscurity of the valley outside the region. Sites of more notable waterworks such as Vyrnwy and Elan attracted walkers from further afield. Cyclists from Todmorden and Tamworth visited Lake Vyrnwy in 1931 and 1935 respectively, while the Chester CHA and Holiday Fellowship Rambling Club organised a ramble to Vyrnwy in 1938. Elan was visited by Kensington Rambling Club in 1928, the South Western branch of the Cyclists' Touring Club, and Cheltenham Motor Club in 1929; and the Newport Ramblers in 1935. Even though rambling around Thirlmere was discouraged, it was still included in accounts of trips to the Lake District by Lancaster Storey Students' Association, Lancaster Cyclists' Touring Club, and the Todmorden Licensed Victuallers' outing, among others during the interwar years. Whether they were waterworks of repute or areas of beauty known more locally, reservoirs were becoming popular sites of leisure during this period.[75]

Unlike angling, rambling was also more inclusive of women. Some forms of rambling, especially harsh all-night rambles, were seen as an activity only for men; however, women were increasingly involved in rambling organisations from the 1900s onwards.[76] Rambling was seen as a form of leisure that was compatible with dominant constructions of femininity, as with cycling and tennis.[77] The increased involvement of women was aided by organisations such as the CHA, which welcomed female participants. Although the CHA allowed women to mingle with the opposite sex, their behaviour was still framed 'within a context of respectability'; for example, women were often castigated for flirting.[78] The CHA played a key role in establishing the moral practices of rambling, particularly on the development of rational behaviour; it is notable that many local CHA groups travelled to reservoirs to help instil this behaviour.[79]

Although commented on less than men's rambling, trips by the Embro [Edinburgh] Ladies Clarion Club to Gladhouse Reservoir in Midlothian, Scotland were noted by newspapers, while members of the Cooperative Women's Guild in Nelson and the Fulledge Wesleyan Mothers' Ramble visited reservoirs around Burnley and Nelson, Lancashire.[80] Pictures were published in newspapers showing women enjoying the idyllic countryside. One photograph showed a group of respectably dressed young women from Armley, a working-class area of Leeds, rambling around Blubberhouses in the middle of the Washburn Valley, taking a keen interest in the ruins of an old mill. Another showed two women looking at a map at Lindley Wood reservoir, dressed in clothing more attributable to middle-class ramblers. Whereas the women in the first photograph are inquisitive of the built environment, the women in the second are using maps to plot their journey, suggesting that they are comfortable with the tools of experienced walkers. Nevertheless, both photographs, published by the *Leeds Mercury*, suggest that regardless of class status, women could and did enjoy rural leisure.

It is clear, then, that waterworks were popular with walkers across the country. Despite this, access to rambling routes in the 1930s, like in many rural areas during this period in Britain, was greatly contested. Rambling groups came into conflict with municipal corporations and private water companies, in addition to private landowners, due to the amount of land purchased in rural areas to supply water to towns and cities.[81] There were clear concerns about how ramblers could potentially affect the quality of the water supply, which saw municipal authorities cordon the edges of the reservoirs and place signs to warn off trespassers as at Thirlmere. There were also concerns from landowners in the surrounding areas of trespassing as these areas became desirable places to visit. The land-owning Fawkes family in the Washburn Valley took it on themselves to close a public right of way in 1883 after several encounters with trespassers and poachers on their estate, with little help offered by Leeds Corporation to negotiate on their behalf.[82] This is a reminder of the strength of statutory powers as well as the delicate relationships water authorities had to engender with local landowners to keep the peace.

Issues over access to rural areas like Thirlmere and the Washburn Valley were already well established as rambling became popular among the working classes in the early twentieth century.[83] This tension reached a peak in the Washburn Valley during the 1930s, mirroring aforementioned national trends. As Leeds Corporation owned much more land in the Washburn Valley than the boundaries of the watersheds, the issue of access was especially contested. An editorial in the *Yorkshire Evening Post* in 1931 highlighted the issue. Responding to a complaint that a public path had been blocked and signs warning trespassers erected, a correspondent was sent to the valley to investigate. A farmer was interviewed, who stated that he had complained to Leeds Corporation that his land was being damaged by ramblers, and that stray dogs had chased two of his sheep into one of the reservoirs where they had drowned. However, it had been the

Leeds Corporation, and not the farmer, that had closed the public path in an attempt to tackle what the *Yorkshire Evening Post* described as the 'hooligan hiker and rampageous picnicker'.[84] The language used by the newspaper set the tone for further interventions on the subject, particularly the use of the word 'hooligan', an early twentieth-century term used to express concerns about the behaviour of urban male working-class youths.[85] The word 'hiker' is also noteworthy, a pejorative Americanism that referred to certain working-class, female and youth cultures that middle-class ramblers had left the city to escape.[86] The distinction between hikers and respectable, middle-class ramblers suggests a concern with the proliferation of working-class ramblers. The use of this distinction is notable, as it set the tone for much of the commentary to come, pointing to a concern with working-class access to the countryside.

Issues regarding access to areas of the countryside owned by municipal corporations were encountered beyond the Washburn Valley, with local branches of the Ramblers' Federation at the forefront of these battles. Concerns were raised in 1935 over the prospect of access to the Derwent Valley following the construction of Ladybower reservoir, a struggle that formed part of a wider critique of what type of landscape was valued by ramblers: namely wilderness, savage grandeur and foreboding rocks.[87] Although signs prohibiting walkers had long been posted around Thirlmere, the Lake District Ramblers' Federation expressed fears around prohibitions on rambling at Haweswater in light of Manchester Corporation's reluctance to admit rights of way. After consulting legal advice, the federation concluded that such an act contravened the Manchester Corporation Act 1919 that gave Manchester permission to construct a waterworks at Haweswater, and that any efforts to obstruct the passage of ramblers should be reported to the federation.[88]

The federation also became involved in access battles in the Washburn Valley. In 1932, the *Yorkshire Post* reported that a popular footpath at Dob Park Bridge in the Washburn Valley, 'regarded by the rambling fraternity for many years as a public right of way', had been closed by the Leeds Corporation's waterworks department, the gate to the path padlocked, and prohibition notices displayed to warn ramblers. A letter received by the West Riding Ramblers' Federation (WRRF) from the waterworks department was 'couched in terms which the Federation considered arbitrary and lacking in courtesy'.[89] A delegation from the WRRF attended a meeting of the waterworks committee to ask for the reopening of the path for public use, which the committee declined, arguing that 'the use of a private footpath by the public would depreciate the value for letting of farm lands through which the footpath runs', especially a concern in the most popular rambling areas in the lower valley such as Dob Park and Lindley Wood.[90]

The reason provided by the committee pertained to financial protection; while precise numbers are difficult to estimate, the popularity of the Washburn Valley as a rambling destination with both rambling clubs and day trippers resulted in a sizeable number of people walking near or over corporation land. Efforts needed to be taken to safeguard the corporation's financial assets from the vast amount of people visiting the area. However, this reasoning may have masked an unease with working-class ramblers.

In the following years, the WRRF, a middle-class organisation, paid much attention to access to the Washburn Valley for ramblers, attempting to work with and, at times, pressure organisations such as Leeds Corporation, Wharfedale Rural District Council (WRDC) and the West Riding County Council in order to provide more access.[91] This was exemplified at a meeting of the WRRF in Keighley in 1934, where it was reported that the owner of the Blubberhouses Moor district had made one path across the moor open to the public; the federation, however, had laid claim to a dozen.[92] Despite this initial impasse, pressure from the federation bore fruit in 1935. At a meeting in Keighley in July, William Shaw, the federation's secretary, was able to report on a compromise that saw seven paths on Blubberhouses moor approved by the WRDC.[93] A map was submitted to the meeting showing 106 paths across the valley that had been identified and agreed between the federation, WRDC, and Leeds Corporation. This was a coup for the federation, which had won greater access to the Washburn Valley. Although limited access to other areas of the countryside occurred during this period, most prominently the granting of limited access to areas of the Peak District owned by Sheffield Corporation a year later, the victory of WRRF was an early step in the direction of open access to the countryside.[94] It is also important to note that not all authorities were so accommodating. The Lake District Ramblers' Federation continued to battle with the Manchester Corporation over access to Haweswater. In response to calls for full access to the area, the Manchester waterworks committee wrote to the federation to note that they considered access provided for following the construction of a new path, at a cost of £1,000, a conclusion the federation rejected.[95] Until legislation on general access to the countryside was passed, battles over access would continue to be fought in an ad hoc and uneven fashion.

Despite the success of the WRRF in gaining access to the Washburn Valley, this access remained couched within the framework of class. An unnamed letter from a member of the WRRF, possibly Shaw, outlined the process undertaken with the Leeds Corporation:

> The Leeds Waterworks people are behaving very handsomely towards ramblers; we sent a deputation to see the clerk to the WRDC last week,

> and he informed them that the Leeds Waterworks Committee have scheduled 106 paths as rights-of-way in their waterworks area. We had a map of these at our meeting on Saturday and so far as we can see there is no serious omission. We were naturally delighted, as we had never anticipated this treatment. The Council Meeting on Saturday had to express agreement in part with the Leeds Waterworks engineer in his denunciation of 'hikers'. Until recently it was possible to travel within walking distance of the Valley by tram from Leeds at a fare of 3d, and consequently the Washburn Valley caught all the rowdy element whose sole object was to get out into the country in the cheapest way possible, and make a row. This service has been taken off now, and the 'hikers' are in consequence now found in other haunts near the City. His statements were probably making the case to appear to be much worse than it really was, but in view of their action in regard to footpaths, we feel we can't quarrel with them about that.[96]

There was clear unease around granting access to the watershed to those deemed unrespectable, emphasised once more by the use of 'hiker'. As Ben Anderson has highlighted, middle-class ramblers and mountaineers had been engaging in this distinction for decades; rambling was seen as a middle-class solution to middle-class problems regarding modernity and the city, so those outside of this specific bourgeois culture could only properly engage with the countryside if they proscribed to middle-class ideas of the ruminative impact of countryside leisure.[97] Members of the working class, and women, who did not enjoy the countryside as a way of combating the trials of urban modernity would fall into the 'hiker' category. This narrative also corresponds to visions of healthy citizenship that David Matless has identified during this period, which were defined as such by the 'anti-citizen' who acted in ways seen as unbecoming.[98] While the unnamed member of the WRRF sought to downplay the extent to which 'hikers' were disrupting rural leisure, they ultimately agreed with the sentiment expressed by the corporation. The removal of the cheap tram fare meant that those deemed undesirable could not reach the valley as easily, thereby solving the issue and making it easier to legitimise granting access to the countryside. Although the WRRF was a key organisation in helping to secure access to the Washburn Valley, the access secured continued to be regulated by middle-class ideals espoused by both organisations.

The unease expressed by the WRRF and the Leeds Corporation extended, once more, to the city's newspapers, demonstrating again the role of the local press as an arena for debate and civic engagement. An article in the *Leeds Mercury* in 1936 highlighted comments by the waterworks committee chairman, Alderman E. J. Clarke, in which he argued that despite the waterworks committee providing a number of footpaths for ramblers, 'the conduct of many ramblers had left a good deal to be desired'. This behaviour had resulted in damage to fences, walls and gates, which increased the risk of the reservoirs becoming polluted from general littering. The article ended with a call to arms: 'The next time you go there keep a sharp look-out for careless or wantonly destructive people [...] If you find any such, give them a piece of your mind!'[99] Further articles on the matter from Frank North and Sydney Moorhouse, both regular columnists of the *Leeds Mercury*, laid the blame on 'an unruly element', stating that they were 'not true ramblers at all'.[100] This characterisation highlights the continued tension with increasing access to areas such as the Washburn Valley. Using terms such as 'unruly element' and 'true ramblers' indicates an unease with ramblers that did not conform to middle-class ideals of rambling, echoing the distinction between rambler and hiker and the social ordering of countryside leisure.[101] This is further evidence of rambling behaviour being defined by how others act improperly. In reality, rambling groups were composed of myriad different social, cultural and political identities. For those like North and Moorhouse, the 'true rambler' was white, middle-class, and most likely male.[102]

However, areas such as the Washburn Valley did become more accessible to the rambler during the 1930s. This was underscored by a survey of public rights of way for the parishes of Fewston and Blubberhouses following the passing of the National Parks and Access to the Countryside Act 1949, which saw the troublesome issue of access to the countryside pass from the ministry of agriculture to the ministry of town and country planning.[103] The survey listed seventeen paths in the parish of Fewston, totalling 7.77 miles of land, while sixteen paths in the parish of Blubberhouses were listed totalling 11.68 miles.[104] The combined figure for both was 19.45 miles, demonstrating that there was much more access to the Washburn Valley than during the interwar period. This was a victory for those who had campaigned as well as those who sought to benefit from better access.

The 1949 Act also had implications for Thirlmere, given the Lake District's new-found status as one of the country's first national parks in 1951, although control over access remained with the local authority. Prohibitive signs remained posted around the reservoir beyond the 1950s, while the North West Water Authority continued to vigorously protect the watershed after it took control of the supply in 1973.[105] The passing of the Act did little to satiate fears from water authorities about the impact of ramblers in catchment areas, as a letter to the editor of the *Yorkshire Post* outlined regarding the formation of a national park in the

Peak District, which cited the lack of protections provided by the national parks legislation against water pollution.[106] Through the construction of reservoirs that appealed to aesthetic sensibilities, a sentiment actively pursued by local newspapers, water authorities helped to create a situation where waterworks became attractive areas for leisure. The discussions over access and the work of organisations like the West Riding Ramblers' Federation eventually encouraged the use of these areas for rambling. The desire for the right sort of behaviour, though, saw authorities engage in a social ordering of the countryside, with tensions over who could or should use these spaces for leisure continuing into the post-war period.

Conclusion

Access to the countryside remained contested into the post-war period, an issue discussed by Tom Stephenson in his account of rambling, *Forbidden Land*. Stephenson highlights the role played by municipal water authorities in continuing to deny access to rural areas due to fears of pollution, despite the efforts of the Ramblers' Association conducting scientific research that showed that ramblers had little to no impact on water supplies. This expanded on a comment Stephenson made in his column for the *Daily Herald* in 1939, in which he specifically cited Thirlmere, Vyrnwy and Elan as areas that should be opened up more to ramblers.[107]

Political responses to the battles for access to the countryside seemed to point to a more optimistic future, with key legislation being passed in the Access to the Mountains Act 1939, the National Parks and Access to the Countryside Act 1949 and the Access to the Countryside Act 1960. However, historians have disputed their effectiveness. John Sheail has argued that the 1939 Act was limited by its status as a private members' bill that helped to further the cause of ramblers without having any tangible effect on access, while Gavin Parker and Neil Ravenscroft have noted that the 1949 Act did little to help ramblers access the countryside but helped landowners to maintain their stranglehold on access routes. For example, of the thirty-five thousand hectares of land that had been brought under access agreements by 1989, over half were in the Peak District, highlighting the limited political impact of the access mechanism within the Act nationwide.[108] Despite the effectiveness or otherwise of legislation, and direct action by ramblers, in 2020 the law of trespass continued to exclude access to ninety-two per cent of English land.[109]

The struggles of leisure seekers throughout the twentieth century make it more important to highlight the actions of some municipal governments in opening up rural areas for leisure. What is clear is that approaches to the development of leisure around reservoirs were far from uniform, once again highlighting the importance of local case studies to unveiling a national story. Although not initially planned, angling was encouraged at the majority of the prominent waterworks schemes, with Manchester's Thirlmere scheme the main outlier. The provision and quality of angling, though, differed, from free fishing for ratepayers in the Washburn Valley to the more expensive comforts of Vyrnwy Hotel. The right to fish in municipal reservoirs was also unevenly debated: in Leeds, the issue caused consternation in the council chamber, whereas in the case of Birmingham, the ability to fish was factored into the planning of Caban Coch reservoir. What was common among municipalities that encouraged fishing was the strengthening of the civic link between reservoirs and their respective cities – the success of fishing spoke to the success of municipal governments in being able to properly manage the activity and, therefore, properly manage the quality of the water supply. Anglers could play their part in not allowing an overabundance of fish, thereby fulfilling their civic duty to manage their water supply. The debate that raged in the pages of the *Yorkshire Post* was also evidence of civic engagement, with those in favour promoting the benefits to the city's water supply as well as their own recreation.

The civic link stretched to ramblers, who, ultimately, wanted to explore areas of the countryside that had been aesthetically improved by urban engineering. As has been demonstrated, reservoirs across the country were popular with ramblers, even Thirlmere, where the Manchester Corporation took steps to disinterest visitors. Like angling, though, engagement with ramblers and water authorities was framed within middle-class ideals, which reflected the composition of urban associational culture more generally during this period. In the case of the Leeds Corporation, this was expressed overtly in its dismissal of 'hikers'. As with angling, which was established as a middle-class pursuit, there remained a tension with members of the working class engaging with rural waterworks. The use of leisure to strength the civic link between the city and the country, then, was exclusionary; only those who behaved within the ideals of middle-class respectability could properly appreciate the significance of municipal achievement in engineering the countryside, something that applied to both fishing and rambling as seen in the debates discussed here. The issue of exclusivity continues to be a problem with modern landscapes and access to the countryside. While more recent research has focused on race and disability, this chapter demonstrates the importance of focusing on waterscapes for historical antecedents to flesh out the story of access and exclusion.[110] It is also notable that ecology was at the forefront of concerns around the management of waterworks, even if these concerns were not expressed within that specific framework. Worries about the effects of fish on the water supply reflected genuine, if perhaps misguided, concerns over adversely affecting the water supply; worries about the polluting effects of ramblers, though, may well have been used to further mask class tensions.

Notes

1. Hugh Cunningham, *Leisure in the Industrial Revolution, c.1780–c.1880* (Croom Helm, 1980), 9–10; Peter Borsay, *A History of Leisure: The British Experience since 1500* (Palgrave Macmillan, 2006), 9; Karl Spracklen, *Constructing Leisure: Historical and Philosophical Debates* (Palgrave Macmillan, 2011), 164

2. Dion Georgiou, 'Redefining the Carnivalesque: The Construction of Ritual, Revelry and Spectacle in British Leisure Practices through the Idea and Model of "Carnival", 1870–1939', *Sport in History* 35, no. 3 (2015): 340, https://doi.org/10.1080/17460263.2015.1088462.

3. See Karen V. Lykke Syse, 'Ideas of Leisure, Pleasure and the River in Early Modern England', in *Perceptions of Water in Britain from Early Modern Times to the Present: An Introduction*, ed. Karen V. Lykke Syse and Terje Oestigaard (BRIC Press, 2010), 35–58; Spracklen, *Constructing Leisure*; Heasim Sul, '*The King's Book of Sports*: The Nature of Leisure in Early Modern England', *The International Journal of the History of Sport* 17, no. 4 (2000): 172, https://doi.org/10.1080/09523360008714153.

4. Research on citizenship has been growing in recent years, particularly as a response to post-structural critiques of urban governmentality. See Helen Meller, 'Urban Renewal and Citizenship: The Quality of Life in British Cities, 1890–1990', *Urban History* 22, no. 1 (1995): 63–84, https://doi.org/10.1017/S096392680001138X; Ben Anderson, 'A Liberal Countryside? The Manchester Ramblers' Federation and the "Social Readjustment" of Urban Citizens, 1929–1936', *Urban History* 38, no. 1 (2011): 84–102, https://doi.org/10.1017/S0963926811000058; Tom Hulme, *After the Shock City: Urban Culture and the Making of Modern Citizenship* (Boydell Press, 2019).

5. Melanie Tebbutt, 'Rambling and Manly Identity in Derbyshire's Dark Peak, 1880s–1920s', *The Historical Journal* 49, no. 4 (2006): 1137, https://doi.org/10.1017/S0018246X06005760; Claire Langhamer, *Women's Leisure in England 1920–60* (Manchester University Press, 2000), 77.

6. Andrew Done and Richard Muir, 'The Landscape History of Grouse Shooting in the Yorkshire Dales', *Rural History*, 12, no. 2 (2001): 195–210, https://doi.org/10.1017/S0956793300002442; Alistair J. Durie, 'Game Shooting: An Elite Sport c.1870–1980', *Sport in History* 28, no. 3 (2008): 431–49, https://doi.org/10.1080/17460260802315504.

7. Marion Sharples, *The Fawkes Family and Their Estates in Wharfedale, 1819–1936* (Thoresby Society, 1997), 51.

8. One example of this was E. W. Dixon, a water engineer for Harrogate Corporation who leased Fewston Grange in 1905 for five years with exclusive fishing rights in the River Washburn between Swinsty and Lindley Wood reservoirs. Another man, Fraser Douglas, who worked in property in Ilkley, paid £75 a year in 1923 for sporting rights that allowed him to shoot in the southern part of the Washburn estate. Leeds Corporation, 'Leeds Waterworks Committee Minutes, volume 8: 1903–1910', West Yorkshire Archive Service (WYAS), LLC22/1/8, 100; Leeds Corporation, 'Leeds Waterworks Committee Minutes, volume 10: 1912–1929', WYAS, LLC22/1/10, 225.

9. John Martin, 'The Transformation of Lowland Game Shooting in England and Wales in the Twentieth Century: The Neglected Metamorphosis', *The International Journal of the History of Sport* 29, no. 8 (2012): 1145–46, https://doi.org/10.1080/09523367.2012.690226.

10. 'The Council and the Vyrnwy Hotel', *Liverpool Echo*, 13 February 1890, 3.

11. An example of this can be seen in 'Grouse Shooting: An Encouraging Opening', *Yorkshire Post*, 13 August 1909, 3.

12. Thomas H. Nelson, *The Birds of Yorkshire: Being A Historical Account of the Avi-Fauna of the County* (A. Brown and Sons, 1907), 517; Durie, 'Game Shooting', 432.

13. Leeds Corporation, 'Leeds Waterworks Committee Minutes, volume 7: 1896–1903', WYAS, LLC22/1/7, 329.

14. Richard Coopey, 'A River Does Indeed Run Through It: Angling and Society in Britain since 1800', in *Perceptions of Water in Britain from Early Modern Times to the Present: An Introduction*, ed. Karen V. Lykke Syse and Terje Oestigaard (BRIC Press, 2010), 59.

15. Richard Coopey and Tim Shakesheff, 'Angling and Nature: Environment, Leisure, Class and Culture in Britain 1750–1975', in *Common Ground: Integrating the Social and Environmental in History*, ed. Geneviève Massard-Guilbaud and Stephen Mosley (Cambridge Scholars Publishing, 2011), 28–9.

16. 'Leeds City Council: The Township Controversy', *Yorkshire Post*, 4 September 1902, 5.

17. Lykke Syse, 'Ideas of Leisure', 38.

18. Marianna Dudley, 'Muddying the Waters: Recreational Conflict and Rights of Use of British Rivers', *Water History* 9, no. 3 (2017): 259–77, https://doi.org/10.1007/s12685-017-0193-2.

19. John Lowerson, 'Angling', in *Sport in Britain: A Social History*, ed. Tony Mason (Cambridge University Press, 1989), 14; Coopey and Shakesheff, 'Angling and Nature', 18.

20. Liverpool Water Committee, 'Liverpool Water Committee Minute Book, October 1895–December 1896', Liverpool Record Office, 352 MIN/WTR/1/35, 99.

21. Manchester Corporation, 'Proceedings of the Waterworks Committee, volume 44: 1895–96', Greater Manchester County Record Office, GB127.M231/2/1/44, 25.

22. Leeds Corporation, 'Leeds Waterworks Committee Minutes, volume 4: 1878–1885', 11 July 1879, WYAS, LLC22/1/4, 52.

23. Special correspondent, 'Elan Valley's Attractions for Midlanders: New Holiday Resort', *Birmingham Daily Gazette*, 14 July 1904, 6.

24. Harriet Ritvo, *The Dawn of Green: Manchester, Thirlmere, and Modern Environmentalism* (University of Chicago Press, 2009), 123–4.

25. 'Untitled', *Huddersfield Chronicle*, 9 February 1886, 10.

26. Special correspondent, 'Elan Valley's Attractions for Midlanders'.

27. Figures collected from *Birmingham Daily Gazette*.

28. Victor Westropp, *The Lake Vyrnwy Fishing Book* (Aberdeen University Press, 1979), 40.

29. Figures collected from *Birmingham Daily Gazette*.

30. Asa Briggs, *Victorian Cities* (Penguin, 1968).

31. 'Editorial', *Liverpool Echo*, 13 December 1888, 3.

32. 'Editorial', *Liverpool Echo*, 2 October 1890, 3

33. 'Lake Vyrnwy Hotel', *Yorkshire Post*, 8 July 1933, 17.

34. Coopey, 'A River Does Indeed Run Through It', 62, 67.

35. Leeds Corporation, 'Leeds Waterworks Committee Minutes, volume 4: 1878–1885', 95, 126.

36. 'City Fisheries: Trout in Good Number and Excellent Condition', *Birmingham Daily Gazette*, 15 December 1913, 10.

37. Leeds Corporation, 'Leeds Waterworks Committee Minutes, volume 4: 1878–1885', 126.

38. Leeds Corporation, 'Leeds Waterworks Committee Minutes, volume 4: 1878–1885', 365.

39. Richard Holt, *Sport and the British: A Modern History* (Oxford University Press, 1989), 56.

40. 'Untitled', *Field*, 12 October 1895, 9; Jack Pike, 'Angling notes', *Cricket and Football Field*, 4 January 1908, 12.

41. Leeds Corporation, 'Leeds Waterworks Committee Minutes, volume 7: 1896–1903', 339–40, 344–45.

42. 'Leeds City Council: The Township Controversy', *Yorkshire Post*.

43. Jeffrey Hill, *Sport, Leisure and Culture in Twentieth-Century Britain* (Palgrave, 2002), 121–22.

44. Peter Bailey, *Leisure and Class in Victorian England: Rational Recreation and the Contest for Control, 1830–1885* (Routledge, 1978), 65; Brad Beaven, *Leisure, Citizenship and Working-Class Men in Britain, 1850–1945* (Manchester University Press, 2005), 88.

45. 'Leeds City Council: The Township Controversy', *Yorkshire Post*.

46. 'Fishing in Vyrnwy Lake', *Liverpool Echo*, 10 April 1889, 4.

47. K. G. Arnold, 'Angling at Fewston and Swinsty Reservoirs', *Yorkshire Post*, 16 September 1902, 8.

48. Arnold, 'Angling at Fewston and Swinsty Reservoirs'.

49. W. Richardson, 'Angling at Fewston and Swinsty Reservoirs', *Yorkshire Post*, 17 September 1902, 5.

50. H. Knight Horsfield, 'Angling in Fewston and Swinsty Reservoirs', *Yorkshire Post*, 18 September 1902, 5.

51. Edmund Barker, 'Angling in Fewston and Swinsty Reservoirs', *Yorkshire Post*, 20 September 1902, 11.

52. W. C. Dawson, 'Fishing in the Leeds Reservoirs', *Yorkshire Post*, 25 September 1902, 9.

53. Dawson, 'Fishing in the Leeds Reservoirs'.

54. Borsay, *A History of Leisure*, 61–2; Leeds Corporation, 'Leeds Waterworks Committee Minutes, volume 10: 1912–1929', 100, 115.

55. A. H. Woodward, 'Otter Had the Laugh: Angling', *Yorkshire Evening Post*, 21 May 1949, 5.

56. 'Women Anglers Banned', *Dundee Courier*, 7 July 1934, 3.

57. Figures gained from the Lake District National Park website, 'Learning: Lake District Facts and Figures', accessed 23 July 2020, https://www.lakedistrict.gov.uk/learning/factsandfigures.

58. David Hey, 'Kinder Scout and the Legend of the Mass Trespass', *Agricultural History Review* 59, no. 2 (2013): 200–201, https://www.jstor.org/stable/23317099.

59. Jeremy Burchardt, *Paradise Lost: Rural Idyll and Social Change since 1800* (I. B. Tauris, 2002), 121.

60. A. W. C., 'Up the Washburn Valley: A Ramble in Winter', *Leeds Mercury*, 4 March 1893, 17.

61. Burchardt, *Paradise Lost*, 125.

62. 'Country Rambles Around Leeds: For Summer Evenings or Holidays', *Leeds Mercury*, 24 June 1905, 17.

63. 'A Whitsuntide Holiday Ramble to Lake Vyrnwy and the Berwyns', *Coventry Herald*, 14 June 1895, 6.

64. 'Fewston', *Wharfedale and Airedale Observer*, 30 March 1894, 5.

65. 'Economical Holidays', *Montgomeryshire Echo*, 21 July 1906, 5.

66. 'Untitled', *Birmingham Daily Gazette*, 23 September 1933, 9; 'Untitled', *Birmingham Daily Gazette*, 5 May 1934, 14.

67. Ritvo, *Dawn of Green*, 130–31.

68. See *The English Lake District, including Furness Abbey, Shap Spa, Seascale, etc., etc.* (George Philip and Son, 1895), 77–8.

69. Ben Harker, '"The Manchester Rambler": Ewan MacColl and the 1932 Mass Trespass', *History Workshop Journal* 59, no. 1 (2005): 220, https://doi.org/10.1093/hwj/dbi016.

70. Burchardt, *Paradise Lost*, 127; Hey, 'Kinder Scout', 199–216; David Prynn, 'The Clarion Clubs, Rambling and the Holiday Associations in Britain since the 1890s', *Journal of Contemporary History* 11, no. 2 (1976): 65–77, https://doi.org/10.1177/002200947601100204.

71. 'A Very Good Friday Out-of-Doors', *Leeds Mercury*, 30 March 1929, 1; also see 'Holiday of Early Risers', *Yorkshire Post*, 10 June 1930, 10; 'Good Send-Off for Easter', *Yorkshire Post*, 15 April 1933, 7; 'Thousands Leave W. Riding Towns', *Yorkshire Post*, 29 May 1939, 9; 'Best Holiday Weather in the North', *Yorkshire Post*, 8 August 1939, 8.

72. Harvey Taylor, *A Claim on the Countryside: A History of the British Outdoor Movement* (Keele University Press, 1997), 228.

73. Countryman, 'A Wayfarer's Diary', *Leeds Mercury*, 12 January 1938, 6; 'Rambling Club Notices', *Yorkshire Evening Post*, 3 September 1932, 6; 'Rambling Club Notices', *Yorkshire Evening Post*, 29 August 1931, 3; 'A Midnight Ramble', *Yorkshire Evening Post*, 27 September 1929, 16.

74. Sydney Moorhouse, 'Rambling Notes', *Leeds Mercury*, 11 September 1935; Countryman, 'A Wayfarer's Diary', *Leeds Mercury*, 26 October 1938, 6; Countryman, 'A Wayfarer's Diary', *Leeds Mercury*, 5 April 1939, 6; Cycling correspondent, 'Record Cycle Ride', *Leeds Mercury*, 9 February 1935, 11.

75. 'Cycling Club', *Todmorden Advertiser and Hebden Bridge Newsletter*, 24 April 1931, 4; Rossignol, 'Cycling Gossip', *Tamworth Herald*, 13 July 1935, 7; 'Chester C.H.A. and H.F. Rambling Club', *Cheshire Observer*, 23 April 1938, 10; 'Brecon', *Brecon County Times*, 20 September 1928, 5; 'C.T.C. Easter Tours', *Birmingham Daily Gazette*, 21 March 1929, 12; 'Cheltenham and County', *Gloucestershire Echo*, 20 May 1929, 4; Hiking correspondent, 'Hiking Notes', *Western Mail*, 18 September 1935, 13; 'To-morrow's Fixtures', *Lancashire Evening Post*, 20 August 1932, 3; 'Cycling C.T.C.', *Lancaster Guardian*, 9 September 1938, 20; 'Local News', *Nelson Leader*, 1 August 1921, 5.

76. Tebbutt, 'Rambling and Manly Identity', 1137.

77. Langhamer, *Women's Leisure in England*, 77, 80.

78. Robert Snape, 'The Co-operative Holidays Association and the Cultural Formation of Countryside Leisure Practice', *Leisure Studies* 23, no. 2 (2004): 152, https://doi.org/10.1080/0261436042000226345.

79. Ben Anderson, 'Partnership or Co-operation? Family, Politics and Strenuousness in the pre-First World War Co-operative Holidays Association', *Sport in History* 33, no. 3 (2013): 274–75, https://doi.org/10.1080/17460263.2013.826434.

80. 'Young Ideas', *Edinburgh Evening News*, 8 July 1932, 12; 'Local News', *Nelson Leader*, 20 May 1921, 5; 'Local News', *Burnley News*, 24 April 1922, 4.

81. Burchardt, *Paradise Lost*, 128.

82. 'Local and District', *Leeds Times*, 30 June 1883, 3; Leeds Corporation, 'Leeds Waterworks Committee Minutes, volume 5: 1885–1890', WYAS, LLC22/1/5, 357; Leeds Corporation, 'Leeds Waterworks Committee Minutes, volume 6: 1890–1896', WYAS, LLC22/1/6, 29.

83. Hey, 'Kinder Scout', 201.

84. 'Closed Footpath Near Dob Park: Why Restrictions Have Been Place on Walkers in Washburn Valley', *Yorkshire Evening Post*, 29 July 1931, 3.

85. Heather Shore, *London's Criminal Underworlds, c.1720–c.1930: A Social and Cultural History* (Palgrave Macmillan, 2015), 147.

86. Anderson, 'A Liberal Countryside?', 96.

87. A. W. H., 'A Rambler's Notebook', *Derby Daily Telegraph*, 26 September 1935, 8; Denis Cosgrove et al. 'Landscape and Identity at Ladybower Reservoir and Rutland Water', *Transactions of the Institute of British Geographers*, 21, no. 3 (1996): 542, https://doi.org/10.2307/622595.

88. Rucksack, 'Rambling Notes', *Lancashire Evening Post*, 14 January 1937, 3.

89. 'Washburn Valley: Yorkshire Ramblers and Closing of Path', *Yorkshire Post*, 18 January 1932, 2.

90. Leeds Corporation, 'Leeds Waterworks Committee Minutes, volume 11: 1930–1948', WYAS, LLC22/1/11, 45.

91. West Riding Ramblers' Federation (WRRF), 'West Riding Ramblers' Federation, 1933–34', WYAS, WYL2412.

92. WRRF, 'West Riding Ramblers' Federation, 1933–34'.

93. WRRF, 'West Riding Ramblers' Federation, 1933–34'.

94. Harker, '"The Manchester Rambler"', 224.

95. 'Refusal of Access to Mardale Fells', *Penrith Observer*, 19 January 1937, 8.

96. WRRF, 'West Riding Ramblers' Federation, 1933–34'.

97. Ben Anderson, *Cities, Mountains and Being Modern in* fin-de-siècle *England and Germany* (Palgrave Macmillan, 2020), 84, https://doi.org/10.1057/978-1-137-54000-3.

98. David Matless, *Landscape and Englishness*, 2nd ed. (Reaktion Books, 2016), 101.

99. 'Damage in Washburndale', *Leeds Mercury*, 25 June 1936, 4.

100. Sydney Moorhouse, 'Rambling Notes', *Leeds Mercury*, 1 July 1936, 7; Frank North, 'Northern Country Gossip', *Leeds Mercury*, 25 June 1936, 4.

101. Anderson, 'A Liberal Countryside?', 96.

102. John Walton, 'The Northern Rambler: Recreational Walking and the Popular Politics of Industrial England, from Peterloo to the 1930s', *Labour History Review* 78, no. 3 (2013): 243–68, https://doi.org/10.3828/lhr.2013.14.

103. John Sheail, 'The Access to Mountains Act 1939: An Essay in Compromise', *Rural History* 21, no. 1 (2010): 72, https://doi.org/10.1017/S095679330999015X.

104. Ministry of Town and Country Planning, 'Survey of Public Rights of Way in Blubberhouses and Fewston', North Yorkshire County Record Office, n.d., PR/FEW 15/3.

105. Ritvo, *Dawn of Green*, 174.

106. Roland H. Wade, 'Peak District National Park', *Yorkshire Post*, 25 October 1950, 2.

107. Tom Stephenson, *Forbidden Land: The Struggle for Access to Mountain and Moorland*, ed. Ann Holt (Manchester University Press, 1989), 105–15; Tom Stephenson, 'Our Birthright', *Daily Herald*, 7 January 1939, 14.

108. Sheail, 'Access to Mountains Act 1939', 59; Gavin Parker and Neil Ravenscroft, 'Benevolence, Nationalism and Hegemony: Fifty Years of the National Parks and Access to the Countryside Act 1949', *Leisure Studies*, 18, no. 4 (1999): 303, https://doi.org/10.1080/026143699374871.

109. Rachel Cooke, 'Forgive Us Our Trespasses: Forbidden Rambles with a Right-to-Roam Campaigner', *Guardian*, 9 August 2020, https://www.theguardian.com/uk-news/2020/aug/09/forgive-us-our-trespasses-forbidden-rambles-with-a-right-to-roam-campaigner.

110. Tom Breen et al., 'Whose Right to Roam? Contesting Access to England's Countryside', *The Journal of Transport History*, 44, no. 2 (2023): 276–307, https://doi.org/10.1177/00225266231174766.

Chapter 6

Urban intrusion: community in the urban/rural hinterland

So far, the impact of reservoirs has been considered from the perspective of the city – the environmental changes caused trying to tame the wilderness, the management of reservoirs, how proponents of cities wrote about these rural areas in positive terms, and how these waterworks became sites of leisure for urban citizens. This final chapter looks at the impact of reservoirs from another perspective: the people who were most affected by the building of waterworks. In relative terms, urban water schemes affected a small number of people; municipal authorities and private waterworks companies would often purposefully target rural areas that had small populations, making parliamentary approval easier to gain. Under two hundred people were affected by the building of the Elan Valley reservoirs, while the population of the parish of Fewston in the Washburn Valley was 310 in 1881 when the reservoirs had been completed.[1]

While few in number compared to the hundreds of thousands who would benefit from such schemes, the impact of the reservoirs on local communities is important to highlight. On the one hand, it seems that depopulating pockets of the countryside for urban improvement would fit into the general narratives of rural decline that had caused concern for centuries. What fuelled this narrative of decline was the fear that people and communities had lost a sense of belonging to modern ways of life that placed less emphasis on supposed traditional values. This belief gained currency in the writings of nineteenth-century novelists, such as Thomas Hardy, who sought to emphasise a fundamental change in rural life, particularly the threat of industrialisation.[2] Additionally, as this chapter will highlight, certain reservoirs represented threats not just to community but to national identity, with Liverpool especially characterised as an invading force taking Welsh resources.

Reservoir schemes undoubtedly had some negative consequences for those who lived in the local area. Some reservoirs, such as Llyn Celyn, were more negatively impactful than others. As set out earlier, this is a contentious and difficult history both in terms of its emotional resonance and also in its complexity. The purpose of this chapter is to assess the broader impact reservoirs made to communities, highlighting negative changes but also how the subsequent management of waterworks allowed local communities to adapt and, in some cases, flourish to an extent that would most likely have not been possible without external stimuli. This fits into a developing historiographical literature that stresses the importance of community spirit as an indicator of rural life rather than demographic rise and fall.[3] In examining reservoirs in the Washburn Valley and those built in Wales, most specifically the Elan Valley reservoirs and Liverpool's Tryweryn scheme, the impact of these schemes to local communities will be shown to have been more nuanced than has perhaps been previously recognised. In remaking the countryside, urban authorities and water companies had an undoubted social impact on local community life. Focusing on individual case studies helps to bring out a more nuanced national picture, one that shows that the community impact of reservoirs was not straightforwardly positive or negative.

Waterworks and the fluidity of community life

Gaining a sense of community life in the nineteenth century can be difficult for the historian, especially in rural areas, as many people could not or did not record their experiences. The diary of John Dickinson, then, provides a rare and valuable insight into how people lived in this period. The diary, published under the title *Timble Man: Diaries of a Dalesman*, chronicles the life of Dickinson, a resident of the hamlet of Timble in the Washburn Valley, between 1878 and his death in 1911. Dickinson was primarily a mason, but also registered births and deaths within the parish of Fewston, salted bacon for local farmers, worked for the Provincial Insurance company, held a position with Wharfedale Rural District Council, and gauged the volume of rainfall in the reservoirs for Leeds Corporation. Through these numerous occupations, some of which he held at different times during his life, he came into contact with many of the families that lived across the valley, and was in a position to judge the development of rural life during the late nineteenth century.

Although Dickinson did not record many entries on the subject of the reservoirs specifically, he often commented on what he saw as the decline of rural life in the valley. In February 1889, he noted that: 'rural life is used up and what spirit there is left in old England concentrates in the great towns where all that is best in everything gradually centres'.[4] This sense of rural decline was linked to nostalgia, a yearning for what was: in this case, the spirit of 'old England', an idea taken up by preservationists in the twentieth century. Perceived urban crisis in the late nineteenth century drew a cultural response from some, resulting in a rise in the proliferation of art, music and architecture that married rurality with Englishness.[5] To some, rural depopulation was emblematic of a cultural shift towards urbanism, which contributed to a remaking of the social fabric of the nation. This strain of thought can be seen in Dickinson's assessment of rural life, which was also characteristic of the work of local residents like the Reverend Thomas Parkinson.[6] While the reservoirs are not mentioned as a cause of this decline, their construction will no doubt have been a factor.

Dickinson continued to be preoccupied with the decline of rural life for much of the following decade. In 1897 he wrote:

> As regards the immediate neighbourhood the state of the community is very dark and depressing. Farming is very unprofitable, the population is decreasing, the best families and the best men and women migrate to the towns. The consequence is that the hopeful zest and spirit which used to prevail 30 or 40 years ago is dead and life has become little more than a mere idle shuffle.[7]

The idea of rural decline pervaded Dickinson's life, so much so that by 1900 he and his family had relocated from Timble to Otley, moving closer to his regular places of work. Otley, a small market town in Lower Wharfedale, was the closet urban area to the Washburn Valley. Ironically, Dickinson wrote that: 'The quiet village life is still in our hearts and the noise and bustle and apparent heartlessness of town life jars on our nerves'.[8] Dickinson longed for a return to a more vibrant rural life, but had himself contributed to the decline of rural community by moving to an urban area. His rural nostalgia developed from what the Washburn Valley had lost to what he had lost; a more intimate sense of belonging. A continual sense of loss for what had been permeated Dickinson's writings as he fulfilled his own observation that the best and brightest migrated to urban centres.

Community life, however, continued across the valley during this period and beyond. Although the population decreased throughout the nineteenth century, no doubt aided by the presence of the reservoirs and their impact on villages like Fewston, remaining residents continued to mark important events in the year. These included the annual feasts, held in July in Timble and August in Fewston, a tradition that was also celebrated in nearby Otley and Yeadon in Wharfedale. It is through these events, which highlighted the centrality of religion to community life, that we can see that the impact of the reservoirs was not wholly negative. While festivities often started with a trip to church, there was more to the feast than sermons. Nearby inns were reportedly filled with drinking and dancing, while swingboats and spice stalls among others added a sense of exoticism to the gala 'at which all the rosy cheeks and pretty faces of the neighbourhood were present, and the usual innocent games [...] were indulged in to the delight of everyone present'.[9] This mirrors the behaviour that took place during other rural festivals such as the Oldham wakes in the early nineteenth century.[10] There was also a game of cricket with a team from nearby Dacre in Nidderdale, an event that mirrored a cricket match at the Yeadon feast, although that game had more glamorous Australian opposition.[11] Despite his notion that rural life was dead, John Dickinson often commented on the vibrancy of life in Timble during the July feasts, one of which included two Frenchmen and a dancing bear, followed by dancing and singing until the early hours of the morning.[12] The presence of a dancing bear was another exotic addition, a tangible link between rural life and the culture of the imperial.[13] It also provided a more sanitised element of entertainment than cockfighting or bull-baiting, key elements of rural festivals during the eighteenth and early nineteenth centuries, thereby maintaining the use of animals for entertainment.[14]

The reporting of the Fewston feast in 1881 further highlighted the presence of a local community spirit. Taking place less than a year after the subsidence of Fewston village, the event remained successful, despite the dilapidated state of the area. Indeed, the perilous state of the village caused more visitors than normal to attend, 'not so much to see the feast, as to look at the subsidence, and gaze upon the beautiful scenery', emphasising that, even after the main subsidence had ceased, it continued to impact on the area.[15] However, the correspondent was more effusive about the activities that occurred during the evening:

> the young folk of the neighbourhood congregated to have a few hours' enjoyment. Reuben had strung his fiddle, and the votaries of the light *[sic]* fantastic toe made hot work of it in the large room in the village inn. In a field near the inn was a 'kissing mill', which, unlike many mills nowadays, was running overtime.[16]

A vibrant community enjoying recreation is presented, drawing euphemistically on the village's past association with industry to illustrate the point. Despite the damage caused by the subsidence, for this one day at least, the village of Fewston was a dynamic area, deserving of the title of 'the metropolis of the Washburn Valley' bestowed on it by the *Wharfedale and Airedale Observer*.

The vibrancy that was noted in 1881 was not long to last. Only a year later the newspaper reported that the feast was in decline: 'The proceedings on Monday were unusually quiet. Of roundabouts, swing-boats, or even spice-stalls, there were none'. A lack of entertainment was met with a lack of participation from residents of the area, with the correspondent only noting the participation of 'two dozen good-looking young men and women [...] a few of the elders [...] quietly looking on and smoking'.[17] In 1880, the *Wharfedale and Airedale Observer* claimed: 'in these degenerate days, when village feasts are fast falling into disrepute, it is some consolation to find that the feast at Fewstone *[sic]*, at all events, remains true to the traditions of the good old days gone by'.[18] Two years later, this consolation had evaporated, with the newspaper noting: 'like nearly all village feasts, it has gradually declined of late years, and the village, with its feast, seems to be gradually sinking'.[19] The effects of subsidence, caused by the construction of Fewston and Swinsty reservoirs on an unstable shale foundation, was having an effect on the local population, demonstrating the socionatural impact of the reservoirs beyond their construction. This decline continued into 1883, when attendance at the village inn was below average, due to a lack of attractions to draw the younger members of the community. One development did occur, though, as the local Methodists decided to use the date to mark the anniversary of their Sunday school. This included a sermon from a popular evangelist from York, followed by a public tea party, attended by over two hundred people.[20] The decision of the Methodists in the area to hold their Sunday school anniversary on the same day as the Fewston feast meant that, despite the decline of its more sociable aspects, it continued to be celebrated by the local community into the twentieth century, evidence of the continued importance that religion played in rural life.[21]

Nonetheless, the vibrancy of the feast days had declined. Fortunately for locals, this was not the only instance of community camaraderie in the Washburn Valley. The construction of the Robinson Library in Timble provided an important social space for the residents of Timble and nearby hamlets. Reading rooms of this kind were common in rural areas, preceding the village hall movement of the interwar period. Their decline during the 1920s was linked to their limited functionality: they were typically small spaces that could not accommodate large events.[22] This does not necessarily apply to the Robinson Library, which functioned as a prominent centre for community life into the twentieth century despite its small size.

This was no doubt aided by the fact that the core population of Timble was small; 109 lived in Timble Great in 1891, with a further 19 living in the accompanying Timble Little.[23] The library, which also acted as a free school, was opened in 1891 and financed by Robinson Gill, a business owner in Brooklyn, New York, who had emigrated from Blubberhouses in the 1850s. Gill was following the example of another expatriate philanthropist, Andrew Carnegie, who established public libraries in several countries. At the opening of the library, Gill hoped that it would stand as 'a perpetual mark of my respect and esteem of the people of the village and the surrounding country' and that it would be a place to 'develop and enlighten the mind and make life more pleasant and cheerful'.[24] It was not long before the Robinson Library came to hold a social as well as didactic purpose.

Two years later, the library started to be used for the anniversary celebrations of the City of Refuge Lodge friendly society. The celebrations were held annually during Whit week, a period of the year that continued to hold cultural significance for rural communities despite the decline of traditional activities related to drinking and debauchery.[25] The success or failure of friendly societies was an indicator of local conditions in individual communities, as friendly societies relied on the community to survive through participation and subscriptions. They were vitally important, though, to rural working class ideals of respectability, especially during anniversary celebrations that focused the community's attention on the civility of the working class.[26] The celebrations, which followed the pattern of club days that Alun Howkins has identified of friendly societies in Oxfordshire, began at the Timble Inn, followed by a procession to Fewston church headed by a brass band.[27] After a service at Fewston church and a short stay at an inn in Fewston, the procession returned to Timble and sat down to a large meal and meeting in the Robinson Library.[28] Like the Fewston feast, the day finished with the youth of the area returning to the Timble Inn to enjoy music and dancing.[29]

As a member of the lodge, John Dickinson noted his attendance at meetings and anniversary celebrations. His entry for the lodge celebration of 1881 gave a flavour of the day's proceedings:

> The Guiseley Brass Band of Musick *[sic]* arrived around 10. There were about 80 men present and it was very busy at the Timble Inn. We walked (in procession) to Fewston Church and made a good show. Club meeting in the evening then a dance which was carried on with great spirit up to 10 o'clock then all turned out.[30]

The presence of a brass band at the front of the procession was not uncommon for friendly society anniversary celebrations or feast days.

The excerpt also highlights the number of people present for the procession, illustrating that the celebration, including the religious element, was popular among the residents of Timble and further afield. A further entry from 1889 emphasised the processional elements of the day as well as its continuing popularity: 'About 100 members of the village lodge started in procession to Fewston Church [...] The Lodge flag was carried in a showy style and all passed off brilliantly'. A series of events took place during the evening, including dancing in the Timble Inn and games such as kissing rings, which led Dickinson to remark, 'altogether a high day for our poor old dull village'.[31]

Unlike the Fewston feast, which decreased in popularity during the 1890s, the lodge anniversary continued to be a popular event into the 1900s. The *Wharfedale and Airedale Observer* commented in 1900 that after the general meeting of the lodge had been held, 'many visitors from a distance and all the young folks of the surrounding districts turned up, and various amusements occupied the time up to close upon the midnight hour'.[32] In 1901, the newspaper hailed the ability of the lodge to maintain its membership and anniversary celebrations 'in face of the general decay of village life'.[33] Indeed, unlike rural events such as the wakes in the provincial Oldham area, which declined steadily during the late nineteenth century, the membership of the lodge increased during the early 1900s, with 120 members in 1900, 134 members in 1902, 150 members in 1903, and 155 members in 1907.[34] This increase was in spite of general malaise around rural depopulation during the early twentieth century.

The pace of rural depopulation in Britain during the late nineteenth century exceeded any other country in Europe, an exodus that undercut forms of community, which was reflected in some newspaper reporting.[35] The opening of an unemployment bureau in Otley in 1906 was attributed to rural depopulation that resulted in an increase of unemployed men in towns and cities.[36] In 1911, the reservoirs were cited as causes for further decline, with compulsory land purchases and afforestation seen as having led to depopulation that had left the valley 'a wilderness'.[37] As with Dickinson's diary, though, the supposed effects of rural depopulation seem a little exaggerated, evidenced by the lodge celebrations that began to incorporate other activities. The anniversary of 1903 included dancing in front of the Timble Inn as well as sociable activities inside the Timble Inn and the chapel.[38] The 1906 anniversary included a cricket match between a team from Timble and a selected eleven from Farnley Hall, demonstrating that different classes engaged with these activities.[39] It is clear, then, that while the size of the Washburn Valley's population decreased, community life in the valley adapted and continued to be celebrated into the twentieth century.

The continuance of community life was further emphasised in 1906 when a scheme to promote the area's farming exploits was put forward, headed by Captain Wakefield, the tenant of Swinsty Hall.[40] The Washburn Valley Farmers' Association sought to promote an agricultural society for the area, which had several benefits for community life. Since the decline of industry in the valley, the primary form of employment was agriculture, aided by the letting of land compulsorily bought by the Leeds Corporation for farming; 185 people were employed in the valley in 1911 as either farmers or farm labourers.[41] Providing a collective society would help to bind the agricultural community of the valley.

A related benefit was the introduction of an annual farming show held in September, which would not only provide an opportunity for the residents of the valley to come together but, with the presence of agricultural competitions such as best mare or heaviest fowl, would also add an element of competition for farmers to engage in and, in theory, raise the stock of farming produce in the valley. Additionally, only those who farmed in the Washburn Valley could enter the farming show. While farming shows were a staple of the agricultural calendar in nearby Otley and Harrogate, these shows were the province of larger and more prestigious farms, at which Washburn Valley farmers were less likely to win awards. Restricting entry to the show gave tenant farmers a chance at winning prizes and stopped the event from becoming larger than was necessary. A further benefit was that, as a society, it was anticipated that events such as talks would be held throughout the year, therefore providing opportunities for the communities of the valley to engage with. One such talk took place in Fewston in 1907 on the prosperity of Danish farming, emphasising that farmers in the valley were interesting in exploring international farming techniques as well as domestic.[42] As older forms of community engagement began to decline, the farming association provided an opportunity to rejuvenate community life.

District agricultural societies such as the Washburn Valley Farmers' Association arguably enjoyed their heyday during the mid-nineteenth century, declining from the 1850s onwards as difficulties were encountered in sustaining regular meetings once favourite topics had been exhausted.[43] The success of the association runs counter to this narrative, not only in starting after many had ceased to exist in the early twentieth century, but in managing to survive until the 1970s. This is, perhaps, due to the nature of agricultural employment in the valley, with farmers only becoming tenants during the 1900s after compulsory land purchases by the Leeds Corporation, meaning that they lacked a unified employment status until then. Additionally, the remote nature of the valley, which was ultimately detrimental to industry during the early nineteenth century, was potentially an advantage in shielding the agricultural community from wider changes, including agricultural shows.

The first Washburn Valley Show, in September 1906, took only five weeks to organise. Meetings with the organising committee, led by Captain Wakefield, were held in all areas of the valley, which lent full support and, more importantly, financial aid to the event. Further support was offered by interested parties from within the valley, such as Captain Wakefield himself and Reverend D. T. Milligan, the vicar of Fewston church. There was also support from wider afield: Joshua Tetley and Sons contributed ten pounds and sixpence, while the Leeds Corporation donated five pounds to the event annually from 1906 onwards for running costs or prize money.[44] The event itself was hailed as a great success for the area by the *Wharfedale and Airedale Observer*, which praised the establishment of the yearly event:

> The chief aim of the association is to promote the betterment of the breeding of stock locally, and during the dreary winter months to arrange for a course of discussions on matters appertaining to the farming industry. Apart from an evening socially spent during the winter season, the exchanging of ideas will have a most beneficial effect, and will tend to cement a good feeling of comradeship between the various townships.[45]

Aside from the agricultural competition itself, which had 123 entries in its first year, entertainment included the performance by a brass band from Otley. As already noted, the presence of brass bands was an integral element of community events in the Washburn Valley, which provided occasions with a sense of dignity.[46] Following the conclusion of the show, a dance was held at the Robinson Library, with refreshments, including beer from Ilkley Brewery Company, provided by the Timble Inn.[47] The show was a success in both providing a space for the tenant farmers of the valley to exhibit their produce and in creating new social events for residents across the valley.

The show continued to grow in popularity over the following years. The second show in 1907, which also took place in Timble, saw an increase in entries, mixed with what was deemed to be a slightly disappointing attendance given the work the association had done in trying to promote the event in towns outside the valley.[48] The third show, held in Norwood, built on the success of the previous two shows, despite being held in a less accessible area of the valley. Entries from farmers increased again on the previous year, and 'there was a large attendance from the more adjunct villages'.[49] The popularity of the event continued to increase. The *Wharfedale and Airedale Observer* remarked of the 1910 show that: 'At the time of opening there was a moderate attendance, and as the afternoon wore on, this was greatly increased by visitors from all parts of the district, even the Metropolis sending its quota' – word of the successful event had evidently spread to Leeds.[50]

This success continued into the interwar period as entries to the competition and visitor numbers increased. This was in spite of the difficulties the agricultural sector encountered during the interwar period, what Alun Howkins has termed the 'locust years' in which the sector was perpetually depressed.[51] The show also continued to draw crowds from outside the valley itself; the *Wharfedale and Airedale Observer* remarked in 1921 that 'the pleasantly-situated show ground was thronged during the afternoon and evening with visitors from the surrounding towns and villages; indeed, the cities of Leeds and Bradford contributed their quota'.[52] In 1925, the newspaper noted that attendance at the show numbered over one thousand, an impressive figure given the relatively inaccessible nature of the Washburn Valley generally and Norwood in particular. Indeed, accessibility became an issue towards the end of the 1920s, prompting the association to move the show from the Sun Inn, Norwood to the Hopper Lane Hotel, situated on the A59 that connects Skipton and Harrogate. Looking back in 1934, the *Wharfedale and Airedale Observer* praised this move: 'The accessibility of the field from the main Harrogate–Skipton Road has resulted in larger number of visitors from further afield, and entries were again a record'.[53] The move also precipitated a change in the entertainment on show. While both venues were situated next to public houses, the shows at Norwood included a roster of sports, such as races for boys, girls, men, single women and married women, three-legged races, a slow bicycle race and an obstacle race, whereas at Blubberhouses the entertainment involved a donkey race and a clay pigeon shooting competition, as well as music provided by brass bands.[54] The show did not provide the same entertainment each year, but sought to evolve in order to maintain the interest of visitors alongside the agricultural competition itself, attempting to capitalise on the valley's popularity as a site of leisure and beauty.

There were some elements of the valley's rural life that warranted John Dickinson's assessment that community life was in decline. The demise of the feast days, important annual cultural events, are an example of this, although the decline of such days in the Washburn Valley occurred slightly later than other local areas.[55] This, in addition to the general reduction in the valley's population, was, to some like Dickinson, evidence that both community and rural life were in terminal decline. However, as K. D. M. Snell has argued, one of the main factors in the expression of community is a sense of belonging.[56] Although the feast days declined in importance, the City of Refuge Lodge anniversary celebrations brought members of the friendly society and others from the wider area together. The success of the Refuge Lodge during this period is an indication that a sense of community remained in the valley, despite Dickinson's contrary assessment. The Washburn Valley Farmers' Association Show, an event that grew through the early twentieth century, played a similar role in bringing together the working community for a day to celebrate both the agricultural produce of the area and the community life of the valley. The Washburn Valley provides an interesting case study to contrast with other areas, such as parts of Wales targeted by Liverpool and Birmingham, as well as the Lake District targeted by Manchester. In those cases, the waterworks schemes ensured that those areas became mostly if not entirely depopulated. In contrast, the Leeds reservoirs had an undoubted impact on the area, as shown in previous chapters, but because the entire valley was not flooded, it meant that life could go on for many, albeit in a different way. As with cultural depictions of the countryside, the coming of reservoirs did not necessarily mean the death of rurality.

The negative impacts of waterworks

While the impact of the reservoirs on the communities of the Washburn Valley was more nuanced than perhaps first envisioned by Dickinson, this does not mean that reservoir projects were not highly disruptive. The subsidence of Fewston village in the Washburn Valley was testament to this, as were the impacts on communities in other areas of the country. Municipal governments purposefully targeted areas of the country for reservoir development that did not have large populations, thereby making parliamentary approval easier to obtain. This led to a somewhat callous regard for those that did live in the affected areas. Little to no mention was made of the impact on local communities during Liverpool's deliberations over the Vyrnwy project, despite the eventual impact that the waterworks would have, with homes for over two hundred residents constructed and a new school built.[57] There was local opposition to the construction of Vyrnwy, although this was ignored by the parliamentary process and the English press. It was also downplayed by the few nationalist publications that did acknowledge local concerns, which Owen Roberts attributes to the nature of Welsh nationalism in the nineteenth century. This form of nationalism saw itself less as oppositional to English modernity and more as wanting to play a full part in the success of the British Empire.[58] Water supply was particularly local in this period, but here we can see the genesis of later ideas around the importance of local efforts to the national supply of water as Denis Cosgrove, Barbara Roscoe and Simon Rycroft have highlighted in the 1970s. For them, people local to the newly built Rutland Water in East Leicestershire saw that reservoir as helping to serve the national need for water, despite the fact that water networks in that period were locally connected and could not transfer water nationally.[59]

Of the several waterworks projects undertaken in the late nineteenth century, Birmingham's Elan and Claerwen Valley schemes had the highest potential impact to rural communities due to the size of the undertaking. While the Claerwen scheme was never realised as planned in the 1890s, what came to pass has been termed by David Lewis Brown as 'the Elan Valley clearance', an evocation of the Highland clearances in Scotland during the eighteenth and nineteenth centuries.[60] Although not as dramatic as those clearances, which saw the decimation of clan culture in the Scottish highlands, the Elan Valley underwent a sizeable population decline because of the reservoirs. As part of the parliamentary Act that authorised the construction of the reservoirs, Birmingham Corporation was given seven years of compulsory purchasing powers.[61] Surveys were undertaken to assess which residents would need to be rehoused and which buildings would need to be rebuilt elsewhere. Of the sixty-seven properties in the Elan and Claerwen valleys, eighteen were demolished or abandoned, with six replacement cottages built in addition to a new school and church for the area. In 1891, there were 298 people living in the Elan and Claerwen valleys, a number that decreased to 103 by 1911. While several families were rehoused by Birmingham Corporation, there was an undoubted impact on the local community of the area, particularly those who spoke only Welsh; by 1911 just five residents in the valleys only spoke Welsh.[62]

While the Elan Valley clearances or the flooding of Llanwddyn to construct Lake Vyrnwy did not provoke outright opposition despite their impact on local people and culture, they were certainly influential, forming part of a longer-term history of displacement and injustice in the minds of many. This was aptly the subject of Emlyn Williams's 1949 film *The Last Days of Dolwyn*, a film notable for being Richard Burton's motion picture debut. The film follows the story of the village of Dolwyn, targeted by industrial interests in Lancashire as a suitable site for a reservoir – a reservoir had been constructed higher up the valley but owing to geological problems that project had to be amended, which meant flooding Dolwyn. The landlords of the area, the Dolwyn family, agree to the project in order to cover several debts, as does the majority of the village in exchange for compensation and the promise of a new home and job in the fictional Liverpool suburb of Hagton. The main character of the story, the elderly widow Merri, is one of the few that fails to accept the move; however, as she is a tenant, she has no power. On discovering that, in fact, she is the leaseholder for her property, Merri refuses to move, turning down hundreds of pounds. In response to his failure to secure the valley for Lord Lancashire, the villainous agent Rob Davis attempts to open the floodgates of the original reservoir further up the valley, but he is unable to do so.[63]

The film has somewhat fantastical elements to it: it concludes with a fight between an enraged Davis trying to set fire to the village and Burton's character Gareth, who accidentally knocks an alcohol-soaked Davis into a fire which causes his death. In order to save her foster-child Gareth from the consequences of his actions, Merri decides to hide the body in her house and go to the reservoir to open the floodgates, which she successfully does. Emlyn's film is woven with relevant themes here. It is notable that opposition to moving from the villagers themselves is largely non-existent – many are happy to move. This is embodied most clearly in Merri's other son Dafydd, who is desperate to leave the dull countryside for the bright lights of Liverpool. Contrasted with him is Burton's Gareth, who at the start of the film returns from Liverpool, unable to bear the noise, the smog, and the seven-storey buildings. Gareth represents the anti-urbanism that would soon be taken up by Plaid Cymru, returning to the land of his forebearers. The film is also notable for the amount of Welsh spoken by characters. There are several occasions where characters like Merri comment on their inability to speak English, emphasising that Dolwyn is a bastion of Welsh language and culture that was under threat.

There is also the theme of progress versus tradition: as well as the traditions of the village being under threat, the viewer is treated to several shots of the already built reservoir at the top of the valley spanning to the rural idyll of Dolwyn, a sign of what was to come. Urban progress is represented by the villainous Rob Davis, played by Williams himself, a former native of the village who had been run out as a twelve-year-old after stealing from the church collection plate. At a meeting of leaseholders to inform them of the scheme, he neatly summarised the urban perspective of rural reservoir development: 'by the miracle of science a few insanitary dwellings will become of use to millions of people'. Ultimately, the message of Williams's film is that progress cannot be stopped, even by the most belligerent of bulwarks. When Davis first tries to flood the village, instead of evacuating following the sounding of the flood alarm, Merri decides to stay in her home, aware that it would mean her death. It is only after Gareth kills Davis that Merri takes it on herself to flood the village to save her son. In the end, the last defender of Dolwyn is the one to flood the village, underlining that modernity is inevitable.

Emlyn's film sits at an interesting nexus point: simultaneous to the construction of Claerwen reservoir and a few short years before Llyn

Celyn, but looking back on projects completed in the late nineteenth century. This suggests that there was continuity of experience. However, constructing reservoirs in Wales in the twentieth century was complicated by the increasingly polarising issue of Welsh nationalism. While this was not as prominent in the nineteenth century as it would become in the twentieth, Wales was conceptualised from the outset as an untapped resource for English cities to utilise.[64] This led to what has been termed as a 'quasi-imperialist' approach to colonising the Welsh rural hinterland by English cities. This was certainly the type of language used by Gwynfor Evans, the leader of Plaid Cymru during the Tryweryn episode, who subsequently became Plaid Cymru's first MP. In a pamphlet published in the 1970s, Evans wrote of Wales as an exploited colony whose natural resources were taken for the benefit of another state. He situated rural depopulation within this framework of colonial exploitation, citing the decline in population in Merioneth between 1881 and 1971. For Evans, the depopulation of rural areas was a symptom of the quasi-imperialist relationship between England and Wales, so a scheme like Tryweryn was not just about appropriating Welsh resources but exploiting depopulated areas caused by English modernity.[65]

The shift in attitude towards Welsh waterworks came not after the Second World War, but during the interwar period. The proposal to dam the River Ceiriog by a group of northern English towns led by Warrington was met with resistance from both conservationists, who worried that the dam would ruin the natural beauty of the Welsh landscape, and nationalists concerned about the weakening of Welsh culture and language. They also argued that Welsh resources should only be for the benefit of the Welsh, while they shared concerns with conservationists over the potential damage that could be wrought to the landscape. While the proposal never went ahead, due more to issues between the English towns than Welsh opposition, it set the stall for the battles to come after the Second World War.[66]

As with other cities in the post-war period, Liverpool was concerned about insufficient water supply. Concerns around the ability of Lake Vyrnwy to continue to meet demand meant that in 1956 Liverpool started to look elsewhere. The council settled on a scheme on the River Tryweryn, a tributary of the River Dee north of Bala Lake. The Tryweryn and Dee was one of the many schemes contemplated by Liverpool Corporation in the 1870s, dismissed at that time because of potential issues with opposition from riparian interests.[67] As rural industry had declined by the 1950s, this was less of an issue. The scheme was projected to supply seventy-five million gallons of water a day, a sizeable increase on the Vyrnwy supply.[68]

Opposition, though, would come to be the defining issue regarding Tryweryn, not from riparian owners but from Welsh nationalists.

The flooding of Capel Celyn and the completion of Llyn Celyn reservoir was seen by Welsh nationalists in particularly morbid terms. As Ed Atkins has highlighted, the continued use of the word 'drowning' when referring to the fate of Capel Celyn reinforced a sense of violence: the village was not being removed or replaced or even erased: it was being killed, submerged against its will. This violent narrative was further reinforced elsewhere. An amateur film produced by staff and students at Friars School (Ysgol Friars) in Bangor in 1965 interwove the language of death. Narrated by a schoolchild, symbolising the lost future of Capel Celyn, there are repeated references to loss and death. One of the earlier scenes was accompanied with the following:

> This tiny village of seventy-four souls under sentence of death since the government Act of 1957 soon will need no longer its stepping stones across its controversial stream.[69]

The reference to souls, as would be used to describe those lost at sea, as well as the more explicit reference to the death sentence of the Liverpool Corporation Act 1957 are indicative of the way that Llyn Celyn reservoir was conceptualised by Welsh nationalists and many Welsh people. After showing scenes of local inhabitants moving out of their homes and shots of the reservoir's construction, the film concludes with what Llyn Celyn meant for Liverpool itself. 'Tryweryn water' – another deliberate semantic tactic used by nationalists to reinforce the impact of the scheme – would be used to provide better housing, access to washing machines, and water for the growing light industries of Merseyside.[70] Following these scenes, the narrator remarked that 'we would do well to remember that progress for many means heartache for the few', followed by shots of the abandoned homes and buildings of Capel Celyn. Modernity came at a cost, a cost that was paid overwhelmingly by those who would benefit the least.

The opposition to Tryweryn was, however, much more complex, as Martin Johnes has highlighted.[71] This speaks to the nature of rural modernity, which presents a more complex framework through which to see social changes to the countryside, as highlighted by Francis Brett Young's *The House Under the Water*. Opposition to the flooding of Capel Celyn also came from the residents of Capel Celyn themselves, who were famously led by Evans to a meeting of the Liverpool Corporation to protest against the scheme. For Trever Fishlock, Tryweryn was a moment of traumatic awakening for many in Wales who saw that Welsh culture and values were under direct threat.[72] However, although residents had been shocked to find surveyors walking around Capel Celyn planning the scheme, the first they had heard about plans to flood the village, by 1957 many had seemingly accepted the inevitable. After all, Liverpool Corporation was obliged to pay compensation to residents and rehouse them, which would mean financial support and better quality housing.[73] This is an issue that is foretold with remarkable prescience in *The Last Days of Dolwyn*, with Williams depicting many of the villagers as being happy and willing to sell up and move to a new estate on the edge of Liverpool, with only Merri holding out. While there was an obvious attachment to place, for many the promise of better housing and a better quality of life will have been attractive. The Friars School film further illustrates this point, showing a couple begrudgingly leaving their home in Capel Celyn only to find them happy and contented in their new home a few miles away.

Although it was a blow to culture in the heartland of Wales, Capel Celyn was not the only village to be submerged to fulfil urban needs. Villages had been flooded for quite some time: indeed, the inspiration for Emlyn Williams' prophetic film was the village of Llanwddyn, which was submerged to construct Lake Vyrnwy. As noted in Chapter 4, the construction of reservoirs in the Elan Valley resulted in submerging several buildings including Nantgwyllt, the one-time home to Percy Shelley. Into the interwar period, the most famous example of a village being flooded for a reservoir was Ashopton, flooded in order to build Ladybower reservoir in Derbyshire.[74] The flooding of rural villages with small populations was a well-established trope of reservoir construction by the 1950s, an act that came to symbolise the political and, to some, moral authority of towns and cities over the countryside, a social dimension to the taming of nature and the Promethean project.

A fruitful example to compare with Llyn Celyn is Thruscross reservoir, built in the Washburn Valley between 1960 and 1966. Not only was this contemporaneous to what was happening in Merionethshire, but Thruscross involved the flooding of West End, a small village in the upper half of the Washburn Valley. In terms of social impact, the two projects share commonalities: both were very disruptive to those that were displaced. Culturally, the impact of Thruscross was far less than Llyn Celyn, for understandable reasons. Furthermore, unlike the residents of Capel Celyn, those living in West End had been expecting to be displaced for nearly one hundred years.

Leeds Corporation had originally planned to build Thruscross in the 1870s with the other Washburn Valley reservoirs. However, due to a lack of money and statutory time granted by the Leeds Waterworks Act 1867, the waterworks committee decided to postpone constructing Thruscross until it was necessary. The moment of necessity was reached in the 1950s, as increased water demand and drought put pressure on the city's supply network. In some respects, the upper Washburn Valley was very similar to that encountered in the 1860s – the flax industry that had sustained life and allowed settlements like West End to develop had already declined by the 1860s, with sheep farming being the predominant form of work. There were some differences, though. First, although the original proposal for Thruscross was not expected to flood West End, residents in the area had long been expecting an impact on their lives. This sense was heightened by a series of compulsory land purchases undertaken by Leeds Corporation in the late nineteenth and early twentieth centuries, ostensibly for the purpose of protecting the Washburn watershed from pollution.[75] In the upper valley, though, where no reservoir yet existed, these purchases could be construed as helping to solve tomorrow's problem. Whatever the rationale, it meant that residents of West End and the surrounding farms became tenants of the corporation.

It is clear that this shift to corporation tenancy, as well as the general decline of the area due to a lack of employment prospects, had an impact on how the village was seen by both residents and urbanites in Leeds. The *Yorkshire Evening Post* continually returned to West End during the twentieth century, utilising the language of Oliver Goldsmith by dubbing it 'the deserted village' as early as 1911; ideas around the death of rural England predated Dickinson's *Timble Man*.[76] Reports in the *Yorkshire Evening Post* often noted the history of West End as an industrial village with a mill that employed two thousand people not fifty years earlier, more likely an accumulative figure stated for effect rather than two thousand employees at any given time. One correspondent to the *Evening Post*, Rightaway, in an article from 1919 revisiting West End, drew a somewhat hyperbolic comparison between the village and war-damaged Belgium: 'A pilgrimage there at the present time might help one to picture some of the ruined villages of Flanders', a comparison also made by J. B. Priestley in his 1934 *English Journey*.[77] The *Yorkshire Evening Post*'s fascination with West End continued throughout the interwar period, with excursions to the village continuing to draw on the village's history as a once thriving industrial village. One article from 1938 pointed to the land purchases by the Leeds Corporation in the 1900s as the final nail in the village's coffin.[78] As already discussed, the decline of West End was precipitated before the corporation sought to build reservoirs in the Washburn Valley. While the corporation undoubtedly capitalised on this decline with land purchases in preparation for the new reservoir, it would be unfair to lay the blame squarely on the Leeds Corporation for West End becoming 'the deserted village'.

Although the waterworks committee did not propose constructing a reservoir at Thruscross until 1952, a *Yorkshire Evening Post* article from 1949 suggested that construction was a distinct possibility. The article provided interviews with the few remaining residents of West End and residents of the nearby village of Thruscross who vehemently argued that, despite the decline of industry and population that had left the area largely unpopulated, a reservoir would spoil the valley. One resident, almost with an air of resignation, stated that 'We know Leeds must have water, but it's heartbreaking to lose our little valley. [...] We hope the borings reveal a mass of solid rock totally unsuitable for reservoirs or embankments'.[79] The article continued the style of reporting employed during the interwar period by once again highlighting the decline of a once bustling industrial village with nothing but 'skeletons' to show for it – another image of death.[80] These comments are indicative of the wider concern during the interwar and post-war years of municipal encroachment into the countryside. They also provide parallels with the experience of Llyn Celyn, which was seen as a threat to Welsh culture. While this was most explicitly expressed by Plaid Cymru as a threat to the Welsh language, the idyllic representation of the valleys as being intrinsic to Welsh culture was also threatened by the imposition of urban engineering. This point is made by Williams in *The Last Days of Dolwyn*, which includes several panoramic shots of the bucolic Welsh countryside before spanning to the dam constructed above the village.

A further article in the *Yorkshire Evening Post* from 1953 once again lamented the future loss of West End, this time interviewing a former school teacher in the village who deplored the decline of schooling in rural villages that, she argued, caused children to lose their sense of place.[81] This is symptomatic of the developing sense during the mid-twentieth century of a 'lost' England, aggravated by the encroachment of towns and cities into the countryside, a theme subsequently deemed to be a myth propagated by groups like the Campaign for the Preservation of Rural England.[82] Thus, the extent to which the countryside was threatened from outside factors has been questioned. Again, there are parallels to be drawn with Llyn Celyn, which was seen by nationalists as a threat to Wales, especially as Plaid Cymru conceptualised Welsh identity as being rural in nature.[83] The difference between the two cases, though, was that West End was largely uninhabited because of previous depopulation. While only a small number of people lived there, there was more significant displacement at Capel Celyn.

Nevertheless, the sense of a lost 'England' remained pervasive. A case in point was the loss of West End village itself, although, according to the *Yorkshire Evening Post's* reporting, the loss would be borne more by visitors who would never see the beauty of West End than the residents themselves, who had long come to terms with the loss of their local idyll.[84]

This, perhaps, is at the heart of the *Yorkshire Evening Post*'s reporting, which, as one resident noted, was not circulated in the Washburn Valley. The concern lay less with the loss of a residential area, but with the loss of a beauty spot on the doorstep of Leeds, which had become more accessible with the increase in motor ownership during the post-war period. While Leeds would be gaining a needed water supply, it would be losing a place of beauty. This demonstrates that, even though a reservoir had not been built, the area was seen within the framework of the 'Leeds Lake District', a key part of the cultural dimension of the civic link between the city and the Washburn Valley. The Leeds Corporation certainly did not directly factor leisure into its planning of Thruscross, a commonality shared with contemporaries such as Cow Green reservoir, Teesdale, and Rutland Water in the East Midlands, the architects of which strictly precluded using the space for recreation.[85] In contrast to narratives of the reservoirs in the lower valley, which were seen to heighten the beauty of the Washburn Valley, the loss of West End was portrayed as a loss to thousands of visitors who would no longer be able to walk over the packhorse bridge or visit Holy Trinity Church. As one correspondent wrote: 'Something will vanish with the Washburn brook. A solitude and a loveliness to spell and an enchantment. You cannot enter the valley without recognising it. You cannot stay without succumbing to it'.[86] This is in contrast to Capel Celyn, which was not seen as a tourist attraction due to its remote location in North Wales. This is where the quasi-imperialist feeling regarding Llyn Celyn separates it from the experiences of those in the Washburn Valley: Thruscross ultimately represented the loss of a leisure spot – few people lived in West End by the 1960s for it to be troublesome. The flooding of Capel Celyn, on the other hand, was seen as a threat to Welsh culture in order to improve the livelihoods of the English in Liverpool.

A final difference between the two examples is in their legacies. Capel Celyn and Llyn Celyn have become synonymous with warnings of threats to national culture. As recently as 2022 during a debate in the House of Commons on the Supreme Court's decision to reject legislation to enable a second Scottish referendum, the group leader of Plaid Cymru, Elizabeth Saville Roberts, referenced Tryweryn to show that nationalist interests in the Union could and would be squashed by Westminster.[87] In contrast, Thruscross escaped controversy like many other reservoirs that sit on flooded villages. Opposition to Thruscross was relatively muted: the main opponents of the scheme were local authorities like the West Riding County Council who were more concerned about transport access than residents being displaced. There also were not that many people living in West End by 1960: the shadow of Thruscross had provoked many to move away. West End is now largely forgotten, remarked on only when drought is sufficient enough to lay bare the old houses and church foundations, as it was in 1995. This shows the importance of focusing on case studies: there are commonalities between each case, but each has its own individual richness.

To return to where this chapter started, it would be reasonable to assume that community life dwindled in the Washburn Valley following the further loss of West End. The local historian Diana Parsons has been scathing of the impact of the reservoirs, saying that the construction of the reservoirs ripped out 'the heart of the valley', and she is especially critical of the decision to prematurely depopulate West End.[88] However, as shown earlier in this chapter, community life adapted and continued after the construction of the original reservoirs in the 1870s, and the same can be said for life during and after the construction of Thruscross. The Washburn Valley Farmers' Association shows continued until 1974, struck down by a lack of financial support rather than a lack of participation. Given the decline of similar types of agricultural show during the late nineteenth century, it is remarkable that the Washburn show lasted as long as it did and emphasises its importance to the farming community.[89] It also helped to bridge the divide between rural tenant and urban landlord. At the show's dinner in 1950, a member of the association, Mr Renton, praised the actions of the outgoing president Mr Forster, a former manager of the Leeds waterworks, who had been able to cultivate close relations with the tenant farmers of the area. Renton remarked that:

> As a boy I used to spend my holidays at Blubberhouses, and the life in the dales is very different to-day from what it was 46 or 47 years ago. On those days if a Corporation official showed his face in the Washburn Valley, everyone went into hiding and peeped round the curtains at him. That does not apply to-day, and it is a good thing.[90]

While only taking place on one day of the year, the Washburn Valley Farmers' Association shows, as well as the activities of other groups like the Washburn Young Farmers' Club, highlight the continuance of community life into the second half of the twentieth century, and shows that rural life was not quite as dead as John Dickinson thought some one hundred years earlier. This can be contrasted for a final time with Llyn Celyn, the village of Capel Celyn lost under the waters of the reservoir. Now all that stands is a graffitied stone wall imploring people to never forget Tryweryn.

Conclusion

Waterworks projects elicited a great number of responses. It would be reasonable to assume that those living in areas targeted for development would feel most negatively about them, and at times this was the case. There was an undeniable sense of loss at the flooding of Capel Celyn as there was with the flooding of West End. Flooding villages for waterworks was not just consigned to England and Wales: it was standard practice in many countries. A few years before Capel Celyn and West End were flooded, the construction of the Bhakra–Nangal dams in India partially or fully flooded 375 villages, showing how Western engineering practices had taken hold across the world even after independence.[91] It is also clear that these schemes could stir up strong emotional responses. Tryweryn became a rallying point for Plaid Cymru, while others moved to action went further still by setting explosive devices around the works.

But as Daniel Haines makes clear in a more international context with Bhakra Nangal, and as this chapter does for England and Wales, the loss of villages did not necessarily mean the death of rural life – positives could come from these developments. As the example of the Washburn Valley shows, the management of the waterworks provided the community with a common occupation and status: the tenant farmer. That allowed residents in the valley to create a sense of collective identity, a rallying point of their own, that celebrated what life had become in the area. The Washburn Valley Farmers' Association continued into the 1970s, well beyond the lifespan of similar agricultural shows. For many later schemes, like Thruscross, a lack of opposition was the result of the scheme being long expected. It is notable that there was a lack of nationalist opposition to the construction of Claerwen reservoir, due in part to geographical factors but also perhaps that the scheme, like Thruscross, was long in the making and expected sooner rather than later. Additionally, the testimony of John Dickinson shows that community life continued to adapt and, in some cases, thrive through local societies and feast days. Johnes's observation of Tryweryn and Plaid Cymru can be applied more widely, then: the relationship between local people and these areas was complex, and responses to reservoir construction were more nuanced than we might assume, a point encapsulated in *The Last Days of Dolwyn*. This chapter has demonstrated the importance of looking at local case studies to telling a more national story, as well as the need to tackle difficult histories. It has also shown that the Promethean project was not just about the urban remaking of the countryside: the social consequences of such actions need to be considered fully. While it is easy to see how reservoir developments would fit into the broader narrative of rural decline, their true impact to local communities was more complex.

Notes

1. David Lewis Brown, *The Elan Valley Clearance: The Fate of the People and Places Affected by the 1892 Elan Valley Reservoir Scheme* (Logaston Press, 2019), 73–150; Census Returns of England and Wales, 1851–1911, Ancestry UK, accessed 25 April 2017, https://www.ancestry.co.uk.

2. K. D. M. Snell, *Spirits of Community: English Senses of Belonging and Loss, 1750–2000* (Bloomsbury, 2016), 19; Martin J. Wiener, *English Culture and the Decline of the Industrial Spirit 1850–1980* (Penguin, 1985), 57.

3. See Snell, *Spirits of Community.*

4. John Dickinson, *Timble Man: Diaries of a Dalesman*, ed. Ronald Harker (Hendon, 1988), 57.

5. Wiener, *English Culture*, 50; Alun Howkins, 'The Discovery of Rural England', in *Englishness: Politics and Culture 1880–1920*, ed. Robert Colls and Philip Dodd (Bloomsbury, 1986), 85–112; Peter Mandler, 'Against "Englishness": English Culture and the Limits to Rural Nostalgia, 1850–1940', *Transactions of the Royal Historical Society* 7 (1997), 155–75, https://doi.org/10.2307/3679274.

6. Jeremy Burchardt, *Paradise Lost: Rural Idyll and Social Change since 1800* (I. B. Tauris, 2002), 141.

7. Dickinson, *Timble Man*, 84.

8. Dickinson, *Timble Man*, 113.

9. 'Fewston', *Wharfedale and Airedale Observer*, 20 August 1880, 3.

10. Robert Poole, 'Oldham Wakes', in *Leisure in Britain 1780–1939*, ed. John K. Walton and James Walvin (Manchester University Press, 1983), 79.

11. 'Yeadon Feast', *Wharfedale and Airedale Observer*, 13 August 1880, 2.

12. Dickinson, *Timble Man*, 22.

13. Helen Cowie, *Exhibiting Animals in Nineteenth-Century Britain: Empathy, Education, Entertainment* (Palgrave Macmillan, 2014), 3, 129.

14. Alun Howkins, 'The Taming of Whitsun: The Changing Face of a Nineteenth-Century Rural Holiday', in *Popular Culture and Class Conflict 1590–1914: Explorations in the History of Labour and Leisure*, ed. Eileen Yeo and Stephen Yeo (Harvester Press, 1981), 191.

15. 'Fewston', *Wharfedale and Airedale Observer*, 19 August 1881, 5.

16. 'Fewston', *Wharfedale and Airedale Observer*, 19 August 1881.

17. 'Fewston', *Wharfedale and Airedale Observer*, 18 August 1882, 5.

18. 'Fewston', *Wharfedale and Airedale Observer*, 20 August 1880, 3.

19. 'Fewston', *Wharfedale and Airedale Observer*, 18 August 1882, 5.

20. 'Fewston', *Wharfedale and Airedale Observer*, 17 August 1883, 4.

21. Bernard Deacon, 'Religion and Community: Frameworks and Issues', *Family and Community History* 5, no. 1 (2002): 41, https://doi.org/10.1179/fch.2002.5.1.004.

22. Burchardt, *Paradise Lost*, 203–4.

23. Information has been collected from the 1891 England census, Ancestry UK, accessed 20 July 2018, https://www.ancestry.co.uk.

24. 'Opening of a Library and Free School at Timble', *Wharfedale and Airedale Observer*, 5 August 1892, 7.

25. Howkins, 'The Taming of Whitsun', 187–209.

26. Audrey Fisk, 'Diversity within the Friendly Society Movement 1834–1911: The Value to Community Studies', *Family and Community History* 3, no. 1 (2000): 23–4, https://doi.org/10.1179/fch.2000.3.1.003; Evelyn Lord, 'The Friendly Society Movement and the Respectability of the Rural Working Class', *Rural History* 8, no. 2 (1997): 172, https://doi.org/10.1017/S0956793300001254.

27. Howkins, 'The Taming of Whitsun', 195–7.

28. 'Timble', *Wharfedale and Airedale Observer*, 26 May 1893, 5.

29. 'Timble', *Wharfedale and Airedale Observer*, 29 May 1896, 5.

30. Dickinson, *Timble Man*, 42.

31. Dickinson, *Timble Man*, 59.

32. 'Timble', *Wharfedale and Airedale Observer*, 8 June 1900, 5.

33. 'Timble', *Wharfedale and Airedale Observer*, 31 May 1901, 5.

34. Poole, 'Oldham Wakes', 87; 'Timble', *Wharfedale and Airedale Observer*, 8 June 1900, 5; 'Timble', *Wharfedale and Airedale Observer*, 23 May 1902, 5; 'Timble', *Wharfedale and Airedale Observer*, 5 June 1903, 5; 'Timble', *Wharfedale and Airedale Observer*, 24 May 1907, 5.

35. K. D. M. Snell, *Parish and Belonging: Community, Identity and Welfare in England and Wales, 1700–1950* (Cambridge University Press, 2006), 387, 497.

36. 'The Unemployment Problem: Labour Bureau to be opened in Otley', *Wharfedale and Airedale Observer*, 23 February 1906, 2.

37. 'Fewston', *Wharfedale and Airedale Observer*, 10 February 1911, 5.

38. 'Timble', *Wharfedale and Airedale Observer*, 5 June 1903, 5.

39. 'Timble', *Wharfedale and Airedale Observer*, 8 June 1906, 5.

40. 'Notes on News', *Wharfedale and Airedale Observer*, 17 August 1906, 4.

41. Information collected from 1911 England and Wales Census for Farnley, Askwith, Fewston, Blubberhouses and Thruscross, Ancestry UK, accessed 20 July 2018, https://www.ancestry.co.uk.

42. 'Farmers and Combination', *Wharfedale and Airedale Observer*, 12 April 1907, 7.

43. Nicholas Goddard, 'Agricultural Institutions: Societies, Associations and the Press', in *The Agrarian History of England and Wales, volume 7: 1850–1914*, ed. E. J. T. Collins (Cambridge University Press, 2000), 668.

44. 'Fewston', *Wharfedale and Airedale Observer*, 31 August 1906, 5; 'Fewston', *Wharfedale and Airedale Observer*, 7 September 1906, 5; see Leeds Corporation, 'Leeds Waterworks Committee Minutes, volumes 8–12', West Yorkshire Archive Service (WYAS), LLC22/1/8–12.

45. 'Washburn Valley Show: A Successful Venture Smartly Arranged', *Wharfedale and Airedale Observer*, 21 September 1906, 7.

46. Lord, 'The Friendly Society Movement', 172; Stephen Etheridge, 'Southern Pennine Brass Bands and the Creation of Northern Identity, c.1840–1914: Musical Constructions of Space, Place and Region', *Northern History* 54, no. 2 (2017): 261, https://doi.org/10.1080/0078172X.2016.1254379.

47. 'Washburn Valley Show: A Successful Venture Smartly Arranged', *Wharfedale and Airedale Observer*, 21 September 1906, 7.

48. 'Washburn Valley Show: The Second Event Proves a Great Success', *Wharfedale and Airedale Observer*, 20 September 1907, 3.

49. 'Norwood Show: Washburn Farmers and Stock Breeding', *Wharfedale and Airedale Observer*, 25 September 1908, 2.

50. 'Washburn Valley Show', *Wharfedale and Airedale Observer*, 16 September 1910, 2.

51. Alun Howkins, *The Death of Rural England: A Social History of the Countryside since 1900* (Routledge, 2003), 45–54.

52. 'Washburn Valley Show: Record Number of Exhibits', *Wharfedale and Airedale Observer*, 16 September 1921, 3.

53. 'Washburn Show Goes Ahead', *Wharfedale and Airedale Observer*, 21 September 1934, 6.

54. 'Washburn Show: Fine Display of Cattle', *Wharfedale and Airedale Observer*, 16 September 1927, 3; 'Washburn Farmers' Show', *Wharfedale and Airedale Observer*, 16 September 1932, 3.

55. 'Fewston', *Wharfedale and Airedale Observer*, 20 August 1880, 3.

56. Snell, *Spirits of Community*, 19.

57. Owen G. Roberts, 'Developing the Untapped Wealth of Britain's "Celtic Fringe": Water Engineering and the Welsh Landscape, 1870–1960', *Landscape Research* 31, no. 2 (2006): 125, https://doi.org/10.1080/01426390600638422.

58. Roberts, 'Developing the Untapped Wealth', 126.

59. Denis Cosgrove et al., 'Landscape and Identity at Ladybower Reservoir and Rutland Water', *Transactions of the Institute of British Geographers* 21, no. 3 (1996): 534–51, https://doi.org/10.2307/622595.

60. Brown, *Elan Valley Clearance*.

61. Birmingham Corporation Water Act 1892, Library of Birmingham, L/F/45/3; 329596.

62. Brown, *Elan Valley Clearance*, 73–150.

63. Emlyn Williams, dir., *The Last Days of Dolwyn*, British Lion Films, 1949.

64. Roberts, 'Developing the Untapped Wealth', 123.

65. Gwynfor Evans, *A National Future for Wales* (John Percy Press, 1975), 31.

66. Roberts, 'Developing the Untapped Wealth', 126–9.

67. John Frederick Bateman, 'New Water Supply: Report of Mr John Frederick Bateman C.E., F.R.S.', 1875, Liverpool Record Office 352.6 WAT, 9.

68. *Echo* municipal correspondent, 'Tryweyrn No Delay', *Liverpool Echo*, 16 December 1959, 19.

69. *Tryweryn, The Story of a Valley* (Friars School, Bangor, 1965), held by National Screen and Sound Archive of Wales, available on YouTube, https://youtu.be/sfTzuZ49u_o.

70. Ed Atkins, 'Building a Dam, Constructing a Nation: The "Drowning" of Capel Celyn', *Journal of Historical Sociology* 31, no. 4 (2018): 463, https://doi.org/10.1111/johs.12186.

71. Martin Johnes, *Wales since 1939* (Manchester University Press, 2012), 214–16.

72. Trevor Fishlock, *Wales and the Welsh* (Cassel, 1973), 102.

73. Johnes, *Wales since 1939*, 214–16.

74. Cosgrove et al, 'Landscape and Identity', 534–51.

75. Power of compulsory purchase was granted in the Leeds Corporation Act 1897. Leeds Corporation, 'Leeds Waterworks Committee Minutes, volume 7: 1896–1903', WYAS, LLC22/1/7, 79–165.

76. Snell, *Spirits of Community*, 4–5; 'Washburn Factory of the Past: The Busy Days of Fifty Years Ago in a Famous Valley', *Yorkshire Evening Post*, 25 November 1911, 4.

77. Rightaway, 'West End Revisited: The Deserted Village of the Washburn', *Yorkshire Evening Post*, 21 June 1919, 4; J. B. Priestley, *English Journey* (Heinemann, 1934), 178.

78. 'Last of "Little Mill" at West End: Washburn Valley's Industries in Days of Water Power', *Yorkshire Evening Post*, 4 June 1938, 8.

79. Con Gordon, 'Reservoir Will Spoil Valley, Say Dalesmen', *Yorkshire Evening Post*, 23 November 1949, 5.

80. Gordon, 'Reservoir Will Spoil Valley'.

81. *Evening Post* reporter, 'A Deserted Village May Be Submerged', *Yorkshire Evening Post*, 24 April 1953, 5.

82. D. N. Jeans, 'Planning and the Myth of the English Countryside in the Interwar Period', *Rural History* 1, no. 2 (1990): 261–62, https://doi.org/10.1017/S0956793300003332.

83. Atkins, 'Building a Dam', 458.

84. *Evening Post* reporter, 'Deserted Village May Be Submerged'.

85. Christine S. McCulloch, 'Political Ecology of Dams in Teesdale', in *Long-Term Benefits and Performance of Dams*, ed. Henry Hewlett (Thomas Telford, 2004), 49–58; Cosgrove et al., 'Landscape and Identity', 548.

86. Gordon, 'Reservoir Will Spoil Valley'.

87. HC Deb (6th series) 23 November 2022 vol. 723 cc.298–99.

88. Diana Parsons, *The Book of the Washburn Valley: Yorkshire's Forgotten Dale* (Halsgrove, 2014), 110, 113.

89. Goddard, 'Agricultural Institutions', 668.

90. 'Rain Affects Attendance at Washburn Show', *Wharfedale and Airedale Observer*, 22 September 1950, 7.

91. Daniel Haines, 'Development, Citizenship, and the Bhakra–Nangal Dams in Postcolonial India, 1948–1952', *The Historical Journal* 65, no. 4 (2022): 1135, https://doi.org/10.1017/S0018246X21000625.

Conclusion

Going back for more: urban demand on the rural environment

Urban growth in the nineteenth and twentieth centuries mandated a simultaneous growth in the water industry. As such, many towns and cities like Leeds, Liverpool and Birmingham undertook waterworks projects to quench the thirsts of their populations and industries. As we've seen, there were a number of similarities and differences that are worth dwelling on in more detail. In terms of similarities, many urban authorities and private water companies took similar approaches to the acquisition of rural water supplies, looking to the uplands of England and Wales to provide pure, soft water. We can also see a conventional wisdom taking hold across the period. Gravitation reservoirs were seen as the most reliable form of water extraction, more expensive than pumping stations in the first instance but more reliable and cheaper in the long term. This altered slightly towards the end of the nineteenth century as new technologies came to the fore, particularly the use of masonry. Liverpool's Vyrnwy reservoir was something of a pioneer in this regard, at least in Britain – Liege's Gileppe dam predated Vyrnwy by some thirteen years. Indeed, it is possible to discern a more unified approach to water engineering towards the end of the nineteenth century, aided by the development of professional associations such as the Association of Water Engineers, established in 1896. In their discussions of how to best cast water pipes, during trips to waterworks and lectures from national and international colleagues, water engineers were starting to conceptualise the city in a more unified way.[1] There were, broadly speaking, also similarities in terms of water management. Many of the larger towns and cities recognised the benefits of afforesting the edges of reservoirs, cultural landscapes were remade in similar ways, and many of these waterscapes were utilised for leisure.

Each city, though, was unique, as were its hinterlands. This meant that each waterworks project was also unique in one way or another, emphasising the need to focus on local case studies to tell a broader story. Different plans were put forward corresponding to local differences, from chains of reservoirs of different sizes in the Washburn and Elan valleys, to one large reservoir project as at Thirlmere or Vyrnwy, or to the larger post-war projects that dispensed with smaller reservoirs for one, much larger structure as at Claerwen and Thruscross. This trend would continue into the 1970s and beyond, encapsulated by the construction of Kielder Water in Northumbria, an enormous scheme designed to provide water not just to Newcastle but also to the thirsty heavy industries of Teesside.[2] Local differences meant that the ability to tame nature was never absolute. Engineers may have begun to conceptualise waterworks in similar ways, but this did not account for the peculiarities of individual landscapes, as Leeds found in the Washburn Valley, or Liverpool along its pipeline from Vyrnwy. As briefly noted early on, Leeds had to almost entirely abandon a scheme in the Ure Valley in the twentieth century after it was discovered that the landscape was largely not fit for purpose, wasting £300,000 in the process.[3]

It is clear that there were similarities beyond the construction of the reservoirs themselves. One of the overarching arguments of this book is that civic identity continued to be linked to waterworks projects well into the twentieth century, more on which below. In the themes looked at here, such as afforestation, cultural landscapes and the development of leisure, this was the case. The second overarching argument, that the hinterland exchange was reciprocal rather than one way, was also the case across the examples cited here. Afforestation schemes further altered the natural landscape but gave resources back to the countryside, while the development of cultural landscapes and leisure conceptualised landscape change in largely positive tones. Waterworks were not just about taking one environmental resource, but became a cultural and environmental give and take. Importantly, this did not just happen at one site or with one city but with several.

That is not to say that approaches to waterworks management were entirely uniform across the country, or within the case studies highlighted here. It is important to stress that many of the examples looked at in *Waterscapes*, particularly Leeds, Liverpool and Birmingham, were all cities with strong civic identities. Not all towns and cities developed such strong identities around civic governance, so it stands to reason that not every town and city would have approached the construction or management of their waterworks in same way, particularly towns with less financial means. As noted in Chapter 3, Manchester Corporation had a very different, or indifferent, approach to afforestation from that of a city like Liverpool that embraced it wholeheartedly. The impact on communities differed greatly across the different examples, as examined in Chapter 6. In some cases, rural displacement was long anticipated and in some ways accepted, while in others, particularly in the case of Capel Celyn, the impact to the community was spotlighted and became symbolic of wider issues of national identity.

The examples looked at here, then, can help to draw out broad similarities and differences. The remainder of this conclusion will look at some of the themes of the book in more detail to help further examine these similarities and differences before turning to the contemporary relevance of this work.

Democratic landscapes?

It is worth commenting on the fact that water authorities privileged particular reservoir development. Many reservoirs were built in uplands so they could utilise gravity to send water down pipes towards towns and cities, rather than rely on expensive pumping systems which required constant fuel to operate. This land was often deemed to not hold agricultural value, particularly in the north where arable land was scarcer than in the south. This also meant that the land was cheaper, as it was mainly used for sheep grazing.[4] This led to tensions, though, which have been hinted at throughout the chapters. Municipal authorities held little regard for the needs of farming land. As such, the process of acquiring land for reservoir development was highly undemocratic: as the nineteenth century progressed, municipal authorities in particular were able to gain powers of compulsory purchase. Leeds Corporation had to negotiate with various landed interests during the passage of their bill in 1867 as seen in Chapter 1. By the time Liverpool and Birmingham came to Parliament to lobby for their own powers in the 1880s and 1890s, seven-year compulsory purchase powers were included in their water Acts.[5] Leeds Corporation gained compulsory purchase powers in the 1890s under the guise of pollution protection. Members of the council felt that local farmers were not taking all the steps they could to prevent effluent entering the reservoirs, so gained powers in an 1897 Improvement Act to compulsorily purchase land.[6] This had an enormous effect on the Washburn Valley, which had until that point largely been populated by smallholdings. Over the turn of the twentieth century, the Washburn Valley became a large landholding for Leeds Corporation, turning residents into tenant farmers. The managing of rural areas in such a way extended the urban footprint, with municipal authorities coming to govern the countryside to improve public health, which led to inevitable tension.

Naturally, these powers could – and did – negatively affect rural areas in some cases. As has already been mentioned, Birmingham's controversial powers in the Birmingham Corporation Water Act 1892 led to a process that David Lewis Brown has compared to the Highland clearances.[7] There is also a national dynamic to bear in mind with Birmingham and Liverpool's schemes: both authorities uprooted local Welsh residents to provide for English cities. It is no surprise that this resulted in a backlash when a scheme was proposed at Tryweryn in the 1960s. In the Washburn Valley, the residents of West End had anticipated a fourth reservoir to submerge their homes for so long that the area was prematurely depopulated, with little surprise when Leeds Corporation eventually built Thruscross Reservoir in the 1960s. The few locals who did stay had little recourse to fight the corporation, with the main opposition coming from rural authorities more concerned with transport links than displacement.

These changes could result in positive consequences for how rural spaces were used. There is an intersection here with ideas around citizenship, which by the end of the nineteenth century focused on people as much as the built environment.[8] Fishing in the reservoirs was conceptualised very literally by urban residents themselves within a narrative of citizenship: fish help to keep the water clean by eating detritus, and by fishing in the Washburn Valley reservoirs, middle-class anglers would be helping to maintain a manageable number of fish. Fishing and rambling were also part of a programme of rational recreation that was promoted as a way to combat the evils of urban life. In promoting the cultural landscapes of areas like Vyrnwy or the Elan Valley, people were encouraged to enjoy these areas themselves, moving outside the city for respectable recreation. Civic improvement was a part of this narrative, but creating and curating a space in rural areas for the pursuit of leisure was also part of a discourse of citizenship. As the focus shifted to working-class participation in narratives of citizenship during the interwar period, the efforts of Liverpool Corporation to educate its residents on the uses of timber from the afforestation scheme at Vyrnwy was important. This can be seen as an extension of the type of civic education undertaken in cities like Manchester during the interwar period, educational programmes favoured by urban planners such as Patrick Geddes as a way of engaging the working class in how the cities operated. This is an example of how cities tried to mould their working-class residents in a way that measured up to the economic ambitions of an increasingly globalised world.[9]

Even here, though, we can see a democratic deficit around these waterscapes. As seen in examples through the nineteenth and twentieth centuries, local opposition was held in little regard until the 1960s. Many could not afford to challenge a scheme in Parliament. Even when schemes were challenged, as with Thirlmere in the 1870s, this was based on cultural and aesthetic grounds rather than economic or political.[10] When reservoir schemes were completed there were issues with inclusion. Chapter 5 demonstrated the issues that some faced accessing areas like the Washburn Valley for leisure. Working-class leisure seekers wanting to fish or ramble were often decried as hikers, their behaviour highlighted by councillors and newspaper correspondents. While rambling was more inclusive in terms of gender than fishing, it is clear that the countryside was conceptualised as a middle-class space where certain behaviours were not tolerated.[11] Problems with access to the countryside continued to be experienced as the twentieth century progressed, particularly for those with disabilities as recent research has highlighted.[12] As such, waterscapes such as these demonstrate the democratic void that was present between the urban and the rural, with urban areas often privileged at the expense of the livelihoods of those living and working in the country. In some cases, local people adapted to this change as in the Washburn Valley, but there was a democratic and inclusionary void nonetheless.

Rural modernism

One of the major themes of the book has been how structures like reservoirs can be seen within a rural modernist framework. The transformative effect of infrastructure built after the Second World War on rural places was profound, resulting in mass electricity networks, pylons, power stations and so on.[13] The reservoirs of the post-war period fit into this framework, but one of the themes of this book has been to highlight how the effect of infrastructural development on the landscape pre-1945 could also fit into a rural modernist way of thinking. Reservoir development in the nineteenth century was conceptualised in Romantic terms, influenced by the upland landscapes that were often targeted as well as the supposed beautifying effects of construction on places of non-outstanding natural beauty.[14] Chapters 4 and 5 focused on how these depictions helped to make areas like the Washburn Valley and Lake Vyrnwy more popular with urban tourists. However, these sites were used and depicted in increasingly modern ways as the twentieth century progressed. Chapter 3 highlighted how these areas became working landscapes for afforestation, which, especially in the case of Liverpool, helped to strengthen the civic link between the city and the countryside.

This book has also traced the development of rural modernism, not as a product of the post-war period but as a sentiment that grew and developed from nineteenth-century Romanticism. Fictional depictions in the form of novels and film were increasingly important to the development of rural modernism. The complexity of Francis Brett Young's *The House Under the Water* speaks to its rural modernist sensibilities. Phil's despair at the loss of Nant Escob and Forest Fawr is remedied in the end by the realisation that the spirit of the place endured. Far from being a maudlin story of rural nostalgia, this conclusion demonstrates the resilience of rural places in the face of modern change, something that is evidenced by the adaptation of community in places like the Washburn Valley seen in Chapter 6.[15] Similarly, *The Last Days of Dolwyn* presents a more complex picture of the social impact of reservoir development, especially in the context of nascent Welsh nationalism. Merri's decision to flood the village she dearly loved to protect her son is an apt metaphor for a rural modernist approach to landscape development, one that recognises the complexity of feeling rural communities endured. While Welsh nationalists suggested that schemes like Tryweryn were an act of English imperialism, Martin Johnes has noted that communities on the ground held more nuanced feelings: some wanted to leave and embrace a more modern life.[16] As with *The House Under the Water*, outputs like *The Last Days of Dolwyn* recognise that changes to the landscape were not solely mired in feelings of loss and nostalgia, again evidenced by community responses to change in the twentieth century looked at in the final chapter. This, then, helps to develop ideas around rural modernism, complimenting recent work that demonstrates a longer lineage of ideas around infrastructure in the countryside.[17] It also contributes to moving studies of landscape away from studies of hedgerows and gardens towards sites that are not as immediately attractive but offer rich potential for social and cultural analysis.[18]

Civic identity

Civic identity has been the central thread of this monograph, with each theme intersecting with civic pride in one way or another. This is important to highlight in and of itself, but especially so for the twentieth century as waterworks have more readily been associated with national rather than local or civic identity. There is logic to this approach. When Denis Cosgrove, Barbara Roscoe and Simon Rycroft explored the spatial and cultural meanings behind Rutland Water, the historical context was somewhat different to that looked at here – water supply was controlled by regional water boards, which would ultimately become privatised regional water companies.[19] As those private companies continue to operate, in spite of their unpopularity, rising water charges and the discharge of sewage into waterways, it is easy to conceptualise water on the regional or national level rather than the local or the civic. But civic identity was a driving force behind much of the development of water infrastructure in British cities well into the 1960s. Commentators continued to link water from disparate rural areas with the city it was destined to serve – 'Birmingham water' rather than water sourced in the Welsh uplands flowing into the River Claerwen that was dammed to provide Birmingham with water. Citizens of Liverpool were educated on what *their* wood from Vyrnwy supported. The Washburn Valley reservoirs were deemed to have contributed to such an idyllic scene that the area was dubbed the 'Leeds Lake District' – all the cultural connotations of one of the most famous rural landscapes of Britain appropriated to describe an area that belonged, both literally and metaphorically, to the people of Leeds.

The continued engagement with civic identity and civic pride, albeit expressed in different ways, demonstrates that wider significance of civic identity in the twentieth century. The nineteenth century was certainly a high point for engagement with civic identity, as Simon Gunn has highlighted by focusing on the development of grand buildings like town halls, as well as civic and funeral processions for local worthies.[20] Waterworks projects were tangible examples of the scientific and technical prowess of the city, as well as proof that the city could provide for ever-growing populations and industries. While the opening of reservoirs as in the Washburn or Elan valleys may not have been as grand as the opening of civic buildings like town halls, they were still inflected with the same tropes, such as the boosterish language and processional culture. In being opened by a monarch, the Elan Valley reservoirs were an example of how the local was increasingly intersecting with the national and international, something echoed in the 1950s when Claerwen reservoir was opened by Elizabeth II. As traditional forms of civic pride declined into the twentieth century, it is reasonable to assume that national and imperial identities took precedence, and there is evidence to suggest this. However, as Brad Beavan has highlighted, the imperial very much intersected with the local in times of war, particularly when there was local involvement in conflicts like the South African Wars.[21] Furthermore, civic identity propelled urban development forward in different ways during the twentieth century, not just in terms of waterworks but also housing, retail and urban planning.[22] The opening of reservoirs in the post-war period continued to link the city with the country, if not in the elaborate and extroverted ways of the nineteenth century – the water fountain of Manchester and Birmingham replaced by the Leeds journalist's coffee cup.

The link between identity and waterworks extended beyond Britain. In some countries, this was linked to imperial identities. This is particularly the case in arid countries such as Australia, where technological modernity could provide abundant water, at least for a time. In Perth, Western Australia, the development of water infrastructure was linked to imperial modernity; the ability to wash a car or keep a lawn green in arid conditions helped residents to consider themselves as part of an imperial hierarchy. This meant that during times of drought residents would flout restrictions in order to keep their gardens green.[23] In Texas, new dams were built to facilitate urban development in Austin. Three structures were built between 1937 and 1941, aided by New Deal funding. Andrew Busch has examined the impact of these reservoirs in detail, including their use in a celebration of water called Aquafest.[24] Like with the reservoirs in Britain explored here, civic pride towards the Austin watershed continued to be expressed throughout the twentieth century. As the waterworks were very literally responsible for the making of modern Austin, it is no surprise that this link between the city and its watershed was celebrated into the 1980s when changing demographics affected the relationship. The reservoirs not only became symbols of Austin's climate resilience, albeit artificially, but also of Austin's independence from private interests.[25] New waterworks in India after independence also underlined a commitment to local over national autonomy, as in the case of Bilaspur, northern India.[26]

Civic identity, then, continued to be an important factor in the development and management of waterworks projects in major cities in and beyond Britain. The extent to which this applied to all cities will, no doubt, have varied, but in the case studies looked at here it is safe to say that the ability of the city to provide and support its citizens and businesses was key, not just in a literal, political sense but in a cultural sense too. As the second half of the twentieth century progressed, changes to waterworks management – from local to regional to private – meant that the civic dimensions of waterworks declined in importance and memory, as in Austin. The importance of waterworks to towns and cities in the late twentieth and twenty-first centuries would be worth investigating. For some cities like Leeds, the Washburn Valley is easily reachable for many, if not all, by car or taxi. The valley continues to be a site of leisure for city dwellers thanks to the efforts of Yorkshire Water in helping to landscape the reservoirs for walking, although the recent implementation of parking charges perhaps challenges this commitment.[27] Additionally, how civic pride intersected with private water companies in cities like Bristol and Newcastle would also be worth further study. While not operated by municipal government, private water companies were often run on behalf of a town or city, and often included prominent civic figures on their boards. How these privately run ventures intersected with civic pride and urban governance awaits future research.

Environment and the Promethean project

In order to secure good supplies of potable water, municipal corporations, as well as private water companies, built waterworks systems that altered rural environments. The construction of reservoirs, both in the nineteenth and twentieth centuries, resulted in a variety of changes to the surrounding landscape. The subsidence of Fewston village in the Washburn Valley was the consequence of building a socio-technology without having a prior requisite understanding of the pressures the landscape could take. This was a relatively minor event – given the scale of disasters at Holmfirth in 1852 and Dale Dyke in 1864, or the subsequent event in Johnstown, Pennsylvania – that caused concern for the structural integrity of the Vyrnwy dam.[28] The floodings of West End and Capel Celyn have been treated here in social terms, but they were also examples of landscape transformation, a loss of rural landscape that had been lived on, worked on and consumed for hundreds of years. However, the thread that runs through all of these examples of environmental change is the enduring attitude towards the rural environment, as encapsulated in the reporting of Claerwen and Thruscross reservoirs; reservoirs were an example of the Promethean project: nature was there to be conquered in order to better serve towns and cities.[29]

As we've seen, municipal governments continued to alter the rural landscape after reservoirs had been constructed. Compulsory land purchases were instigated to ostensibly better protect the reservoirs from pollution. The subsequent afforestation schemes also altered the rural environment, introducing new, non-native trees. However, the treatment of unemployed workers on the Washburn Valley afforestation scheme further emphasised attitudes to the environment. As the *Yorkshire Post* reported in 1913, more than sixty per cent of the trees planted had failed.[30] The corporation did not provide the unemployed men with the training or the tools to properly attempt the work, highlighting that the social and political ramifications of the scheme were more important than the ecological consequences. Once more, the purpose of nature was to better serve urban settlements in order to provide resources and, in this case, social provision.

This attitude towards nature, which was prevalent across the period under study despite a growing interest in ecology, was linked to the wider conceptualisation of nature.[31] Maria Kaika has argued that the city/nature dialectic encapsulated positive and negative connotations of both: either the city was the place of technological modernity set against wild nature that had to be tamed to better serve urban interests, or the city was the place of industry, dirt and poverty set against the pristine rural idyll.[32] Indeed, the creation of 'second nature' in cities – that is, artificial sites of nature – is linked to this dialectic, as Matthew Gandy has shown in the case of New York City's Central Park, with its recreation of supposed pristine wilderness that echoed the Catskill Mountains.[33] Both of these conceptions of nature have been analysed here. While Chapter 2 highlighted the desire of local authorities and engineers to conquer the wilderness of nature, Chapters 4 and 5 examined how nature in places like the Washburn or Elan valleys was positively conceptualised, viewed through the prism of the Romantic rambler and the pursuer of leisure.

It is clear that reservoirs were sites of socionature, their construction the result of social forces mixing with natural agency. The landscape was an active agent in the formation of the reservoirs, both in how the contours of the land were used for the siting of the reservoirs and in the problems faced during construction that resulted in amendments to the original plans. Similarly, the reservoirs, as socionatural sites, impacted negatively on nature and society locally. Not only was the land on which Fewston village was built damaged by the water pressure of Swinsty Reservoir, but homes were rendered uninhabitable. Local people were displaced by reservoir projects, loudly in the case of Capel Celyn, more quietly in the Elan, Claerwen and Washburn valleys. Afforestation schemes altered the watershed of the reservoirs, with the introduction of non-native trees to the valley, but also had social implications for how the unemployed labourers of Leeds were treated. Indeed, the writings of newspaper correspondents and guidebook writers, who sought to promote these rural areas as improved by urban engineering, exaggerated the romantic elements of their cultural landscapes, and so also participated in the remaking of nature.

Thus, the impact of the reservoirs on the rural environment was multifaceted, a conclusion made possible by approaching the study from the perspective of socionature. Viewing the reservoirs as sites of socionature can help in moving beyond the nature/city dialectic emphasised by contemporaries to see them as an amalgam of urban and rural and, therefore, part of a wider urban ecology. This also helps us to see that the hinterland relationship is reciprocal rather than a one-way process. As William Cronon has shown, cities cannot be separated from their environments, and the environmental impact of cities reaches well beyond municipal borders.[34] But in looking at issues like afforestation, how cultural landscapes were remade and how these waterscapes were used for leisure, we can see that this hinterland exchange went both ways. Approaching the history of water supply and reservoir construction from the perspective of socio-nature can aid historians in viewing the ways in which urban and rural settings are interdependent, to better reconcile the relationship between nature and the city.[35]

The here and now

To return to where *Waterscapes* began, examples and debates on the history of reservoir development over the past one hundred and fifty years have currency in the present. Record temperatures were noted in the summer of 2022 in the United Kingdom, while much of Europe and the rest of the world suffered incredibly hot summers in 2023 and 2024, even if the United Kingdom did not.[36] Increased water consumption as well as a lack of reservoir development since the 1990s has led the sector to become vulnerable to drought, which will be experienced with more regularity as the effects of climate change increasingly take hold. This has brought renewed focus on the supply of water but also the governance of the sector more generally.

There are a number of issues to point to here. First, the increase in consumption in 2023 points to the failure of water companies to reinforce the need to restrict water usage during times of shortage. Second, and perhaps more seriously, it reflects a failure on the part of the water companies themselves, which have been accused of taking record profits but not investing in key infrastructure, with some water loss attributed to outdated and inadequate infrastructure. In December 2022, Thames Water posted profits of nearly £500 million despite an increase in the number of burst pipes.[37] More seriously, it was reported in June 2023 that the United Kingdom's water regulator Ofwat and the government were preparing to take Thames Water into temporary national ownership after it was revealed that the company had a £10 billion financial hole amid accusations of asset stripping.[38] This all comes at a difficult time for the water industry amidst public outrage at dumping of sewage into waterways as well as increased water rates during a cost-of-living crisis. At the start of 2025, Thames Water continues to be plagued by financial difficulties, while investigations have revealed that money earmarked for environmental clean-up was diverted to pay bonuses and dividends to shareholders.[39]

As drought is set to become a more regular occurrence in Britain, the attitude of water companies seems to have shifted on how to cope with such extreme weather. For the first time since the 1990s, water companies are considering building new reservoirs to help meet increased demand. As noted at the start of this book, in March 2023 Ofwat gave the green light to further consultation on three new reservoirs in Oxfordshire, Lincolnshire and Cambridgeshire.[40] This change in attitude is perhaps linked to the political milieu of 2022, an extension of the then UK government's disposition for announcing big solutions to big problems – forty new hospitals to help reduce waiting lists in the NHS, eight new nuclear reactors to help the energy crisis – without providing reassurances or substance as to whether they will actually happen or discussing the potential issues with such schemes. The reports produced by Ofwat that began this book point to the multiple issues that these reservoir schemes face, not least because water companies have not adequately engaged with heritage organisations and local stakeholders.[41] As the battles against Thirlmere in the 1870s, Ullswater in the 1950s, and Tryweryn in the 1960s highlight, there are social, ecological and cultural costs to building new reservoirs which need to be seriously considered by water authorities, regulators and the UK government. As this book shows, though, reservoirs can be beneficial to rural areas, drawing in leisure seekers, stimulating local economies, and further developing cultural conceptions of the countryside. Additionally, there are no easy answers as to how to provide safe, potable water in the twenty-first century, as Joe Williams, Stefan Bouzarovski and Eric Swyngedouw, as well as Ruth Morgan, have highlighted regarding the energy-intensive nature of desalination in hotter countries like Australia and the USA.[42] There is always a cost to socionatural structures like reservoirs to both society and ecology. It is striking that in California, pressure has been building to restore the Hetch Hetchy Valley in Yosemite National Park, controversially dammed by San Francisco in the early twentieth century, while maintaining the water and power usage that comes from the valley.[43] Regulators and policy makers need to be sure that building new reservoirs, furthering our dependence on ever-increasing water supply rather than rationing what we already have access to, is the right way to approach our future, which is set to become ever more unstable. Learning about the impact of reservoirs in a more holistic fashion, as set out here, might be a place to start.

Notes

1. Andrew McTominey, 'Water and the Modern Engineered City: The Association of Water Engineers in a British and Transnational Context, 1896–1914', *Water History* 12, no. 2 (2020): 131–49, https://doi.org/10.1007/s12685-020-00249-1.

2. Jill Payne, 'Constructing the Kielder Landscape: Plantations, Dams and the Romantic Ideal', in *Local Places, Global Processes: Histories of Environmental Change in Britain and Beyond*, ed. Peter Coates et al. (Oxbow Books, 2016), 97–108.

3. Andrew McTominey, 'Waterworks, Municipal Government and the Environment in Twentieth-Century Britain', *Urban History* 51, no. 3 (2024): 600–615, https://doi.org/10.1017/S0963926823000597.

4. Matthew Kelly, *Quartz and Feldspar: Dartmoor – A British Landscape in Modern Times* (Vintage, 2016), 278.

5. Liverpool Corporation Waterworks Act 1880, 43 & 44 Vict. c. cxliii, 7–32. Available at https://www.legislation.gov.uk/ukla/Vict/43-44/143/contents/enacted; Birmingham Corporation Water Act 1892, 55 & 56 Vict. c. clxxiii, held by Library of Birmingham, L/F/45/3; 329596.

6. Leeds Corporation Act 1897, 60 & 61 Vict. c. cxcix, held by Leeds Central Library, LQ352, 20. Available at https://www.legislation.gov.uk/ukla/Vict/60-61/199/contents/enacted.

7. David Lewis Brown, *The Elan Valley Clearance: The Fate of the People and Places Affected by the 1892 Elan Valley Reservoir Scheme* (Logaston Press, 2019).

8. Helen Meller, 'Urban Renewal and Citizenship: The Quality of Life in British Cities, 1890–1990', *Urban History* 22, no. 1 (1995): 64, https://doi.org/10.1017/S096392680001138X.

9. Tom Hulme, *After the Shock City: Urban Culture and the Making of Modern Citizenship* (Boydell Press, 2019), 9.

10. Harriet Ritvo, *The Dawn of Green: Manchester, Thirlmere, and Modern Environmentalism* (University of Chicago Press, 2009).

11. Ben Anderson, 'A Liberal Countryside? The Manchester Ramblers' Federation and the 'Social Readjustment' of Urban Citizens, 1929–1936', *Urban History* 38, no. 1 (2011): 84–102, https://doi.org/10.1017/S0963926811000058.

12. Tom Breen et al., 'Whose Right to Roam? Contesting Access to England's Countryside', *The Journal of Transport History*, 44, no. 2 (2023): 276–307, https://doi.org/10.1177/00225266231174766.

13. Linda M. Ross et al., 'Introduction', in *New Lives, New Landscapes Revisited: Rural Modernity in Britain*, ed. Linda M. Ross et al. (British Academy, Oxford University Press, 2023), 8.

14. Katrina Navickas, 'Building Amenity in Areas of Non-Outstanding Natural Beauty in the Southern Pennines', in *New Lives, New Landscapes Revisited: Rural Modernity in Britain*, ed. Linda M. Ross et al. (British Academy, Oxford University Press, 2023), 112.

15. Kristin Bluemel, 'Rural Modernity in Britain: Landscape, Literature, Nostalgia' in *New Lives, New Landscapes Revisited: Rural Modernity in Britain*, ed. Linda M. Ross et al. (British Academy, Oxford University Press, 2023), 58.

16. Martin Johnes, *Wales since 1939* (Manchester University Press, 2012), 214–16.

17. Linda M. Ross et al., eds., *New Lives, New Landscapes Revisited: Rural Modernity in Britain* (British Academy, Oxford University Press, 2023).

18. Tom Williamson, 'Landscape: The Configured Space', in *History Beyond the Text: A Student's Guide to Approaching Alternative Sources*, ed. Sarah Barber and Corinna M. Peniston-Bird (Routledge, 2009), 136–54; W. G. Hoskins, *The Making of the English Landscape* (Hodder and Stoughton, 1955).

19. Denis Cosgrove et al., 'Landscape and Identity at Ladybower Reservoir and Rutland Water', *Transactions of the Institute of British Geographers* 21, no. 3 (1996): 534–51, https://doi.org/10.2307/622595.

20. Simon Gunn, *The Public Culture of the Victorian Middle Class: Ritual and Authority in the English Industrial City, 1840–1914* (Manchester University Press, 2004).

21. Brad Beaven, 'The Provincial Press, Civic Ceremony and the Citizen-Soldier During the Boer War, 1899–1902: A Study of Local Patriotism', *Journal of Imperial and Commonwealth History* 37, no. 2 (2009): 207–28, https://doi.org/10.1080/03086530903010350.

22. Tom Hulme, 'Urban Materialities: Citizenship, Public Housing and Governance in Modern Britain', in *New Approaches to Governance and Rule in Urban Europe since 1500*, ed. Simon Gunn and Tom Hulme (Routledge, 2020), 190–210; Peter Shapely, 'Civic Pride and Redevelopment in the Post-War British City', *Urban History* 39, no. 2 (2012): 310–28, https://doi.org/10.1017/S0963926812000077.

23. Andrea Gaynor, 'Lawnscaping Perth: Water Supply, Gardens, and Scarcity, 1890–1925', *Journal of Urban History* 46, no. 1 (2020): 63–78, https://doi.org/10.1177/0096144217692991.

24. Andrew M. Busch, 'Dams and the Age of Abundance: Hydraulic Boosterism, Regional Growth, and the Reemergence of Water Scarcity in Central Texas', *Journal of Urban History* 49, no. 2 (2023): 310, https://doi.org/10.1177/00961442211008865.

25. Busch, 'Dams and the Age of Abundance', 314.

26. Daniel Haines, 'Development, Citizenship and the Bhakra–Nangal Dams in Postcolonial India, 1948–1952', *The Historical Journal* 65, no. 4 (2022): 1124–44, https://doi.org/10.1017/S0018246X21000625.

27. Lesley Tate, 'Parking Charges Are Coming says Yorkshire Water – Even Though Its Yet to Get Council Approval', *Telegraph and Argus*, 17 August 2022, https://www.thetelegraphandargus.co.uk/news/20668370.parking-charges-coming-says-yorkshire-water—even-though-yet-get-council-approval/.

28. Shane Ewen, 'Socio-Technological Disasters and Engineering Expertise in Victorian Britain: The Holmfirth and Sheffield Floods of 1852 and 1864', *Journal of Historical Geography*, 46 (2014): 15–20, https://doi.org/10.1016/j.jhg.2014.05.021; Emily Godbey, 'Disaster Tourism and the Melodrama of Authenticity: Revisiting the 1889 Johnstown Flood', *Pennsylvania History* 73, no. 3 (2006): 273–315; Patty Wharton-Michael, 'The Johnstown Flood of 1889: The *Johnstown Tribune*'s Commonsense Coverage vs. Common-Practice Sensationalism', *Journalism History* 38, no. 1 (2012): 23–33, https://doi.org/10.1080/00947679.2012.12062869.

29. Malcolm Barker, 'The Birth of a Reservoir ... A Nightmare of Sound in the Quiet Valley', *Yorkshire Evening Post*, 24 August 1962, 10; Maria Kaika, 'Dams as Symbols of Modernization: The Urbanization of Nature Between Geographical Imagination and Materiality', *Annals of the Association of American Geographers* 96, no. 2 (2006): 276, https://doi.org/10.1111/j.1467-8306.2006.00478.x.

30. Special correspondent, 'Leeds Afforestation: Its Bearing on the Water Supply', *Yorkshire Post*, 11 January 1913, 10.

31. John Sheail has explored the writings of Thomas Woodhead, an ecologist who compiled a history of Huddersfield's waterworks in 1939 that considered the ecological impact of the town's water catchment area, arguing that ecology could provide the solutions to problems arising from waterworks schemes. See John Sheail, 'T. W. Woodhead and the Study of Vegetation and Man in the Huddersfield District', *The Naturalist* 113 (1988): 137, https://www.biodiversitylibrary.org/page/50376549; T. W. Woodhead, *History of the Huddersfield Water Supplies* (Tolson Memorial Museum, 1939), 123.

32. Maria Kaika, *City of Flows: Modernity, Nature, and the City* (Routledge, 2005), 14.

33. Matthew Gandy, *Concrete and Clay: Remaking Nature in New York City* (MIT Press, 2003), 93.

34. William Cronon, *Nature's Metropolis: Chicago and the Great West* (Norton, 1991).

35. Martin V. Melosi, 'Humans, Cities, and Nature: How Do Cities Fit in the Material World?', *Journal of Urban History* 36, no. 1 (2010): 3–21, https://doi.org/10.1177/0096144209349876.

36. Mark Poynting and Erwan Rivault, '2023 Confirmed as World's Hottest Year on Record', *BBC News*, 9 January 2024, https://www.bbc.co.uk/news/science-environment-67861954; Simon King, 'Summer 2024 Was World's Hottest on Record', *BBC News*, 6 September 2024, https://www.bbc.co.uk/weather/articles/c93p5kz9elro.

37. Mark Sweney and Helena Horton, 'Thames Water Reports Profits Boom Despite Surge in Burst Pipes During Drought', *Guardian*, 5 December 2022, https://www.theguardian.com/environment/2022/dec/05/thames-water-reports-profits-boom-despite-surge-in-burst-pipes-during-drought.

38. Anna Isaac et al., 'Thames Water in Crisis Talks Over Potential £10bn Black Hole', *Guardian*, 28 June 2023, https://www.theguardian.com/business/2023/jun/28/thames-water-in-crisis-talks-over-potential-10bn-black-hole-cost-possible-collapse.

39. Anna Issac, 'Revealed: Thames Water Diverted "Cash for Clean-Ups" to Help Pay Bonuses', *Guardian*, 23 December 2024, https://www.theguardian.com/business/2024/dec/23/revealed-thames-water-diverted-cash-for-clean-ups-to-help-pay-bonuses.

40. 'Plans for Three New Reservoirs Move a Step Closer', *Ofwat*, 30 March 2023, https://www.ofwat.gov.uk/plans-for-three-new-reservoirs-move-a-step-closer/.

41. Ofwat, *Strategic Regional Water Resource Solutions: Standard Gate Two Final Decision for South East Strategic Reservoir Option*', 28 June 2023, 7–26, https://www.ofwat.gov.uk/consultation/strategic-regional-water-resource-solutions-standard-gate-two-draft-decision-for-south-east-strategic-reservoir-option/; Ofwat, *Strategic Regional Water Resource Solutions: Standard Gate Two Final Decision for Fens Reservoir*, 28 June 2023, 8–9, 12, https://www.ofwat.gov.uk/consultation/strategic-regional-water-resource-solutions-standard-gate-two-draft-decision-for-fenland-reservoir/; Ofwat, *Strategic Regional Water Resource Solutions: Standard Gate Two Final Decision for South Lincolnshire Reservoir*, 28 June 2023, 8, https://www.ofwat.gov.uk/consultation/strategic-regional-water-resource-solutions-standard-gate-two-draft-decision-for-south-lincolnshire-reservoir/.

42. Joe Williams et al., 'The Urban Resource Nexus: On the Politics of Relationality, Water–Energy Infrastructure and the Fallacy of Integration', *Environment and Planning C: Politics and Space* 37, no. 4 (2018): 652–69, https://doi.org/10.1177/0263774X18803370; Ruth Morgan, 'The Allure of Climate and Water Independence: Desalination Projects in Perth and San Diego', *Journal of Urban History* 46, no. 1 (2020): 113–28, https://doi.org/10.1177/0096144217692990.

43. Robert L. Righter, *The Battle over Hetch Hetchy: America's Most Controversial Dam and the Birth of Modern Environmentalism* (Oxford University Press, 2005).

Bibliography

Primary sources

British parliamentary papers

Birmingham Corporation Water Act 1892, 55 & 56 Vict. c. clxxiii. Held by Library of Birmingham, L/F/45/3; 329596.

HC Deb (4th series) 19 March 1907 vol. 171, c.662.

HC Deb (6th series) 23 November 2022 vol. 723 cc.298–99.

HL Deb (5th series) 19 October 1949 vol. 164 cc.949–1010.

Leeds Corporation Act 1897, 60 & 61 Vict. c. cxcix. Available at https://www.legislation.gov.uk/ukla/Vict/60-61/199/contents/enacted.

Leeds Waterworks Act 1837, 7 Will. 4 & 1 Vict. c. lxxxiii. Available at https://www.legislation.gov.uk/ukla/Will4and1Vict/7/83/contents/enacted

Liverpool Corporation Waterworks Act 1880, 43 & 44 Vict. c. cxliii. Available at https://www.legislation.gov.uk/ukla/Vict/43-44/143/contents/enacted.

National Archives, London

Leeds CB Thruscross Reservoir: Water Order 1960, National Archives, HLG 127/29.

County record offices and university archive collections

Library of Birmingham

Anonymous. 'Feat of Engineering: Three Great Dams at Elan Valley'. *Birmingham Newspaper Scrapbook, part 2, 1867–1907*. Library of Birmingham LF 71.061 243371.

City of Birmingham Waterworks Department. 'Visit of Their Majesties the King and Queen to the Elan Valley Works, Rhayader: Official Programme'. 1904. Library of Birmingham L/./45/31; 202633.

Liverpool Record Office

Bateman, John Frederick. 'New Water Supply: Report of Mr John Frederick Bateman C.E., F.R.S.' 1875. Liverpool Record Office 352.6 WAT.

Campbell Brown, J. 'Appendix to Supplementary Report of the Borough and Water Engineer as to a Supply of Water from the Upper Waters of the River Vyrnwy in North Wales'. 1878. Liverpool Record Office 352.6 WAT.

Deacon, George. 'Report of the Borough and Water Engineer as to a Supply from the Upper Waters of the Vyrnwy in North Wales'. 1877. Liverpool Record Office 352.6 WAT.

Forwood, W. B. 'Water Supply: Notes and Observations'. 1879. Liverpool Record Office 352.6 WAT.

Hawksley, Thomas. 'New Water Supply: Report of Mr. T. Hawksley, C.E.' 1875. Liverpool Record Office 352.6 WAT.

Liverpool Corporation, 'Liverpool Water Committee Minutes' 1880–1889, Liverpool Record Office, 352 MIN/WTR/1/16-25.

North Yorkshire County Record Office

Ministry of Town and Country Planning, 'Survey of public rights of way in Blubberhouses and Fewston', North Yorkshire Country Record Office, n.d., PR/FEW 15/3.

West Yorkshire Archive Service

Leeds Corporation. 'Leeds Waterworks Committee Minutes, volumes 2–12: 1861–1961'. West Yorkshire Archive Service. LLC22/1/2-12.

West Riding Ramblers Federation. 'West Riding Ramblers Federation 1934–36'. West Yorkshire Archive Service. WYL2412.

University of Leeds, Brotherton Library, Special Collection

Fisher, W. R., and Samuel Margerison. 'Reports on the Afforestation of the Washburn Valley Estate'. City of Leeds Waterworks (1905), held by Special Collections, Brotherton Library, University of Leeds, Sheppard Pamphlets FIS.

Newspapers and other news sources

BBC News
Birmingham Daily Post
Birmingham Gazette
Birmingham Mail
Brecon County Times
Buckinghamshire Examiner
Burnley News
Cheshire Observer
Crewe Examiner
Cricket and Football Field
Daily Herald

Derbyshire Times
Dundee Courier
Edinburgh Evening News
Field
Gloucestershire Echo
Guardian
Illustrated Sporting and Dramatic News
Lancashire Evening Post
Lancaster Evening Post
Lancaster Guardian
Leeds Intelligencer
Leeds Mercury
Leeds Times
Liverpool Echo
Manchester Evening News
Manchester Guardian
Market Harborough Advertiser and Midland Mail
Montgomeryshire Echo
Montgomeryshire Express
Morning Post
Nelson Leader
Newry Reporter
Northants Evening Telegraph
Northern Whig
Observer
Oswestry Advertiser
Penrith Observer
Scotsman
Sunderland Daily Echo
Telegraph and Argus
Todmorden Advertiser and Hebden Bridge Newsletter
Wharfedale and Airedale Observer
Weekly Dispatch
Western Chronicle
Western Mail
Yorkshire Post
Yorkshire Evening Post

Primary source publications pre-1900

Anonymous. *The English Lake District, including Furness Abbey, Shap Spa, Seascale, etc., etc.* George Philip and Son, 1895.

Barclay, Thomas. *The Future Water Supply of Birmingham.* Cornish Brothers, 1892.
Bradley, Tom. *The Washburn.* Old Hall Press, 1988 [first published 1895].
Filliter, Edward. 'Report on the Best Mode of Obtaining an Additional and Purer Supply of Water for the Borough of Leeds'. 1866.
Parkinson, Rev. Thomas. *An Idyll and Ballads of Washburn-dale.* East Kent Works, n/d, edition held by Leeds Library.
White, William. *Directory of Leeds, Bradford, Huddersfield [...] Woolen and Worsted Manufactures.* William White, 1866.

Printed primary materials, 1900 to 1950

Anonymous. *The English Lake District; Being the Fourth Edition of 'Morecambe and the Lake District Illustrated'.* William Mate and Sons, 1905.
Bogg, Edmund. *Two Thousand Miles in Wharfedale.* James Miles, 1904.
Grenfell, Arthur P. 'Afforestation and Unemployment', *Fabian Society Tracts, nos. 134–166.* Fabian Society, 1912.
Morton, H. V. *In Search of Wales.* Methuen, 1932.
Parry, Joseph. 'Afforestation', *British Waterworks Association: Proceedings 1918–1920, volume 2.* British Waterworks Association, 1920, 121–7.
Pope, Alexander. 'The Washburn Valley Afforestation Scheme of the Leeds City Council'. Reprinted from the *Quarterly Journal of Forestry.* Laughton and Company, 1914.
Priestley, J. B. *English Journey.* Heinemann, 1934.
Speight, Harry. *Upper Wharfedale.* Elliot Stock, 1900.
Woodhead, T. W. *History of the Huddersfield Water Supplies.* Tolson Memorial Museum, 1939.
Young, Francis Brett. *The House Under the Water.* Heinemann, 1932.

Printed primary material post-1950

Birmingham Corporation. *The Elan Valley Works of the Birmingham Corporation.* Birmingham Corporation, 1968.
Birmingham Corporation. *City of Birmingham Waterworks.* James Upton Ltd., 1967.
Dickinson, John. *Timble Man: Diaries of a Dalesman.* Edited by Ronald Harker. Hendon, 1988.
Evans, Gwynfor. *A National Future for Wales.* John Percy Press, 1975.
Fishlock, Trevor. *Wales and the Welsh.* Cassel, 1973.
Ofwat. 'Strategic Regional Water Resource Solutions: Standard Gate Two Final Decision for Fens Reservoir'. 28 June 2023.

Ofwat. 'Strategic Regional Water Resource Solutions: Standard Gate Two Final Decision for South East Strategic Reservoir Option'. 28 June 2023.

Ofwat. 'Strategic Regional Water Resource Solutions: Standard Gate Two Final Decision for South Lincolnshire Reservoir'. 28 June 2023.

Westropp, Victor. *The Lake Vyrnwy Fishing Book*. Aberdeen University Press, 1979.

Filmography

Friars School, Bangor. *Tryweryn, The Story of a Valley*. 1965. National Screen and Sound Archive of Wales. Available on YouTube, https://youtu.be/sfTzuZ49u_0

Rotha, Paul, dir. *A City Speaks*. Manchester Corporation, 1947, https://player.bfi.org.uk/free/film/watch-city-speaks-1947-online

Williams, Emlyn, dir. *The Last Days of Dolwyn*. British Lion Films, 1949.

Web sources

1891 England census. Ancestry UK. Accessed 20 July 2018. https://www.ancestry.co.uk/.

1911 England and Wales census. Ancestry UK. Accessed 20 July 2018. https://www.ancestry.co.uk/.

'Driest July in England since 1935', *Met Office*, 1 August 2022, https://www.metoffice.gov.uk/about-us/press-office/news/weather-and-climate/2022/driest-july-in-england-since-1935.

Ofwat. 'Plans for Three New Reservoirs Move a Step Closer'. Ofwat. 30 March 2023. https://www.ofwat.gov.uk/plans-for-three-new-reservoirs-move-a-step-closer/

Ordnance Survey. 'Yorkshire sheet CLXX', 1893. National Library of Scotland. https://maps.nls.uk/view/102344800.

Ordnance Survey. 'Yorkshire sheet CLXX.NW', 1910. National Library of Scotland. https://maps.nls.uk/view/100945598.

Secondary sources, post-1900

Monographs

Albritton, Vicky, and Fredrik Albritton Jonsson. *Green Victorians: The Simple Life in John Ruskin's Lake District*. University of Chicago Press, 2016.

Anderson, Ben. *Cities, Mountains and Being Modern in* fin-de-siècle *England and Germany*. Palgrave Macmillan, 2020.

Bailey, Peter. *Leisure and Class in Victorian England: Rational Recreation and the Contest for Control, 1830–1885*. Routledge, 1978.
Bate, Jonathan. *The Song of the Earth*. Harvard University Press, 2000.
Beaven, Brad. *Leisure, Citizenship and Working-Class Men in Britain, 1850–1945*. Manchester University Press, 2005.
Binnie, G. M. *Early Victorian Water Engineers*. Thomas Telford, 1981.
Borsay, Peter. *A History of Leisure: The British Experience since 1500*. Palgrave Macmillan, 2006.
Briggs, Asa. *Victorian Cities*. Penguin, 1968.
Broich, John. *London: Water and the Making of the Modern City*. University of Pittsburgh Press, 2013.
Brown, David Lewis. *The Elan Valley Clearance: The Fate of the People and Places Affected by the 1892 Elan Valley Reservoir Scheme*. Logaston Press, 2019.
Burchardt, Jeremy. *Paradise Lost: Rural Idyll and Social Change since 1800*. I. B. Tauris, 2002.
Cannedine, David. *In Churchill's Shadow: Confronting the Past in Modern Britain*. Penguin, 2003.
Cook, Margaret, Lionel Frost, Andrea Gaynor, Jenny Gregory, Ruth A.Morgan, Martin Shanahan, and Peter Spearritt. *Cities in a Sunburnt Country: Water and the Making of Modern Australia*. Cambridge University Press, 2022. https://doi.org/10.1017/9781108917698.
Cowie, Helen. *Exhibiting Animals in Nineteenth-Century Britain: Empathy, Education, Entertainment*. Palgrave Macmillan, 2014.
Croll, Andy. *Civilising the Urban: Popular Culture and Public Space in Merthyr, c.1870–1914*. University of Wales Press, 2000.
Cronon, William. *Nature's Metropolis: Chicago and the Great West*. Norton, 1991.
Cunningham, Hugh. *Leisure in the Industrial Revolution, c.1780–1880*. Croom Helm, 1980.
Evans, David. *A History of Nature Conservation in Britain*. Routledge, 1997.
Ewen, Shane. *What Is Urban History?*. Polity, 2016.
Field, John. *Learning through Labour: Training, Unemployment and the State 1890–1939*. University of Leeds, 1992.
Gandy, Matthew. *Concrete and Clay: Reworking Nature in New York City*. MIT Press, 2003.
Goubert, Jean-Pierre. *The Conquest of Water: The Advent of Health in the Industrial Age*. Polity Press, 1989.
Grove, Richard. *Green Imperialism: Colonial Expansion, Tropical Island Edens and the Origins of Environmentalism, 1600–1860*. Cambridge University Press, 1996.

Gunn, Simon. *The Public Culture of the Victorian Middle Class*. Manchester University Press, 2000.

Hamlin, Christopher. *Public Health and Social Justice in the Age of Chadwick: Britain, 1800–1854*. Cambridge University Press, 1998.

Hassan, John. *A History of Water in Modern England and Wales*. Manchester University Press, 1998.

Hennock, E. P. *Fit and Proper Persons: Ideal and Reality in Nineteenth-Century Urban Government*. Edward Arnold, 1973.

Hill, David. *In Turner's Footsteps: Through the Hills and Dales of Northern England*. John Murray Ltd, 1984.

Hill, Jeffrey. *Sport, Leisure and Culture in Twentieth-Century Britain*. Palgrave, 2002.

Holt, Richard. *Sport and the British: A Modern History*. Oxford University Press, 1989.

Hoskins, W. G. *The Making of the English Landscape*. Hodder and Stoughton, 1955.

Howkins, Alun. *The Death of Rural England: A Social History of the Countryside since 1900*. Routledge, 2003.

Hulme, Tom. *After the Shock City: Urban Culture and the Making of Modern Citizenship*. Boydell Press, 2019.

Jensen, Lotte. *Water: A Dutch Cultural History*. Radboud University Press, 2024.

Johnes, Martin. *Wales since 1939*. Manchester University Press, 2012.

Josephson, Paul R. *Industrialised Nature: Brute Force Technology and the Transformation of the Natural World*. Island Press, 2002.

Joyce, Patrick. *The Rule of Freedom: Liberalism and the Modern City*. Verso, 2003.

Kahrl, William L. *Water and Power: The Conflict over Los Angeles' Water Supply in the Owens Valley*. University of California Press, 1982.

Kaika, Maria. *City of Flows: Modernity, Nature, and the City*. Routledge, 2005.

Kelly, Matthew. *The Women Who Saved the English Countryside*. Yale University Press, 2022.

Kelly, Matthew. *Quartz and Feldspar: Dartmoor – A British Landscape in Modern Times*. Vintage, 2016.

Langhamer, Claire. *Women's Leisure in England 1920–60*. Manchester University Press, 2000.

Levine-Clark, Marjorie. *Unemployment, Welfare, and Masculine Citizenship: 'So Much Honest Poverty' in Britain, 1870–1930*. Palgrave Macmillan, 2015.

Luckin, Bill. *Pollution and Control: A Social History of the Thames in the Nineteenth Century*. Adam Hilger, 1986.

Matless, David. *Landscape and Englishness*. 2nd ed. Reaktion Books Ltd, 2016.
McCarthy, Jeffrey Mathes. *Green Modernism: Nature and the English Novel, 1900 to 1930*. Palgrave, 2015.
McNeil, John. *Something New Under the Sun: An Environmental History of the Twentieth Century*. Penguin, 2001.
Millward, Robert. *Private and Public Enterprise in Europe: Energy, Telecommunications and Transport, 1830–1990*. Cambridge University Press, 2005.
Morgan, Marjorie. *National Identities and Travel in Victorian Britain*. Palgrave, 2001.
Mosley, Stephen. *The Environment in World History*. Routledge, 2010.
Nelson, Thomas H. *The Birds of Yorkshire: Being A Historical Account of the Avi-Fauna of the County*. A. Brown and Sons, 1907.
O'Hara, Glen. *The Politics of Water in Post-War Britain*. Palgrave Macmillan, 2017.
Otter, Chris. *The Victorian Eye: A Political History of Light and Vision in Britain, 1800–1910*. University of Chicago Press, 2008.
Parsons, Diana. *The Book of the Washburn Valley: Yorkshire's Forgotten Dale*. Halsgrove, 2014.
Platt, Harold L. *Shock Cities: The Environmental Transformation and Reform of Manchester and Chicago*. University of Chicago Press, 2005.
Righter, Robert L. *The Battle over Hetch Hetchy: America's Most Controversial Dam and the Birth of Modern Environmentalism*. Oxford University Press, 2005.
Ritvo, Harriet. *The Dawn of Green: Manchester, Thirlmere, and Modern Environmentalism*. University of Chicago Press, 2009.
Sampson, Fiona. *Starlight Wood: Walking Back to the Romantic Countryside*. Corsair, 2022.
Sharples, Marion. *The Fawkes Family and Their Estates in Wharfedale, 1819–1936*. Thoresby Society, 1997.
Sheail, John. *An Environmental History of Twentieth-Century Britain*. Palgrave, 2002.
Shore, Heather. *London's Criminal Underworlds, c.1720–1930: A Social and Cultural History*. Palgrave Macmillan, 2015.
Smith, Norman. *A History of Dams*. Peter Davies, 1971.
Snell, K. D. M. *Spirits of Community: English Senses of Belonging and Loss, 1750–2000*. Bloomsbury, 2015.
Snell, K. D. M. *Parish and Belonging: Community, Identity and Welfare in England and Wales, 1700–1950*. Cambridge University Press, 2006.
Spracklen, Karl. *Constructing Leisure: Historical and Philosophical Debates*. Palgrave Macmillan, 2011.

Stephenson, Tom. *Forbidden Land: The Struggle for Access to Mountain and Moorland*. Edited by Ann Holt. Manchester University Press, 1989.

Taylor, Harvey. *A Claim on the Countryside: A History of the British Outdoor Movement*. Keele University Press, 1997.

Ward, Stephen V. *Selling Places: The Marketing and Promotion of Towns and Cities 1850–2000*. E. & F. N. Spon, 1998.

Wiener, Martin J. *English Culture and the Decline of the Industrial Spirit 1850–1980*. Penguin, 1985.

White, Richard. *The Organic Machine: The Remaking of the Columbia River*. Hill & Wang, 1995.

Wildman, Charlotte. *Urban Redevelopment and Modernity in Liverpool and Manchester, 1918–39*. Bloomsbury Academic, 2016.

Winter, James. *Secure from Rash Assault: Sustaining the Victorian Environment*. University of California Press, 1999.

Wohl, Anthony. *Endangered Lives: Public Health in Victorian Britain*. J. M. Dent & Sons, 1983.

Journals

Adorno, Theodor W. 'The idea of natural history', *Telos* 1984, no. 60 (1984): 123–4, https://doi.org/10.3817/0684060111.

Atkins, Ed. 'Building a Dam, Constructing a Nation: The "Drowning" of Capel Celyn', *Journal of Historical Sociology*, 31, no. 4 (2018): 455–68, https://doi.org/10.1111/johs.12186.

Anderson, Ben. 'Partnership or Co-operation? Family, Politics and Strenuousness in the pre-First World War Co-operative Holidays Association', *Sport in History* 33, no. 3 (2013): 260–81, https://doi.org/10.1080/17460263.2013.826434.

Anderson, Ben. 'A Liberal Countryside? The Manchester Ramblers' Federation and the "Social Readjustment" of Urban Citizens, 1929–1936', *Urban History* 38, no. 1 (2011): 84–102, https://doi.org/10.1017/S0963926811000058.

Beaven, Brad. 'The Provincial Press, Civic Ceremony and the Citizen-Soldier During the Boer War, 1899–1902: A Study of Local Patriotism', *Journal of Imperial and Commonwealth History* 37, no. 2 (2009): 207–28, https://doi.org/10.1080/03086530903010350.

Breen, Tom, Abbi Flint, Clare Hickman, and Glen O'Hara. 'Whose Right to Roam? Contesting Access to England's Countryside', *The Journal of Transport History* 44, no. 2 (2023): 276–307, https://doi.org/10.1177/00225266231174766.

Busch, Andrew M. 'Dams and the Age of Abundance: Hydraulic Boosterism, Regional Growth, and the Reemergence of Water Scarcity in Central Texas', *Journal of Urban History* 49, no. 2 (2023): 309–34, https://doi.org/10.1177/00961442211008865.

Cosgrove, Denis, Barbara Roscoe, and Simon Rycroft. 'Landscape and Identity at Ladybower Reservoir and Rutland Water', *Transactions of the Institute of British Geographers* 21, no. 3 (1996): 534–51, https://doi.org/10.2307/622595.

Cronon, William. 'A Place for Stories: Nature, History, and Narrative', *Journal of American History* 78, no. 4 (1992): 1347–76, https://doi.org/10.2307/2079346.

Cronon, William. 'Modes of Prophecy and Production: Placing Nature in History', *Journal of American History* 76, no. 4 (1990): 1122–31, https://doi.org/10.2307/2936590.

Deacon, Bernard. 'Religion and Community: Frameworks and Issues', *Family and Community History* 5, no. 1 (2002): 33–44, https://doi.org/10.1179/fch.2002.5.1.004.

Done, Andrew, and Richard Muir. 'The Landscape History of Grouse Shooting in the Yorkshire Dales', *Rural History* 12, no. 2 (2001): 195–210, https://doi.org/10.1017/S0956793300002442.

Dudley, Marianna. 'Muddying the Waters: Recreational Conflict and Rights of Use of British Rivers', *Water History* 9, no. 3 (2017): 259–77, https://doi.org/10.1007/s12685-017-0193-2.

Durie, Alistair J. 'Game Shooting: An Elite Sport c.1870–1980', *Sport in History* 28, no. 3 (2008): 431–49, https://doi.org/10.1080/17460260802315504.

Edgerton, David. 'The "White Heat" Revisited: The British Government and Technology in the 1960s', *Modern British History* 7, no. 1 (1996): 53–82, https://doi.org/10.1093/tcbh/7.1.53.

Etheridge, Stephen. 'Southern Pennine Brass Bands and the Creation of Northern Identity, c.1840–1914: Musical Constructions of Space, Place and Region', *Northern History* 54, no. 2 (2017): 244–61, https://doi.org/10.1080/0078172X.2016.1254379.

Evenden, Matthew. 'Beyond the Organic Machine? New Approaches to River Historiography', *Environmental History* 23, no. 4 (2018): 698–720, http://dx.doi.org/10.1093/envhis/emy054.

Ewen, Shane. 'Socio-Technological Disasters and Engineering Expertise in Victorian Britain: The Holmfirth and Sheffield Floods of 1852 and 1864', *Journal of Historical Geography*, 46 (2014): 13–25, https://doi.org/10.1016/j.jhg.2014.05.021.

Ewen, Shane. 'Sheffield's Great Flood of 1864: Engineering Failure and the Municipalisation of Water', *Environment and History* 20, no. 2 (2014): 177–207, https://doi.org/10.3197/096734014X13941952680954.

Fisk, Audrey. 'Diversity within the Friendly Society Movement 1834–1911: The Value to Community Studies', *Family and Community History* 3, no. 1 (2000): 19–31, https://doi.org/10.1179/fch.2000.3.1.003.

Foster, Ann-Marie. 'The Barry Urban District Council, Disaster Relief Funds and Civic Society, 1913–1934', *Urban History*, 48, no. 4 (2021): 685–700, https://doi.org/10.1017/S0963926820000577.

Gaynor, Andrea. 'Lawnscaping Perth: Water Supply, Gardens, and Scarcity, 1890–1925', *Journal of Urban History* 46, no. 1 (2020): 63–78, https://doi.org/10.1177/0096144217692991.

Georgiou, Dion. 'Redefining the Carnivalesque: The Construction of Ritual, Revelry and Spectacle in British Leisure Practices through the Idea and Model of "Carnival", 1870–1939', *Sport in History* 35, no. 3 (2015): 335–63, https://doi.org/10.1080/17460263.2015.1088462.

Godbey, Emily. 'Disaster Tourism and the Melodrama of Authenticity: Revisiting the 1889 Johnstown Flood', *Pennsylvania History* 73, no. 3 (2006): 273–315.

Goodwin, Gráinne and Gordon Johnston. 'Guidebook Publishing in the Nineteenth Century: John Murray's *Handbooks for Travellers*', *Studies in Travel Writing* 17, no. 1 (2013): 43–61, https://doi.org/10.1080/13645145.2012.747791.

Haines, Daniel. 'Development, Citizenship, and the Bhakra–Nangal Dams in Postcolonial India, 1948–1952', *The Historical Journal* 65, no. 4 (2022), 1124–44, https://doi.org/10.1017/S0018246X21000625.

Hamlin, Christopher. 'Muddling in Bumbledom: On the Enormity of Large Sanitary Improvements in Four British Towns, 1855–1885', *Victorian Studies*, 32, no. 1 (1988): 55–83, https://www.jstor.org/stable/3828289.

Harker, Ben. '"The Manchester Rambler": Ewan MacColl and the 1932 Mass Trespass', *History Workshop Journal* 59, no. 1 (2005): 219–28, https://doi.org/10.1093/hwj/dbi016.

Hassan, John. 'The Growth and Impact of the British Water Industry in the Nineteenth Century', *Economic History Review* 38, no. 4 (1985): 531–47, https://doi.org/10.1111/j.1468-0289.1985.tb00387.x.

Hassan, John, and Peter Taylor. 'The Politics of Water in Early and Mid-Victorian Britain: The Experience of Bolton', *Transactions of the Historical Society of Lancashire and Cheshire* 148 (1998): 119–45.

Hey, David. 'Kinder Scout and the Legend of the Mass Trespass', *Agricultural History Review* 59, no. 2 (2013): 199–216, https://www.jstor.org/stable/23317099.

Hillier, Joseph. 'Implementation without Control: The Role of Private Water Companies in Establishing Constant Water in Nineteenth-Century London', *Urban History* 41, no. 2 (2014): 228–46, https://doi.org/10.1017/S0963926813000278.

Hopkins, Jeffrey. 'Signs of the Post-Rural: Marketing Myths of a Symbolic Countryside', *Geografiska Annaler: Series B, Human Geography* 80, no. 2 (1998): 65–81, https://doi.org/10.1111/j.0435-3684.1998.00030.x.

Hulme, Tom. '"A Nation of Town Criers": Civic Publicity and Historical Pageantry in Inter-War Britain', *Urban History* 44, no. 2 (2017): 270–92, https://doi.org/10.1017/S0963926816000262.

Jay, L. J. 'The Black Country of Francis Brett Young', *Transactions of the Institute of British Geographers* 66 (1975): 57–72, https://doi.org/10.2307/621621.

Jeans, D. N. 'Planning and the Myth of the English Countryside in the Interwar Period', *Rural History* 1, no. 2 (1990): 261–62, https://doi.org/10.1017/S0956793300003332.

Jones, Peter. 'Posting the Future: British Stamp Design and the "White Heat" of a Technological Revolution', *Journal of Design History* 17, no. 2 (2004): 163–76, https://doi.org/10.1093/jdh/17.2.163.

Kaika, Maria. 'Dams as Symbols of Modernization: The Urbanization of Nature Between Geographical Imagination and Materiality', *Annals of the Association of American Geographers* 96, no. 2 (2006): 276–301, https://doi.org/10.1111/j.1467-8306.2006.00478.x.

Kelly, Matthew. 'The Politics of the British Environment Since 1945', *The Political Quarterly* 94, no. 2 (2023): 208–15, https://doi.org/10.1111/1467-923X.13275.

Larkham, Peter J. and Keith D. Lilley. 'Plans, Planners and City Images: Place Promotion and Civic Boosterism in British Reconstruction Planning', *Urban History* 30, no. 2 (2003): 183–205, https://doi.org/10.1017/S0963926803001123.

Lord, Evelyn. 'The Friendly Society Movement and the Respectability of the Rural Working Class', *Rural History* 8, no. 2 (1997): 165–73, https://doi.org/10.1017/S0956793300001254.

Luckin, Bill. 'Revisiting the Idea of Degeneration in Urban Britain, 1830–1900', *Urban History* 33, no. 2 (2006): 234–52, https://doi.org/10.1017/S0963926805003275.

Mandler, Peter. 'Against "Englishness": English Culture and the Limits to Rural Nostalgia, 1850–1940', *Transactions of the Royal Historical Society* 7 (1997): 155–75, https://doi.org/10.2307/3679274.

Martin, John. 'The Transformation of Lowland Game Shooting in England and Wales in the Twentieth Century: The Neglected Metamorphosis', *The International Journal of the History of Sport* 29, no. 8 (2012): 1141–58, https://doi.org/10.1080/09523367.2012.690226.

McCulloch, Christine S. 'The Water Resources Board: England and Wales' Venture into National Water Resources Planning, 1964–1973',

Water Alternatives 2, no. 3 (2009): 461–75, https://www.water-alternatives.org/index.php/alldoc/articles/vol2/v2issue3/59-a2-3-10.

McTominey, Andrew. 'Waterworks, Municipal Government and the Environment in Twentieth-Century Britain', *Urban History* 51, no. 3 (2024): 600–15, https://doi.org/10.1017/S0963926823000597.

McTominey, Andrew. 'Water and the Modern Engineered City: The Association of Water Engineers in a British and Transnational context, 1896–1914', *Water History* 12, no. 2 (2020): 131–49, https://doi.org/10.1007/s12685-020-00249-1.

McTominey, Andrew. 'Bad Neighbours? Water Supply and the Civic Rivalry of Leeds and Bradford, *c*.1850–1887', *International Journal of Regional and Local History* 12, no. 1 (2017): 24–41, https://doi.org/10.1080/20514530.2017.1353769.

Meehl, Gerald A., Haiyan Teng, Nan Rosenbloom, Aixue Hu, Claudia Tebaldi, and Guy Walton. 'How the Great Plains Dust Bowl Drought Spread Heat Extremes Around the Northern Hemisphere', *Scientific Reports* 12, article 17380 (2022), https://doi.org/10.1038/s41598-022-22262-5.

Meller, Helen. 'Urban Renewal and Citizenship: The Quality of Life in British Cities, 1890–1990', *Urban History* 22, no. 1 (1995): 63–84, https://doi.org/10.1017/S096392680001138X.

Melosi, Martin V. 'Humans, Cities, and Nature: How Do Cities Fit in the Material World?', *Journal of Urban History* 36, no. 1 (2010): 3–21, https://doi.org/10.1177/0096144209349876.

Millward, Robert and Sally Sheard. 'The Urban Fiscal Problem, 1870–1914: Government Expenditure and Finance in England and Wales', *Economic History Review* 48, no. 3 (1995): 501–35, https://doi.org/10.2307/2598179.

Morgan, Ruth. 'The Allure of Climate and Water Independence: Desalination Projects in Perth and San Diego', *Journal of Urban History* 46, no. 1 (2020): 113–28, https://doi.org/10.1177/0096144217692990.

Mosley, Stephen. 'Common Ground: Integrating Social and Environmental History', *Journal of Social History* 39, no. 3 (2006): 915–33, https://doi.org/10.1353/jsh.2006.0007.

Navickas, Katrina. 'Conflicts of Power, Landscape and Amenity in Debates over the British Super Grid in the 1950s', *Rural History* 30, no. 1 (2019): 87–103, https://doi.org/10.1017/S0956793319000013.

Parker, Gavin and Neil Ravenscroft. 'Benevolence, Nationalism and Hegemony: Fifty Years of the National Parks and Access to the Countryside Act 1949', *Leisure Studies* 18, no. 4 (1999): 297–313, https://doi.org/10.1080/026143699374871.

Pollard, Eileen. '"When the Reservoir Comes": Drowned Villages, Community and Nostalgia in Contemporary British Fiction', *C21 Literature: Journal of 21st-Century Writings* 5, no. 3 (2017): 1–21, https://doi.org/10.16995/c21.9.

Prynn, David. 'The Clarion Clubs, Rambling and the Holiday Associations in Britain since the 1890s', *Journal of Contemporary History* 11, no. 2 (1976), 65–77, https://doi.org/10.1177/002200947601100204.

Ramesh, Aditya. 'Indian Rivers, "Productive Works", and the Emergence of Large Dams in Nineteenth-Century Madras', *The Historical Journal* 64, no. 2 (2021): 281–309, https://doi.org/10.1017/S0018246X20000163.

Roberts, Ben. 'Entertaining the Community: the Evolution of Civic Ritual and Public Celebration, 1860–1953', *Urban History* 44, no. 3 (2017): 444–63, https://doi.org/10.1017/S0963926816000511.

Roberts, Owen. 'Waterworks and Commemoration: Purity, Rurality, and Civic Identity in Britain, 1880–1921', *Continuity and Change* 22, no. 2 (2007): 305–25, https://doi.org/10.1017/S0268416007006352.

Roberts, Owen. 'Developing the Untapped Wealth of Britain's "Celtic Fringe": Water Engineering and the Welsh Landscape, 1870–1960', *Landscape Research* 31, no. 2 (2006): 121–33, https://doi.org/10.1080/01426390600638422.

Roberts, Owen. 'The Politics of Health and the Origins of Liverpool's Lake Vyrnwy Water Scheme, 1871–92', *Welsh History Review* 20, no. 2 (2000): 308–35.

Rosen, Christine Meisner and Joel Arthur Tarr. 'The Importance of an Urban Perspective in Environmental History', *Journal of Urban History* 20, no. 3 (1994): 299–310, https://doi.org/10.1177/009614429402000301.

Shapely, Peter. 'Civic Pride and Redevelopment in the Post-war British City', *Urban History* 39, no. 2 (2012): 310–28, https://doi.org/10.1017/S0963926812000077.

Sharples, M. 'The Fawkes-Turner Connection and the Art Collection at Farnley Hall, Otley, 1792–1937: A Great Estate Enhanced and Supported', *Northern History* 26, no. 1 (1990): 131–59, https://doi.org/10.1179/007817290790175935.

Sheail, John. 'The Access to Mountains Act 1939: An Essay in Compromise', *Rural History* 21, no. 1 (2010): 59–74, https://doi.org/10.1017/S095679330999015X.

Sheail, John. 'Local Legislation: Its Scope and Context', *Archives* 30, no. 113 (2005): 36–50, https://doi.org/10.3828/archives.2005.3.

Sheail, John. 'The "Amenity" Clause: An Insight into Half a Century of Environmental Protection in the United Kingdom', *Transactions of the*

Institute of British Geographers 17, no. 2 (1992): 152–65, https://doi.org/10.2307/622543.

Sheail, John. 'T. W. Woodhead and the Study of Vegetation and Man in the Huddersfield District', *The Naturalist* 113 (1988): 125–39, https://www.biodiversitylibrary.org/page/50376549.

Sheard, Sally. 'Water and Health: The Formation and Exploitation of the Relationship in Liverpool, 1847–1900', *Transactions of the Historic Society of Lancashire and Cheshire* 143 (1994), 141–64, https://www.hslc.org.uk/wp-content/uploads/143-8-Sheard.pdf.

Snape, Robert. 'The Co-operative Holidays Association and the Cultural Formation of Countryside Leisure Practice', *Leisure Studies* 23, no. 2 (2004): 143–58, https://doi.org/10.1080/0261436042000226345.

Stobart, Jon. 'Identity, Competition and Place Promotion in the Five Towns', *Urban History* 30, no. 2 (2003), 163–82, https://doi.org/10.1017/S0963926803001111.

Strang, Veronica. 'Fluidscapes: Water, Identity, and the Senses', *Worldviews* 10, no. 2 (2006), 147–54, https://www.jstor.org/stable/43809682.

Sul, Heasim. '*The King's Book of Sports*: The Nature of Leisure in Early Modern England', *The International Journal of the History of Sport* 17, no. 4 (2000): 167–79, https://doi.org/10.1080/09523360008714153.

Swyngedouw, Erik. '"Not a Drop of Water ...": State, Modernity, and the Production of Nature in Spain, 1898–2010', *Environment and History* 20, no. 1 (2014): 67–92, https://doi.org/10.3197/096734014X13851121443445.

Swyngedouw, Erik. 'Modernity and Hybridity: Nature, *Regeneracionismo*, and the Production of the Spanish Waterscape, 1890–1930', *Annals of the Association of American Geographers*, 89, no. 3 (1999): 443–65 https://doi.org/10.1111/0004-5608.00157.

Taylor, Vanessa, Heather Chappells, Will Mead, and Frank Trentmann. 'Drought is Normal: The Socio-Technical Evolution of Drought and Water Demand in England and Wales, 1893–2006', *Journal of Historical Geography* 35, no. 3 (2009): 568–91, https://doi.org/10.1016/j.jhg.2008.09.004.

Taylor, Vanessa, and Frank Trentmann. 'Liquid Politics: Water and the Politics of Everyday Life in the Modern City', *Past and Present* 211, no. 1 (2011): 199–241, https://doi.org/10.1093/pastj/gtq068.

Tebbutt, Melanie. 'Rambling and Manly Identity in Derbyshire's Dark Peak, 1880s–1920s', *The Historical Journal* 49, no. 4 (2006): 1125–53, https://doi.org/10.1017/S0018246X06005760.

Thornton, Judith and Peter Pearson. 'Bristol Water Works Company: A Study of Nineteenth Century Resistance to Local Authority Purchase

Attempts', *Water History* 5, no. 3 (2013): 307–30, https://doi.org/10.1007/s12685-013-0083-1.

Walton, John K. 'The Northern Rambler: Recreational Walking and the Popular Politics of Industrial England, from Peterloo to the 1930s', *Labour History Review* 78, no. 3 (2013): 243–68, https://doi.org/10.3828/lhr.2013.14.

Wharton-Michael, Patty. 'The Johnstown Flood of 1889: The *Johnstown Tribune*'s Commonsense Coverage vs. Common-Practice Sensationalism', *Journalism History* 38, no. 1 (2012): 23–33, https://doi.org/10.1080/00947679.2012.12062869.

Wildman, Charlotte. '*A City Speaks*: The Projection of Civic Identity in Manchester', *Modern British History* 23, no. 1 (2012): 80–99, https://doi.org/10.1093/tcbh/hwr067.

Williams, Joe, Stefan Bouzarovski and Erik Swyngedouw. 'The Urban Resource Nexus: On the Politics of Relationality, Water–Energy Infrastructure and the Fallacy of Integration', *Environment and Planning C: Politics and Space* 37, no. 4 (2018): 652–69, https://doi.org/10.1177/0263774X18803370.

Edited collections

Ross, Linda M., Katrina Navickas, Matthew Kelly and Ben Anderson, eds. *New Lives, New Landscapes Revisited: Rural Modernity in Britain*. British Academy, Oxford University Press, 2023.

Soens, Tim, Dieter Schott, Michael Toyka-Seid, and Bert De Munck, eds. *Urbanising Nature: Actors and Agency (Dis)Connecting Cities and Natures since 1500*. Routledge, 2019.

Book chapters

Bluemel, Kristin. 'Rural Modernity in Britain: Landscape, Literature, Nostalgia'. In *New Lives, New Landscapes Revisited: Rural Modernity in Britain*, edited by Linda M. Ross et al., 37–60. British Academy, Oxford University Press, 2023.

Caunce, Stephen. 'Yorkshire Post Newspapers Ltd: Perseverance Rewarded'. In *Leeds City Business 1893–1993: Essays Marking the Centenary of the Incorporation*, edited by John Chartres and Katrina Honeyman, 24–56. Leeds University Press, 1993.

Coopey, Richard, and Tim Shakesheff. 'Angling and Nature: Environment, Leisure, Class and Culture in Britain 1750–1975'. In *Common Ground: Integrating the Social and Environmental in History*, edited by Geneviève Massard-Guilbaud and Stephen Mosley, 16–41. Cambridge Scholars Publishing, 2011.

Coopey, Richard. 'A River Does Indeed Run Through It: Angling and Society in Britain since 1800'. In *Perceptions of Water in Britain from Early Modern Times to the Present: An Introduction*, edited by Karen V. Lykke Syse and Terje Oestigaard, 59–82. BRIC Press, 2010.

Goddard, Nicholas. 'Agricultural Institutions: Societies, Associations and the Press'. In *The Agrarian History of England and Wales, volume 7: 1850–1914*, edited by E. J. T. Collins, 650–90. Cambridge University Press, 2000.

Gruffudd, Pyrs. 'Selling the Countryside: Representations of Rural Britain'. In *Place Promotion: The Use of Publicity and Marketing to Sell Towns and Regions*, edited by John R. Gold and Stephen V. Ward, 247–64. Wiley, 1994.

Hanley, Keith. 'The Imaginative Visitor: Wordsworth and the Romantic Construction of Literary Tourism in the Lake District'. In *The Making of a Cultural Landscape: The English Lake District as Tourist Destination, 1750–2010*, edited by John K. Walton and Jason Wood, 113–32. Ashgate, 2013.

Howkins, Alun. 'The Discovery of Rural England'. In *Englishness: Politics and Culture 1880–1920*, edited by Robert Colls and Philip Dodd, 85–112. Bloomsbury, 1986.

Howkins, Alun. 'The Taming of Whitsun: The Changing Face of a Nineteenth-Century Rural Holiday'. In *Popular Culture and Class Conflict 1590–1914: Explorations in the History of Labour and Leisure*, edited by Eileen Yeo and Stephen Yeo, 187–209. Harvester Press, 1981.

Hulme, Tom. 'Urban Materialities: Citizenship, Public Housing and Governing the Body'. In *New Approaches to Governance and Rule in Urban Europe since 1500*, edited by Simon Gunn and Tom Hulme, 190–210. Routledge, 2020.

Lowerson, John. 'Angling'. In *Sport in Britain: A Social History*, edited by Tony Mason, 12–43. Cambridge University Press, 1989.

Lykke Syse, Karen V. 'Ideas of Leisure, Pleasure and the River in Early Modern England'. In *Perceptions of Water in Britain from Early Modern Times to the Present: An Introduction*, edited by Karen V. Lykke Syse and Terje Oestigaard, 35–58. BRIC Press, 2010.

McCulloch, Christine S. 'Political Ecology of Dams in Teesdale'. In *Long-Term Benefits and Performance of Dams* edited by Henry Hewlett, 49–58. Thomas Telford, 2004.

Meller, Helen. 'Gender, Citizenship and the Making of the Modern Environment'. In *Women and the Making of Built Space in England, 1870–1950*, edited by Elizabeth Darling and Lesley Whitworth, 13–32. Ashgate, 2007.

Millward, Robert. 'The Political Economy of Urban Utilities'. In *The Cambridge Urban History of Britain, volume 3: 1840–1930*, edited by M. Daunton, 315–50. Cambridge University Press, 2000.

Navickas, Katrina. 'Building Amenity in Areas of Non-Outstanding Natural Beauty in the Southern Pennines'. In *New Lives, New Landscapes Revisited: Rural Modernity in Britain*, edited by Linda M. Ross, Katrina Navickas, Matthew Kelly and Ben Anderson, 92–114. British Academy, Oxford University Press, 2023.

Nicholson, Bob. 'Transatlantic Connections'. In *The Routledge Handbook of Nineteenth-Century British Periodicals and Newspapers*, edited by Andrew King, Alexis Easley and John Morton, 163–74. Routledge, 2016.

Payne, Jill. 'Constructing the Kielder Landscape: Plantations, Dams and the Romantic Ideal'. In *Local Places, Global Processes: Histories of Environmental Change in Britain and Beyond*, edited by Peter Coates, David Moon and Paul Warde, 97–108. Oxbow Books, 2016.

Poole, Robert. 'Oldham Wakes'. In *Leisure in Britain 1780–1939*, edited by John K. Walton and James Walvin, 71–98. Manchester University Press, 1983.

Ross, Linda M., Katrina Navickas, Matthew Kelly and Ben Anderson. 'Introduction'. In *New Lives, New Landscapes Revisited: Rural Modernity in Britain*, edited by Linda M. Ross, Katrina Navickas, Matthew Kelly and Ben Anderson, 1–14. British Academy, Oxford University Press, 2023.

MacLeod, Roy. 'Introduction'. In *Government and Expertise: Specialists, Administrators and Professionals, 1860–1919*, edited by Roy MacLeod, 1–26. Cambridge University Press, 1988.

Williamson, Tom. 'Landscape: The Configured Space'. In *History Beyond the Text: A Student's Guide to Approaching Alternative Sources*, edited by Sarah Barber and Corinna M. Peniston-Bird, 136–54. Routledge, 2009.

Worster, Donald. 'Appendix: Doing Environmental History'. In *The Ends of the Earth: Perspectives on Modern Environmental History*, edited by Donald Worster, 289–308. Cambridge University Press, 1998.

Unpublished Masters and PhD theses

Dalton, Raymond David. 'Labour and the Municipality: Labour Politics in Leeds 1900–1914'. Unpublished doctoral thesis, University of Huddersfield, 2000.

Pepperd, Richard Samuel. 'The Growth and Development of Leeds Waterworks Undertakings, 1694–1852'. Unpublished doctoral thesis, University of Leeds, 1973.

Index

www.ingramcontent.com/pod-product-compliance
Lightning Source LLC
LaVergne TN
LVHW052016300826
846742LV00019B/70

9781915249111